The Rise of Contemporary in the United States

The Rise of Contemporary Conservatism in the United States offers students an accessible introduction to the history of modern American conservatism. Author Kenneth J. Heineman provides a concise but substantial discussion of modern conservatism from its origins in opposition to Franklin D. Roosevelt's New Deal up until the 2016 election of Donald J. Trump.

The text examines electoral coalitions and politics as connected to economic and foreign policy as well as ideology. Conservative ideas and values are addressed directly, both on their own terms and in the context of contemporary political applications. A robust collection of primary documents offers students and instructors the opportunity to examine directly the views of both conservatives and their critics. Supported by a range of study tools including a glossary of key figures and terms, a detailed chronology, and ample suggestions for further reading, *The Rise of Contemporary Conservatism in the United States* is the ideal introduction for students interested in the forging and fracturing of modern conservative coalitions and ideologies.

Kenneth J. Heineman is Professor of History at Angelo State University in Texas, and the author of *Civil War Dynasty: The Ewing Family of Ohio* (2012).

Introduction to the series

History is the narrative constructed by historians from traces left by the past. Historical enquiry is often driven by contemporary issues and, in consequence, historical narratives are constantly reconsidered, reconstructed, and reshaped. The fact that different historians have different perspectives on issues means that there is often controversy and no universally agreed version of past events. *Seminar Studies* was designed to bridge the gap between current research and debate, and the broad, popular general surveys that often date rapidly.

The volumes in the series are written by historians who are not only familiar with the latest research and current debates concerning their topic, but who have themselves contributed to our understanding of the subject. The books are intended to provide the reader with a clear introduction to a major topic in history. They provide both a narrative of events and a critical analysis of contemporary interpretations. They include the kinds of tools generally omitted from specialist monographs: a chronology of events, a glossary of terms, and brief biographies of 'who's who'. They also include bibliographical essays in order to guide students to the literature on various aspects of the subject. Students and teachers alike will find that the selection of documents will stimulate the discussion and offer insight into the raw materials used by historians in their attempt to understand the past.

Clive Emsley and Gordon Martel
Series Editors

The Rise of Contemporary Conservatism in the United States

Kenneth J. Heineman

Routledge
Taylor & Francis Group
NEW YORK AND LONDON

First published 2019
by Routledge
711 Third Avenue, New York, NY 10017

and by Routledge
2 Park Square, Milton Park, Abingdon, Oxon, OX14 4RN

Routledge is an imprint of the Taylor & Francis Group, an informa business

© 2019 Taylor & Francis

The right of Kenneth J. Heineman to be identified as author of this work has been asserted by him in accordance with sections 77 and 78 of the Copyright, Designs and Patents Act 1988.

All rights reserved. No part of this book may be reprinted or reproduced or utilised in any form or by any electronic, mechanical, or other means, now known or hereafter invented, including photocopying and recording, or in any information storage or retrieval system, without permission in writing from the publishers.

Trademark notice: Product or corporate names may be trademarks or registered trademarks, and are used only for identification and explanation without intent to infringe.

Library of Congress Cataloging-in-Publication Data
Names: Heineman, Kenneth J., 1962– author.
Title: The rise of contemporary conservatism in the United States / by Kenneth J. Heineman.
Description: New York, NY : Routledge, 2019. |
Series: Seminar studies | Includes bibliographical references.
Identifiers: LCCN 2018015516 (print) | LCCN 2018029349 (ebook) |
ISBN 9780429456442 (ebook) | ISBN 9781138096257
Subjects: LCSH: Conservatism–United States–History. |
Right and left (Political science)–United States–History. |
United States–Politics and government.
Classification: LCC JC573.2.U6 (ebook) |
LCC JC573.2.U6 .H397 2019 (print) | DDC 320.520973–dc23
LC record available at https://lccn.loc.gov/2018015516

ISBN: 978-1-138-09625-7 (hbk)
ISBN: 978-1-138-09626-4 (pbk)
ISBN: 978-0-429-45644-2 (ebk)

Typeset in Sabon
by Out of House Publishing

Printed and bound in Great Britain by
TJ International Ltd, Padstow, Cornwall

Contents

List of Figures ix
Acknowledgments x
Chronology xi
Who's Who xvii

PART I
Analysis and Assessment 1

Prologue 3

1 The New Deal and Conservative Reaction, 1933–1945 6
   Conservative Economic and Social Policies before the Great Depression 6
   The Limits of Conservative Economic and Social Policies before the Great Depression 8
   The Fall of the Conservative Order, 1929–1932 9
   The Rise of Franklin Roosevelt 11
   The New Deal 12
   Creating New Deal Democrats: The Southern Front 14
   Creating New Deal Democrats: The Northern Front 16
   Conservative Reaction: The Business Response 18
   Conservative Reaction: The Challenge from Within the Democratic Party 22
   Foreign Policy Dissent 24

2 Conservatism Adrift, 1946–1960 29
   Conservative Resurgence? 29
   The 1948 Election 32
   Hitting Back 35
   The Rise of Modern Republicans 39
   Conservatives Regroup 41

    Conservative Fusion 44
    Reagan's Journey 46
    The 1960 Election: Modern Republicans and Conservatives 48
    The 1960 Election: Democrats 50

3 Crisis and Opportunity, 1961–1972   53
    Racial Issues, North and South, 1961–1963 53
    Civil Rights Reaction, 1961–1964 55
    The 1964 Election 58
    The Great Society 61
    Vietnam 63
    Youth Movement 66
    Reagan's Rise 68
    Nixon 70
    Electoral Realignment. Again? 73

4 Conservative Advance, 1973–1980   76
    Falling, 1973–1975 76
    Fighting for Control, 1973–1976 78
    The Crisis of the 1970s: Domestic Policy 82
    The Crisis of the 1970s: Foreign Policy 84
    Conservatives' Response: Foreign Policy in the 1970s 86
    Conservatives' Response: Economic Policy in the 1970s 88
    Conservatives' Response: Social Policy in the 1970s 90
    The 1980 Election: The Battle 92
    The 1980 Election: The Judgment 95

5 The Reagan Revolution and Its Discontents, 1981–1992   97
    Reagan the Underestimated 97
    Reagan and the Economy, 1981–1988 100
    Reagan and National Security, 1981–1988 103
    Reagan and Social Policy, 1981–1988 105
    Culture and Politics in the Reagan Era, 1981–1988 107
    The Conservative Retreat, 1986–1988 109
    The Triumph of George H.W. Bush, 1988 111
    The Agonies of George H.W. Bush, 1989–1992 113
    The Conservative Break-Up, 1992 115

6 The Politics of Division, 1993–2016   118
    Bill Clinton's Successes and Set-Backs, 1993–1994 118
    Conservative Bipartisanship, 1995–1998 119
    Ideological Combat: The 1990s 122
    George W. Bush and the 2000 Election 125
    George W. Bush and Domestic Policy, 2001–2003 126

George W. Bush and National Security, 2001–2003 127
George W. Bush's Reelection and the Foreign Policy Fallout,
  2004–2007 131
George W. Bush and the Domestic Policy Crash, 2005–2008 132
Conservatives Flounder, 2008–2010 134
Conservatives Win and Lose, 2011–2016 136

PART II
Primary Documents 141

1 Herbert C. Hoover, "Address of President Herbert Hoover Accepting the Republican Nomination for President, August 11, 1932" 143
2 J. Howard Pew, "Which Road to Take?" Speech delivered in Washington, D.C., for the American Liberty League, 1935 144
3 Jouett Shouse, "The New Deal vs. Democracy," Speech delivered in Washington, D.C., for the American Liberty League, 1936 145
4 Hatton Sumners, "Extension of Remarks of Hon. Hatton W. Sumners of Texas in the House of Representatives, Monday, March 11, 1946" 146
5 Charles Lindbergh, "Who Are the War Agitators?" Speech delivered in Des Moines, Iowa, September 11, 1941 147
6 Robert A. Taft, *A Foreign Policy for Americans*, 1951 (selection) 149
7 Joseph McCarthy, "The History of George Catlett Marshall," remarks delivered during the 82nd Congress, June 14, 1951 150
8 "Declaration of Constitutional Principles, 1956," (also known as the "Southern Manifesto") delivered during the 84th Congress, March 12, 1956 151
9 Barry Goldwater, *The Conscience of a Conservative*, 1960 (selection) 152
10 George C. Wallace, "Inaugural Address of Governor George Wallace, January 14, 1963, Montgomery, Alabama" 153
11 Barry Goldwater, "Remarks," delivered at the 88th Congress, June 18, 1964 154
12 Barry M. Goldwater, "Acceptance Speech, Republican National Convention, July 16, 1964" 155
13 Ronald Reagan, "A Time for Choosing," address on behalf of Barry M. Goldwater presidential campaign, October 27, 1964 156
14 Phyllis Schlafly, "What's Wrong with 'Equal Rights' for Women?" 1972 158
15 Jude Wanniski, "Taxes, Revenues, and the 'Laffer Curve,'" 1978 159
16 Jerry Falwell, *Listen, America! The Conservative Blueprint for America's Moral Rebirth*, 1980 (selection) 160

17 Ronald Reagan, "Neshoba County Fair Speech," delivered August 3, 1980	161
18 Ronald W. Reagan, "Presidential Inaugural Address, January 20, 1981"	162
19 Ronald W. Reagan, "Address to the Nation on the Economy, October 13, 1982"	163
20 Ronald W. Reagan, "Address to the Nation on Defense and National Security, March 23, 1983"	164
21 Ronald W. Reagan, "Remarks at the Veterans Day Ceremony at the Vietnam Veterans Memorial, November 11, 1988"	165
22 Ronald W. Reagan, "Remarks on East–West Relations at the Brandenburg Gate in West Berlin, June 12, 1987"	166
23 Newt Gingrich, "Contract with America, 1994"	167
24 George W. Bush, "Fact Sheet: Compassionate Conservatism, April 30, 2002"	169
25 George W. Bush, "President Delivers State of the Union Address, January 29, 2002"	170
26 Donald J. Trump, "Inaugural Address, January 20, 2017"	171
Glossary	173
Further Reading	177
References	181
Index	191

Figures

1.1	Franklin D. Roosevelt	12
1.2	J. Howard Pew	20
1.3	Aviator Charles Lindbergh	27
2.1	Robert A. Taft	30
2.2	Strom Thurmond	35
2.3	Joseph R. McCarthy	37
2.4	William F. Buckley	44
3.1	University of Mississippi ("Ole Miss") Riot	54
3.2	Barry Goldwater	57
3.3	George C. Wallace	72
4.1	Phyllis Schlafly	79
4.2	Jesse Helms	80
4.3	Jerry Falwell	90
4.4	David Koch	95
5.1	Ronald W. Reagan	98
5.2	Oliver North	110
5.3	Pat Robertson	112
6.1	Newt Gingrich and Bill Clinton	120
6.2	World Trade Center, September 11, 2001	129
6.3	Donald J. Trump	138

Acknowledgments

I wish to express my appreciation first for the series editor, Gordon Martel, and then for Ted Meyer, who has overseen the manuscript preparation and assisted with obtaining copyright permissions. I am also indebted to the many foundations and archives who have given me permission to use a portion of their materials in the primary documents section. Additionally, Vincent Cannato aided me immensely in locating and obtaining one very important permission.

At Angelo State University, Jason Pierce, my friend and colleague, generously reviewed a draft of this manuscript and provided insightful suggestions and caught errors. Two students in Kevin Garrison's Professional Editing class, Hunter Stabeno and Daniel Biasatti, also reviewed the manuscript and provided helpful observations.

Finally, I appreciate Theresa Heineman's assistance in locating photographs, reading the manuscript, and putting up with my obsessive writing bouts.

Chronology

1932	In the third year of the Great Depression, voters ejected Republican president Herbert Hoover from office.
1933	Democratic president Franklin D. Roosevelt gave Americans a "New Deal."
1934	Conservatives founded the American Liberty League to oppose Roosevelt.
1935	Democrats created Social Security, gave workers the right to organize labor unions, and built an electoral coalition that dominated politics for two generations.
1936	Roosevelt won reelection in a historic landslide that virtually wiped out the Republican Party in Congress.
1937	Organized labor's struggle to unionize the automobile and steel industries aroused middle-class anger. World War II began in Asia.
1938	Conservative southern Democrats helped establish the anti–New Deal House Committee on Un-American Activities. Voter backlash against the Democrats in the midterm elections revitalized the Republican Party. J. Howard Pew of Sun Oil helped found the nation's first conservative domestic policy think tank, the American Enterprise Association.
1939	World War II began in Europe.
1940	Roosevelt ran for an unprecedented third term as president and tried to prepare the United States for entry into World War II. Conservatives formed the anti-interventionist America First Committee.
1941	American First Committee speaker Charles Lindbergh warned that Roosevelt, the British, and Jews were plotting to drag the U.S. into the European war. Republican senator Robert A. Taft of Ohio denounced Roosevelt's efforts to assist the British in fighting Germany. Japan attacked the U.S. Pacific Fleet at Pearl Harbor and Germany subsequently declared war on America.

1942–1945	The U.S., in an alliance with Great Britain, the Soviet Union, and China, defeated the "Axis Powers" of Germany, Japan, and Italy. Roosevelt died in 1945, elevating Vice President Harry Truman to the White House.
1946	The World War II alliance between the U.S. and the Soviet Union collapsed, leading to the "Cold War." Republicans captured the House and the Senate for the first time since the beginning of the Great Depression.
1947	The Truman Doctrine oriented U.S. foreign policy toward the containment of communism in western Europe. Senator Taft sponsored legislation to place limits on union organizing. Ronald Reagan became president of the Screen Actors Guild.
1948	Many southerners, upset with Truman's support for civil rights, broke off from the Democratic Party to champion South Carolina governor Strom Thurmond for president. Democrats who rejected the Truman Doctrine rallied behind the presidential campaign of former vice president Henry Wallace. Former Soviet spy Whittaker Chambers exposed the extent of communist infiltration in the federal government during Roosevelt's presidency. The Chambers' case turned congressman Richard Nixon, a Republican from California, into a national figure.
1949	China fell to communist insurgents. The Soviet Union acquired the atomic bomb.
1950	Republican senator Joseph McCarthy of Wisconsin announced that the State Department was riddled with communist agents. Communist North Korea invaded South Korea. Truman intervened in the Korean War. China's subsequent military intervention in the Korean War led to a stalemate.
1951–1952	Senator McCarthy denounced Truman's former Secretary of State, George Marshall, as an agent of the Soviet Union. War-weary Americans turned against Truman. Taft wrote a controversial book denouncing the interventionist foreign policies of Roosevelt and Truman. Moderate Republicans blocked Taft from receiving the Republican presidential nomination. Republican presidential nominee Dwight Eisenhower won the election.
1953	Eisenhower championed "Modern Republicanism," urging his party to embrace the New Deal's domestic programs, promote civil rights, and contain communist expansion overseas.
1954	Republicans lost Congress in the 1954 midterm elections and remained a minority for a generation. Eisenhower

marginalized Senator McCarthy. The Supreme Court ruled in *Brown v. Board of Education* that racial segregation in public schools was unconstitutional. Clarence Manion founded the first conservative radio (later television) talk show.

1955   William F. Buckley, Jr., founded the *National Review* magazine, which became the intellectual center of the conservative movement. Buckley argued that conservative factions must repudiate isolationists and unite behind opposition to federal power. Nearly all southern Democrats in Congress pledged to resist racial integration.

1956–1959   Conservative disgust with Eisenhower grew because of his support for the 1957 Civil Rights Act. Some conservatives formulated an early version of the "Southern Strategy," arguing that Republicans needed to oppose civil rights and seek to break white southerners off from the Democratic Party.

1960–1963   Nixon's defeat in the 1960 presidential election convinced conservatives that it was time to overthrow Modern Republicans. Conservatives criticized President John F. Kennedy's decision in 1962 to deploy U.S. soldiers to the University of Mississippi to protect a black student from a segregationist mob. The American Enterprise Association renamed itself the American Enterprise Institute in 1962. Kennedy was assassinated in 1963 and Vice President Lyndon Johnson became president.

1964   Lyndon Johnson proclaimed a "War on Poverty." Arizona senator Barry Goldwater denounced the 1964 Civil Rights Act. Conservatives nominated Goldwater for president, leading many liberal Republicans to vote for Johnson or not vote at all. Reagan gained national political exposure for a broadcast endorsing Goldwater. Johnson won a historic landslide victory.

1965–1967   Johnson escalated the Vietnam War and pushed Congress to pass social-welfare legislation, including Medicare and Medicaid. Violent antiwar protest on college campuses increased. Cities from Los Angeles to Detroit experienced rioting. Reagan was elected governor of California in 1966 on a platform of cracking down on campus and urban riots.

1968   Civil rights leader Martin Luther King, Jr., was assassinated and rioting broke out in 100 cities. North Vietnam launched the Tet Offensive, convincing Johnson that the war was not winnable. Former Alabama governor George Wallace ran for president as an independent, vowing to crush campus and urban rioters. Nixon won a close election.

1969–1971	Nixon established the Selective Service lottery in 1969, reducing college students' concern that they might have to fight in Vietnam. Campus antiwar protest largely evaporated. Nixon expanded federal regulatory powers, creating the Environmental Protection Agency (1970).
1972	Antiwar Democrats captured the Democratic Party and repudiated the Truman Doctrine. Nixon's decisive landslide reelection cracked apart the New Deal electoral coalition. Conservative activist Phyllis Schlafly established the Eagle Forum to prevent ratification of the Equal Rights Amendment. Jesse Helms of North Carolina was elected to the Senate as a conservative Republican.
1973	Conservative businessmen, including Joseph Coors, founded a new think tank based in Washington, D.C., the Heritage Foundation. Nixon established the Drug Enforcement Agency (DEA). The Supreme Court in *Roe v. Wade* recognized abortion as a constitutional right.
1974	Nixon resigned in disgrace due to the Watergate scandal. Democrats scored decisive victories in the House and Senate elections, largely by defeating liberal Republicans.
1975	South Vietnam fell to North Vietnamese communists.
1976	Reagan nearly defeated incumbent president Gerald Ford for the Republican presidential nomination. Ford lost to Democratic presidential nominee Jimmy Carter.
1977	Libertarians established the CATO Institute think tank in Washington, D.C.
1978–1979	American unemployment and inflation mounted while plants shut down across the Midwest. The Soviet Union invaded Afghanistan (1979) and Islamic militants seized the U.S. Embassy in Iran in 1979. Jerry Falwell founded the Moral Majority in 1979.
1980	Republican presidential nominee Reagan defeated Carter. Republicans won control of the Senate.
1981–1983	Southern Democrats in the House helped pass Reagan's domestic legislation and supported increased defense expenditures.
1984	Democratic presidential nominee Walter Mondale pledged to raise taxes, cut defense spending, and increase social-welfare spending. Reagan won a landslide reelection.
1985–1987	Advisers inside Reagan's National Security Council defied Congress by negotiating an arms deal with the Iranians and using the profits to aid anti-communist insurgents in Nicaragua. The Iran-Contra scandal damaged Reagan's presidency. Democrats won back control of the Senate

in the 1986 midterm elections and subsequently denied Robert Bork a seat on the Supreme Court. Reagan went to West Berlin in 1987 and challenged the Soviet Union to tear down the Berlin Wall. Rush Limbaugh launched new era of conservative talk radio in 1987.

1988 Conservatives reluctantly supported Vice President George H.W. Bush's presidential candidacy.

1989 Jerry Falwell disbanded the Moral Majority. Pat Robertson founded the Christian Coalition. The Soviet Union withdrew from Afghanistan.

1990–1991 President George H.W. Bush launched a war against Iraq in response to its invasion of Kuwait. Bush angered conservatives by raising taxes and expanding federal regulatory powers. The Soviet Union collapsed in 1991, ending the Cold War.

1992 Conservatives, no longer having a common Soviet enemy, fractured over economic and social policies. Isolationist and anti-interventionist conservatives reasserted themselves. Voters rejected Bush.

1993–1994 Democratic president Bill Clinton unsuccessfully promoted a national health care program. Clinton was more successful in passing the North American Free Trade Agreement (NAFTA) in 1993, but only because of Republican support. Conservatives in the House, led by Newt Gingrich of Georgia, announced a legislative reform agenda which they called "The Contract with America." Republicans won control of the House and the Senate in the 1994 midterm elections. They had not led both branches at the same time in forty years.

1995–1998 Gingrich and Bill Clinton worked together to reform welfare, reduce federal spending, fight crime, and balance the federal budget. Media tycoon Rupert Murdoch established a conservative news network, the Fox News Channel, in 1996. Conservatives, disgusted with Gingrich's partnership with Clinton, forced him out as House Speaker in 1998.

1999 Conservative senator Phil Gramm of Texas eliminated New Deal-era regulations (Glass-Steagall) that kept Wall Street and financial institutions apart. Efforts failed to impeach Clinton for lying under oath that he had not engaged in sexual acts with a White House intern.

2000 George W. Bush, the Republican governor of Texas and son of former president George H.W. Bush, narrowly won the 2000 presidential election. During the campaign, Bush announced that he believed in "compassionate conservatism," which many conservatives regarded as an attack on Reagan's legacy.

2001   The terrorist attack on September 11, 2001, killed more Americans than the Imperial Japanese assault on Pearl Harbor nearly sixty years earlier. Bush pushed Congress to pass the PATRIOT Act and destroy the terrorists' base of operations in Afghanistan.

2002–2003   Bush warned of an "Axis of Evil" and convinced Congress to authorize an invasion of Iraq. In addition to increased spending on the War on Terror, Bush's domestic policy agenda added further to the federal deficit even as he cut federal taxes. Bush set historic records in deficit spending and added more to the national debt than all his predecessors combined.

2004   Increased public skepticism of the war in Iraq, as well as a lack of progress in Afghanistan, resulted in Bush barely winning reelection against an antiwar Democratic presidential candidate.

2005–2007   Hurricane Katrina devastated New Orleans. The Federal Emergency Relief Administration failed to deal adequately with the loss of life from the hurricane. Voters, weary of war and the Katrina disaster, gave Congress to the Democrats in the 2006 midterm elections. In 2007, Wall Street, the housing market, and financial institutions collapsed because of the earlier repeal of federal financial regulations.

2008   Democratic nominee Barack Obama became the first African-American elected president.

2009–2010   Obama, through the Affordable Care Act and "stimulus" spending, added more to the national debt than had George W. Bush. Conservatives organized the Tea Party movement and helped Republicans capture Congress in the 2010 midterm elections.

2011–2016   Unending war, mounting debt, rising crime rates, and stagnant wages fueled voter anger and political alienation, especially among working-class whites and young voters. Republican presidential nominee Donald Trump, a New York real estate developer and reality television series star, won election. Most conservatives disliked Trump as much as their liberal counterparts because of his criticism of the War on Terror and Wall Street.

Who's Who

Anderson, John B. (1922–2017): Republican U.S. representative, Illinois, 1961–1981; identified with the liberal, "Modern Republican," wing of his party; failed to win 1980 Republican presidential nomination; ran as an independent candidate for president in 1980.

Boot, Max (1969–): Neoconservative political journalist; writer for the *Weekly Standard* and the *Wall Street Journal*; advocate of the 2003 invasion of Iraq; affiliated with the neoconservative Council on Foreign Relations and the American Enterprise Institute.

Bork, Robert (1927–2012): Conservative jurist; critical of 1960s civil rights legislation; aroused liberal Democratic and Republican opposition to his nomination to the U.S. Supreme Court by President Ronald Reagan in 1987; the term "borked" came to be used to identify judicial nominees who suffered career-ending Senate attacks.

Bozell, L. Brent, Jr. (1926–1997): Conservative Catholic writer and intellectual; brother-in-law of, and co-author with, William F. Buckley, Jr.; speechwriter for 1964 Republican presidential nominee Barry Goldwater.

Buchanan, Patrick J. (1938–): Socially conservative, economically populist Catholic writer; served as a communications strategist for Richard Nixon and Ronald Reagan; ran unsuccessfully in the 1992 and 1996 Republican presidential primaries; opponent of the Persian Gulf War (1990–1991) and the 2003 invasion of Iraq; ran unsuccessfully as an independent presidential candidate in 2000.

Buckley, William F., Jr. (1925–2008): Conservative Catholic writer; founder in 1955 of the chief political magazine of the Right, the *National Review*; promoter of conservative "fusion," uniting anti-communists, economic conservatives, and social conservatives.

Bush, George Herbert Walker "H.W." (1924–): Republican U.S. President, 1989–1993; denounced Ronald Reagan's tax reforms as "voodoo economics;" repudiated his liberal Republican beliefs to serve as Reagan's vice president, 1981–1989; ran for president as a conservative in 1988; defeated for reelection in 1992.

Bush, George W. (1946–): Republican U.S. President, 2001–2009; the son of President George H.W. Bush; the "War on Terror" crippled his presidency; federal deficits and the national debt rose to historic heights; Democrats regained control of Congress in the 2006 midterm elections; the financial collapse of 2007–2008 made it possible for Democrats to win the White House in 2008.

Chambers, Whittaker (1901–1961): Soviet espionage agent during the 1930s; repudiated his allegiance to the Soviet Union; testified before the House Committee on Un-American Activities against Alger Hiss in 1948; Regnery published his best-selling memoir, *Witness*, in 1952; became an occasional writer for the *National Review*.

Clinton, Hillary Rodham (1947–): Democratic U.S. senator, New York, 2001–2009; "Goldwater Girl" in 1964, became a liberal afterward; married Yale Law School classmate Bill Clinton; First Lady, 1993–2001; served as Secretary of State in the Obama administration; unsuccessful Democratic presidential candidate in 2016.

Clinton, William Jefferson "Bill" (1946–): Democratic U.S. president, 1993–2001; governor of Arkansas prior to the 1992 presidential election; worked with conservative Republicans in Congress to pass reform legislation; balanced the federal budget during his second presidential term; survived a Senate impeachment trial in 1999.

Coors, Joseph (1917–2003): President of Coors Brewing; major donor to the conservative Heritage Foundation; supporter of social conservatives, including Phyllis Schlafly; cheered presidential campaigns of Barry Goldwater and Ronald Reagan.

Dies, Martin, Jr. (1901–1972): Democratic U.S. representative, Texas, 1931–1944, 1953–1958; established the House Committee on Un-American Activities in 1938; pioneer in using congressional hearings to depict supporters of social reform as communists.

Eisenhower, Dwight D. (1890–1969): Republican U.S. president, 1953–1961; Supreme Commander of Allied Forces in the European Theater in World War II; advocate of "Modern Republicanism" – which meant accepting New Deal reforms and urging Republicans to bring African-Americans back to their party.

Ford, Gerald R. (1913–2006): Republican U.S. president, 1974–1976; identified with the Eisenhower wing of the Republican Party; elected to the House from Michigan in 1948 and remained in Congress until 1973, when he became Richard Nixon's vice president; became president following Nixon's resignation in 1974; lost 1976 presidential election.

Frumm, David (1960–): Neoconservative political journalist; speechwriter for President George W. Bush, coined the phrase, "Axis of Evil"; advocate of the 2003 invasion of Iraq; supported Democrat Hillary Rodham Clinton for president in 2016.

Goldwater, Barry (1909–1998): Republican U.S. senator, Arizona, 1952–1986; Phoenix, Arizona, department store heir and anti-New Deal businessman; ally of Senator Joseph McCarthy; conservative foe of Franklin Roosevelt, Harry Truman, and Dwight Eisenhower; unsuccessful Republican presidential nominee in 1964.

Gorbachev, Mikhail (1931–): General secretary of the Soviet Communist Party; oversaw the end of the Soviet Union, 1985–1991; Gorbachev opened discussions with President Ronald Reagan; with the collapse of the Soviet Union, American conservatives no longer had a common enemy to unite them.

Graham, Billy (1918–2018): Southern Baptist minister; anti-communist evangelist; preached to several million Americans at revivals in the 1950s and 1960s; social conservative; friend of Dwight Eisenhower and Richard Nixon; largely withdrew from politics following the Watergate scandal and Nixon's resignation as president.

Gramm, William "Phil" (1942–): Republican U.S. senator, Texas, 1983–2002; elected as a Democrat to the House in 1978; mobilized conservative House Democrats to support President Ronald Reagan's economic reforms; joined the Republican Party and became an advocate of libertarian economics.

Helms, Jesse (1921–2008): Republican U.S. senator, North Carolina, 1973–2003; embodied William F. Buckley, Jr.'s, vision of a "conservative fusionist," combining economic and social conservatism with anti-communism; segregationist southern Democrat in the 1950s and 1960s; moved into the Republican Party in the 1970s.

Hess Karl (1923–1994): Staffer with the conservative American Enterprise Institute in the early 1960s; joined the Barry Goldwater 1964 presidential campaign as a speechwriter.

Hiss, Alger (1904–1996): U.S. diplomat, friend of powerful New Dealers, and Soviet spy; exposed by former Soviet courier Whittaker Chambers before the House Committee on Un-American Activities in 1948; convicted of lying under oath; Hiss's downfall boosted the career of Un-American Activities Committee member Richard Nixon.

Hoover, Herbert (1864–1964): Republican U.S. president, 1929–1933; Great Depression began early in his term and worsened every year; inability to improve economy led to his defeat by Franklin Roosevelt in 1932.

Johnson, Lyndon B. (1908–1973): Democratic U.S. president, 1963–1969; elected to the House from Texas in 1937; elected to Senate in 1948; served as John Kennedy's vice president until Kennedy's assassination in 1963; expanded social-welfare programs, escalated Vietnam War, and pushed for civil rights in the 1960s.

Kennedy, John F. (1917–1963): Democratic U.S. president, 1961–1963; elected to the House and the Senate from Massachusetts; first and only Catholic to be elected president; assassinated in 1963.

King, Martin Luther, Jr. (1929–1968): African-American Baptist minister and civil rights activist; founder of the Southern Christian Leadership Conference in 1957; worked with President Lyndon Johnson to pass civil rights legislation; assassinated in 1968.

Kirkpatrick, Jeane (1926–2006): Georgetown University professor of political science; author of influential essay on American foreign policy that shaped President Ronald Reagan's thinking; one of the original neoconservatives; served as Reagan's ambassador to the United Nations.

Koch, Charles (1935–) and **Koch, David** (1940–): Sons of a Wichita, Kansas, businessman; billionaire funders of libertarian organizations and causes since the 1970s, including the CATO Institute, the American Legislative Exchange Council, and the Tea Party movement; David Koch ran for vice president on the Libertarian Party ticket in 1980.

Kristol, Irving (1920–2009): Member of the founding generation of neoconservatives; edited one of the first neoconservative journals, *The Public Interest*; blamed liberal Democrats for ignoring escalating crime rates; believed that liberals were too willing to negotiate with the Soviet Union.

Kristol, William "Bill" (1952–): Neoconservative journalist and son of Irving Kristol; editor of the *Weekly Standard*; commentator on the Fox News Channel; affiliated with the neoconservative American Enterprise Institute; advocate of the 2003 invasion of Iraq.

Laffer, Arthur (1940–): Economics professor at the University of Chicago; advocate of the free market; rebranded the Mellon Tax Plan of the 1920s as "supply-side economics" in the 1970s; inspired President Ronald Reagan to cut taxes.

Landon, Alfred "Alf" (1887–1987): Governor of Kansas and Republican presidential nominee in 1936; despite funding from the anti-New Deal Liberty League, Landon suffered the worst Electoral College defeat in American history—winning only Maine and Vermont.

Limbaugh, "Rush" Hudson III (1951–): Pioneer of conservative talk radio with over 15 million listeners; an experienced disc jockey and sports announcer, Limbaugh made the transition to political talk radio in the 1980s; by the 1990s he had become a leading voice of the conservative opposition to liberalism.

Lindbergh, Charles (1902–1974): First person to fly by himself with no stops across the Atlantic Ocean in 1927; anti-New Deal businessman; received honors and recognition from Nazi Germany; spokesman for the isolationist America First Committee in 1941; helped to discredit non-interventionist movement in the U.S.

Manion, Clarence E. (1896–1979): Star of *The Manion Forum*, which he established in 1954 and which was the first national conservative radio (and television) talk show; served on board of directors of the America First Committee.

McCarthy, Joseph R. (1908–1957): Republican U.S. senator, Wisconsin, 1946–1957; so notorious for making unsubstantiated charges of communism against supporters of the New Deal and Harry Truman that "McCarthyism" became a term for slanderous red-baiting; inspired many conservatives in the 1950s; censured by the Senate in 1954.

Mellon, Andrew (1855–1937): Leader of Pittsburgh-based Gulf Oil and ALCOA, the Aluminum Corporation of America; Secretary of the Treasury under presidents Warren Harding, Calvin Coolidge, and Herbert Hoover; advocate of the 1920s "Mellon Plan" of federal tax reform which became the basis for "supply-side economics" in the 1980s.

Murdoch, Rupert (1931–): Australian-born billionaire media baron; founder of the conservative Fox News Channel and *Weekly Standard* in the 1990s; owner of the *Wall Street Journal* since 2007.

Nixon, Richard Milhouse (1913–1994): Republican U.S. president, California, 1969–1974; served as President Dwight Eisenhower's vice president, 1953–1961; champion of "Modern Republicanism" in the 1950s; failed to win presidency in 1960; elected president in 1968; expanded federal regulatory powers; resigned in 1974 after covering up his operatives' wiretapping of the Democratic National Committee's offices in Washington's Watergate Hotel.

Norquist, Grover (1956–): Libertarian activist; built Americans for Tax Reform in the mid-1980s; assisted in drafting the conservative 1994 Contract with America; demanded that Republican office holders and candidates sign pledges never to raise taxes or face well-financed primary election challengers; critical of the 2003 invasion of Iraq.

North, Oliver L. (1943–): Deputy director of the National Security Council under President Ronald Reagan; former Marine and dedicated anti-communist; implicated in the 1980s Iran-Contra Scandal; Fox News Channel correspondent.

Obama, Barack H. "Barry" (1961–): Democratic U.S. president, 2009–2017; first African-American president; known for health care initiative and adding trillions of dollars to the national debt; popular enough to score decisive victories in 2008 and 2012, while Democrats lost the House and hundreds of state-level offices across the nation.

O'Neill, Thomas Phillip "Tip," Jr. (1912–1994): Democratic U.S. representative, Massachusetts, 1953–1987; entered politics during the Great Depression as a Franklin Roosevelt Democrat; served as Speaker of the House (1977–1986); unsuccessfully fought Ronald Reagan's legislative agenda.

Perot, Henry "Ross" (1930–): Texas-born billionaire; Republican-turned independent; disgusted with President George H.W. Bush, he ran as an independent presidential candidate in 1992, earning 19 percent of the popular vote and assuring Bill Clinton's victory; critical of Democratic president Bill Clinton and his support for NAFTA; ran again for president as an independent, performing worse than he had in 1992.

Pew, J. Howard (1882–1971): President of the Philadelphia-based Sun (later Sunoco) Oil, 1912–1947; helped establish the anti-New Deal Liberty League in 1934; assisted in funding the conservative think tank the American Enterprise Association (later known as the American Enterprise Institute); provided funding to the conservative magazine *Human Interest*, the religiously traditionalist publication *Christianity Today*; and conservative broadcaster Clarence Manion.

Reagan, Ronald W. (1911–2004): Republican U.S. president, 1981–1989; inspired by Franklin Roosevelt, Reagan served as president of the Screen Actors Guild after World War II; left acting for politics; became a Republican; campaigned for Barry Goldwater in 1964; elected governor of California; with the U.S. facing its worst economic crisis since the 1930s, Reagan followed the leadership example of his liberal idol, Roosevelt.

Regnery, Henry (1912–1996): Conservative anti-New Deal activist and publisher; on the board of directors of the America First Committee; published the conservative political magazine *Human Events* and established Regnery Publishing; leading publisher of conservative books since the 1940s.

Rehnquist, William (1924–2005): Legal and political adviser to Arizona senator Barry Goldwater in the early 1960s; appointed to the Supreme Court in 1971 by President Richard Nixon and made chief justice in 1986 by President Ronald Reagan.

Robertson, Marion Gordon "Pat" (1930–): Conservative religious activist; son of Senator A. Willis Robertson of Virginia; established the Christian Broadcast Network (CBN) in 1960; founded the Christian Coalition in 1989; unsuccessfully sought the Republican presidential nomination in 1988.

Roosevelt, Franklin D. (1882–1945): Democratic U.S. president, 1933–1945; launched the New Deal; changed the federal government's relationship with the American people; built Democrats into a national party which dominated politics through the twentieth century; only president to be elected to four terms in office.

Schlafly, Phyllis (1924–2016): Conservative activist; born Phyllis Stewart; rose to prominence as a promoter of Barry Goldwater in the early 1960s; fought against the ratification of an Equal Rights Amendment to the Constitution in the 1970s; founded the Eagle Forum in 1975 to champion traditional family values.

Sumners, Hatton (1875–1962): Democratic U.S. representative, Texas, 1913–1946; chair of the House Judiciary Committee; critic of the New Deal; opponent of labor unions and civil rights; led fight in 1937 against Franklin Roosevelt's initiative to enlarge the Supreme Court so that he could appoint more liberal justices.

Taft, Robert A. (1889–1953): Republican U.S. senator, Ohio; elected to Senate as part of anti-New Deal backlash in 1938; known as "Mr. Republican" for his opposition to Franklin Roosevelt and Harry Truman; opposed U.S. entry into World War II and Korea; leader of the conservative opposition to the expansion of federal power.

Thurmond, Strom (1902–2003): Democratic governor of South Carolina, 1947–1951; ran for president on segregationist states' rights "Dixiecrat" ticket in 1948; anti-communist, anti-labor union conservative; served in U.S. Senate from 1954 to 2003; became a Republican in 1964; supported Barry Goldwater for president.

Truman, Harry S. (1884–1972): Democratic U.S. president, 1945–1953; elected to the Senate from Missouri in 1934; joined the Democratic national ticket as vice president in 1944; completed Franklin Roosevelt's fourth term; launched the Truman Doctrine, committing the U.S. to containing the expansion of communism.

Trump, Donald J. (1946–): Republican U.S. president, 2017–; New York real estate and Atlantic City casino developer; reality television series star; life-long Democrat turned Republican; critical of NAFTA, the War on Terror, and the escalating national debt; earned scorn of neoconservatives and liberals for his policy ideas and blunt attacks on critics; scored an unexpected victory in the 2016 presidential election.

Viguerie, Richard (1933–): An officer in the Young Americans for Freedom during its early years; compiled database of conservative-leaning voters which led to his idea of "direct mail," soliciting campaign donations from a targeted audience; honed his fundraising skills in the 1968 George Wallace independent presidential run; went on to become a major conservative fundraiser and marketing strategist in the 1970s and 1980s.

Wallace, George (1919–1998): Democratic Alabama governor, 1963–1967; New Deal Democrat; segregationist in the early 1960s; ran for president as an independent in 1968, condemning antiwar protesters and urban crime; paralyzed from an assassination attempt in 1972.

Part I
Analysis and Assessment

Prologue

In politics, as with physics, for every action there is a reaction—and the more powerful the action, the more dramatic is the reaction. The era of the Great Depression and World War II altered the relationship of the American people to the federal government. Before 1932, most Americans, if they looked to government at all for aid, directed attention toward their state capitals and county seats. The federal government had few responsibilities and even fewer employees. All this changed in 1932 with the election of **Franklin D. Roosevelt** as President of the United States.

Roosevelt's domestic policies, collectively known as the **New Deal**, made Washington, D.C., the epicenter of American politics and created a vast array of entitlement programs and regulations. In turn, the beneficiaries of the New Deal became welded into an electoral coalition that dominated national politics for sixty years (if not longer). Southern white Protestants, northern black Protestants, urban Catholics and Jews, and northern industrial workers all became **New Deal Democrats**.

The Republican Party's inability to defeat Roosevelt led to the formation of a conservative faction determined to undo the New Deal and force their party to become a center of political opposition. Over the next decades, conservatives struggled with Republicans who were prepared to make peace with the New Deal, and tried to persuade voters that the expanding, activist federal government was their enemy. Their goal, which proved elusive until the 1970s, was to break apart the New Deal electoral coalition and build a Republican majority with Democratic defectors.

Conservatives found their presidential champion in 1964 with Arizona senator **Barry Goldwater**—until he went down in humiliating defeat. They then turned to former Hollywood actor and California governor Ronald Reagan.

One of the fundamental problems confronting conservatives, whether in the 1940s or since the 1990s, has been their factional divisions. There are varieties of conservatism that are in conflict. **Social conservatives**, also known as moral traditionalists and the Religious Right, emphasize domestic moral issues: crime, narcotics use, and sexual behavior, to list a few. Among this conservative faction, foreign and economic policy issues can be less important than social issues. Further complicating matters, social conservatives are not necessarily always Republican voters. Their ranks have included southern white Democrats and northern working-class white Catholics.

Economic conservatives, especially **libertarians**, denounce the federal government's role in promoting labor unions, regulating corporate activities, and raising taxes. Libertarians are often in conflict with social conservatives since they do not believe the federal government should regulate the boardroom or the bedroom.

On foreign policy issues, there are isolationist, or anti-interventionist, conservatives, as well as militarily interventionist conservatives. Some anti-interventionist conservatives, along with libertarians, oppose the expansion of federal power which came with the increased emphasis on national security during and after World War II.

In the mid-1950s, conservative journalist and intellectual **William F. Buckley, Jr.**, formulated a concept to meld conservatism's conflicting factions into one potentially powerful movement. He called his idea "**conservative fusionism**." All conservative factions, Buckley argued, shared a suspicion of federal power. They also shared a distaste for international communism. Buckley proposed focusing on conservatives' common ground—though the price would be expelling, or diminishing, isolationists. Conservative fusionism proved successful, until the end of the **Cold War** in the early 1990s once again exposed all the fractures within the conservative faction.

This text will focus on conservative politics from 1932 to 2016. There are six narrative chapters, discussing America's political history from the 1930s through the 2016 presidential election. We live in the world Franklin Roosevelt made, which is why he will appear in all six chapters. In death, Roosevelt looms as large as he did in life. There is another figure who will also appear in all six chapters: **Ronald Reagan**. Roosevelt inspired Reagan's political career. Although Reagan was the most conservative president elected since World War II, he saw himself as carrying on the legacy of Roosevelt, not erasing it. In death, Reagan has become for conservatives what Roosevelt was for liberals: the irreplaceable, sanctified leader.

While many analyses of American conservatism focus on ideas and intellectuals, I look at politicians and electoral coalitions. Most Americans, at all points in our history, have seldom followed political debates—and when they did it was often not very deeply. For most Americans, when they say that they are engaged with politics what they mean is that they vote—for the president and, less often, for members of Congress.

Politicians, whether partisans of Roosevelt or Reagan, must appeal to voters on a basic level. On the campaign trail that translates into discussing how domestic and foreign policy affects voters' lives. Politicians who quote great thinkers, whether those thinkers are liberal or conservative, have one thing in common: they seldom get elected and if they do, they are not in office long.

In addition to the narrative chapters, a glossary of terms, a who's who section to identify the political players, recommendations for further reading, and a list of references, there is a primary documents section. The works I have chosen are mainly what conservative politicians stated for the public record. There are some documents from conservative activists who typically did not hold political office, but who wanted to influence the thinking of elected officials. Sometimes politicians followed their advice; often they did not. The most successful conservative politicians knew when to listen to their policy experts and when not to listen.

Conservative activists' record of electoral success is at best a mixture of failure and some achievement. If you want absolute political success, look to dictatorships. In a dictatorship, policies are adopted and the society functions smoothly—until the violent end. Democracies, in contrast, plod along, citizens argue bitterly over compromises and, ultimately, achieve little—except for irritating nearly everyone at home and abroad.

If the history of American conservatism since the 1930s tells us anything, it is that shrewd politicians such as Reagan maintained their faith in the democratic process despite fierce legislative and news media opposition. Moreover, as the truism goes, Reagan, like Roosevelt, never allowed "the perfect to be the enemy of the good."

1 The New Deal and Conservative Reaction, 1933–1945

Conservative Economic and Social Policies before the Great Depression

To corporation executives, post-World War I America was an economic paradise. Secretary of the Treasury **Andrew Mellon**, whose Pittsburgh-based empire included Gulf Oil, championed a new federal taxation policy. The 1923 "**Mellon Plan**" reduced tax rates at the top income brackets from 73 percent to 25 percent. Mellon, and the three successive Republican presidents he served—Warren Harding, Calvin Coolidge, and **Herbert Hoover**—believed that the wealthy, freed from their heavy tax burden, would increase their investments. That, in turn, would stimulate production and economic growth. Ultimately, the benefits of a super-charged economy would trickle down to all Americans in the form of less expensive consumer goods and more jobs. Later conservatives rebranded the Mellon Plan as "**supply-side economics**" and hailed it as a model of superior tax policy.

Industrialists went on a capital-intensive spending spree, building 22,800 factories between 1925 and 1929. As Mellon predicted, expanded production lowered per-unit costs to consumers. Henry Ford's Model T, for instance, which had cost $600 in 1912, could be purchased for $290 by the mid-1920s. Meanwhile, the Pittsburgh District produced more steel than nearly all of America's overseas competitors combined, while Texas accounted for 20 percent of the world's oil production. Unemployment averaged 4 percent annually.

Expenditures on consumer goods increased 25 percent between 1923 and 1929. The number of American automobiles went from 6.7 million in 1919 to 23 million in 1929. Radio sales, which amounted to $60 million in 1922, ballooned to $842 million by 1929. The newly-born film industry not only became one of the nation's most lucrative businesses, but Hollywood achieved global cultural influence. Ninety-five percent of the films shown in the United Kingdom were Hollywood productions.

On the social front, the 1920s were years of victory for morally conservative, rural Protestants. Since the second half of the nineteenth century, organizations such as the Women's Christian Temperance Union had crusaded against "demon rum." Prohibitionists argued that eliminating alcohol would eradicate urban crime and poverty, since immoral behavior, not low wages, bred America's social ills. With America's entry into World War I in 1917, prohibitionists linked their cause to anti-German patriotism. (Most of America's brewers had ethnic German backgrounds.) Their tactics resulted in three-quarters of the states ratifying the Eighteenth Amendment which embedded **Prohibition** in the Constitution.

As did alcohol, unrestricted Catholic and Jewish immigration from southern and eastern Europe horrified many Protestants. Between 1890 and 1914, the U.S. experienced the largest immigration wave in its history. Forty million immigrants entered America, of which half remained and the other half returned to Europe.

Socially conservative Protestants blamed low-paid immigrants for replacing native-born Protestants in the industrial workforce and identified them with such ills as drunkenness and prostitution. President Theodore Roosevelt fretted that America was committing "racial suicide." Catholics and Jews, whose mental inferiority was an article of faith in small-town America, were reproducing at a higher rate than Protestants. Inevitably, immigration foes argued, southern and eastern Europeans would pollute America's racial pool.

The fear of racial pollution did not penetrate the corporate boardroom. Industrialists sent recruiters to impoverished villages in the Austro-Hungarian and Russian empires. It took $15 to sail across the Atlantic. (Even adjusted for inflation, a modern-day trans-Atlantic trip would be more expensive.) Most companies fronted the cost of the tickets and then deducted the amount from immigrants' wages. Half the immigrants were transients who sought to earn enough money to return home and buy land. They had no intention of acquiring citizenship, voting, or joining labor unions. Immigrant steel workers labored seventy-two hours a week, inhaling sulfur and losing their hearing. In the Pennsylvania coal mines, immigrant Italians made a pithy observation about safety conditions: "Wops are cheaper than props."

Corporate leaders' attitudes toward immigration shifted with the outbreak of World War I in 1914. With their labor pool trapped in a war zone, executives turned to a domestic source for inexpensive workers: destitute African-Americans from the South. Not only would they work cheaply, they were Protestant and, once registered to vote, supported Republicans—the heirs of the "Party of Lincoln."

What finally convinced automakers and steel mill operators to embrace immigration restriction was the 1919 strike wave. Twenty-two percent of the U.S. labor force, the highest proportion in American history, went on strike. To the industrialists' shock, a quarter of a million immigrant steel workers in the Pittsburgh District joined the uprising. War-time inflation had devoured their wages while workplace speed ups had led to mounting injuries. Once immigrants walked away from their jobs, they lost their usefulness.

The immigration restriction laws of 1921 and 1924 established national origins quotas. Congressional Republicans drew upon the U.S. Census for data on how many people of each ethnic group resided in the nation. The

1921 law established a 3 percent admissions quota for each group, but relied upon the 1910, rather than the 1920, Census. Since there was an upsurge of immigration between 1910 and 1914, the 1920 Census would have registered a higher number of Croatians, Slovaks, and so on, than would have been true of the 1910 Census. The 1924 law lowered the admissions quota to 2 percent and drew upon the 1890 Census, which predated the immigration wave from southern and eastern Europe. Even though business considerations motivated immigration restriction, social conservatives nonetheless claimed that they had achieved the victory.

The Limits of Conservative Economic and Social Policies before the Great Depression

Social and economic conservatives' triumph was less than total. Prohibition did not reduce urban crime. Before Prohibition, New York City had 8,000 saloons. After Prohibition, the number of illegal saloons, or "speakeasies," in New York rose to 32,000. Worse, the illegal distribution and production of alcohol led to the formation of criminal syndicates which operated on a national scale. Fiscal conservatives who advocated limited federal government in the 1920s had no choice but to enlarge the national law enforcement bureaucracy to deal with organized crime.

As for conservative economic policy, fixating on the supply side of the production equation, and allowing the free market to operate with little federal oversight, had a downside. The annual subsistence-level income for a family of four in the 1920s was $2,000. Subsistence meant sufficient income to pay for rent, food, and clothing. It did not mean income to purchase homes, let alone save for retirement. Sixty percent of Americans (70 million) lived at or below the level of subsistence. Forty-two percent of families earned less than $1,000 a year. Conditions in the South were the worst in the nation, with 5.5 million white and 3 million black landless tenant farmers and sharecroppers making less than $100 annually.

Since the Mellon Plan did not address the demand side of the economic equation, businesses sought to boost consumer spending by providing credit. Three-quarters of the automobiles purchased in the 1920s were on an "installment" plan, as customers paid a little down and then made small payments with interest attached. Americans had never taken on so much debt—and never had so little prospect of getting out of debt.

The reality of over-production could be seen most clearly in construction. In 1925, residential construction stood at 124 percent of capacity, while industrial construction was at 120 percent of capacity. Put differently, this meant that 24 percent of the houses built and 20 percent of the new plants erected stood unsold and empty. Rather than aligning inventory with demand, by 1928 residential construction was at 128 percent of capacity and industrial construction was at 142 percent of capacity. Conservative economic policy made it possible to build an enormous amount of housing and commercial structures, but did not put sufficient income in peoples' pockets to acquire them.

There was also the problem of stock market speculation. The Mellon Plan freed up millions of dollars which would have otherwise gone into the Federal Treasury. While many businessmen invested in plants and created jobs, others pursued quick profits. Brokers took out large short-term loans from banks with little collateral and then bought stocks. They were betting that the price of the stock would rise quickly—an outcome made more likely as other brokers flocked to what they thought was a hot investment. Speculators would then sell off, pay their loans with interest, and rejoice in their profits.

The allure of easy money led banks to participate directly in stock speculation, with many branching off into real estate and oil-drilling speculation. Thanks to speculation, shares of DuPont rose from $310 in October 1928 to $525 in December 1928, while Wright Aeronautic went from $69 a share to $289 a share in the same three-month period. None of that increase in stock price represented an actual increase in value.

The Fall of the Conservative Order, 1929–1932

Stock speculation and over-production culminated in Wall Street's crash in October 1929. While America had experienced "boom and bust" economic cycles since the early years of industrialization, the Great Depression proved to be the worst. The crash was of such magnitude that it wounded democracy and capitalism in the U.S. and around the world. Germany embraced National Socialism and embarked on the road to genocide, while Japan opted for the military conquest of Asia. Even if neither pre-Depression Germany nor Japan had been models of capitalist democracy, both had representative government of a kind.

In the U.S., unemployment doubled between 1930 and 1931, and then nearly doubled again between 1931 and 1932. Fifteen million Americans, 25 percent of the nation's workforce, was unemployed. If the millions working part-time for reduced hours and wages were included in the labor data, the unemployment rate would have been 40 percent. Bank failures rose from 659 in 1929 to 2,294 in 1931. Industrial production, which stood at 80 percent of capacity in 1930, fell to 55 percent of capacity by 1932.

The industrial sector took devastating hits. Between 1929 and 1932, American steel production fell 59 percent. U.S. Steel, which claimed 60 percent of the domestic market, operated at 12 percent of capacity by 1932. A year earlier, U.S. Steel had cut wages 10 percent. Within ten days other industries followed U.S. Steel's example, reducing the pay of 2 million workers. Rather than lay off workers, U.S. Steel began converting full-time positions into part-time jobs. By 1933, 100 percent of the U.S. Steel workforce was employed part-time.

Coal operators had laid off 300,000 miners by 1932. Of the 300,000 miners remaining employed, they worked 146 days out of the year, earning

$2.50 a day. Meanwhile, General Electric and Westinghouse cut their labor force in half between 1929 and 1933. In New York City, the number of residents seeking public assistance for food and rent rose from 500,000 in 1931 to 1.25 million in 1933—18 percent of the population. Detroit, home of the "Big Three" automakers, registered an unemployment rate of 50 percent by 1932, twice the national average. The "Motor City" did not have the resources to feed and shelter so many destitute people. Nationally, factory closings, wage cuts, and conversion of full-time jobs to part-time resulted in blue-collar income falling 40 percent between 1929 and 1932.

The collapse of American industry sent the agricultural sector into a downward economic spiral. In Cimarron County, Oklahoma, for instance, the 1931 wheat harvest brought in a $1 million. Two years later, virtually the same amount of wheat in Cimarron County generated $7,000. The 1929 market value of Texas and Oklahoma cotton had been $1.5 billion. In 1930, the value of Texas and Oklahoma cotton was $826 million—a 55 percent reduction. As financially distressed Americans in the urban-industrial centers bought less food and clothing, the agricultural sector lost money with every harvest. Often farmers compensated by increasing their production, which only drove prices lower. Farm income fell 50 percent in the four years following the stock market crash.

President Hoover, whose 1928 electoral victory had been the product of a booming economy and the defection of several southern Democratic states that refused to vote for the Catholic nominee of their party, proved to be inept. Initially, Hoover denied that there was an economic crisis. Then he pushed for the creation of the Reconstruction Finance Corporation (RFC). The RFC loaned federal money to banks so they could then loan to businesses and, hopefully, stimulate economic expansion. Hoover also persuaded the Republican Congress to cut corporate and individual taxes by 1 percent. Middle-class Americans with a $4,000 income saw their federal taxes cut from $5.63 a year to $1.88. (In today's currency, that represented a tax reduction of $62.03.)

Once it became obvious that Hoover's tax cuts had failed to stimulate economic expansion and consumer spending, other Republicans took the lead. Republican representative Hamilton Fish of New York held House hearings in 1931 at which he blamed "red [communist] immigrant troublemakers" for creating public unrest. At the state level, Republican legislators urged voters to focus on America's real problems: alcohol, gambling, pornography, and narcotics.

Republican Party leaders could not deny Hoover's re-nomination in 1932 without admitting their failure. At the 1932 Republican National Convention, Hoover acknowledged that there were economic challenges facing the nation [Document 1: p. 143]. He pledged more tax cuts and promised to reduce the size and cost of the federal government. Hoover also devoted much time to defending Prohibition against Democratic repeal efforts.

The Rise of Franklin Roosevelt

The 1932 presidential election represented a decisive rejection of Hoover—not an endorsement of Democratic nominee Franklin Roosevelt. Even sympathetic commentators regarded Roosevelt as an intellectual lightweight. Living on inherited wealth, Roosevelt had glided through Harvard with "Gentlemen's C's" and briefly practiced as an attorney following graduation from Columbia Law School.

He encouraged people to think he was closely related to Theodore Roosevelt, a perception which helped him get elected to the New York legislature. The outgoing young man married Theodore Roosevelt's shy niece, Eleanor Roosevelt. When Woodrow Wilson won the presidency in 1912 after the Republican Party split into irreconcilable Theodore Roosevelt and William Howard Taft factions, Franklin Roosevelt became Assistant Secretary of the Navy. Wilson thought it would be funny to have a Roosevelt in his administration. Roosevelt played upon his name again for political advancement in 1920, receiving the Democratic Party's nomination for vice president.

In 1921, Franklin Roosevelt's life changed. Roosevelt contracted polio and lost the use of his legs. Rather than surrendering to his illness, Roosevelt rallied. Few outside his immediate circle knew the extent of his paralysis. His personality evolved. Far from losing his finely tuned social skills, Roosevelt's self-confidence deepened, as did his perspective on life's challenges. A friend once asked him how he could be so calm when faced with so many storms. Roosevelt replied that if you spent seven years of your life trying to wiggle your toes—and failing—you learned a lot about patience.

His political ambition had not diminished. Roosevelt did not want to be pitied, and, understanding that at no time in world history had a leader ever been chosen from among the ranks of the paralyzed, he kept the severity of his physical condition hidden. Only once during his presidency did Roosevelt let down his guard. While visiting a hospital in the European Theater of combat, Roosevelt learned of a pilot who, to escape from a crashed and burning plane, had cut off his legs. Roosevelt rolled his wheelchair over to the airman, revealed the extent of his disability, and told him that he could do anything with enough determination.

Elected governor of New York in 1928, and winning a landslide reelection in 1930, Roosevelt promised a "New Deal" for Americans during the 1932 presidential election. Few people knew what Roosevelt meant by "New Deal," but it was a catchy phrase and soon received its popular rendition: "The New Deal." Roosevelt exuded confidence at his 1933 inauguration. His condemnation of conservative economic and political leadership was ringing:

> True they have tried, but their efforts have been cast in the pattern of an outworn tradition ... Stripped of the lure of profit by which to

Figure 1.1 Franklin Delano Roosevelt (1882–1945), President of the United States, 1933–1945
Source: Courtesy of the Library of Congress Prints and Photographs Division

induce our people to follow their false leadership, they have resorted to exhortations, pleading tearfully for restored confidence. They know only the rules of a generation of self-seekers. They have no vision, and when there is no vision the people perish.

Afterward, as family and friends sipped cocktails and celebrated the ratification of the Twenty-First Amendment repealing Prohibition, a cousin warned Roosevelt that if he failed he would not be reelected in 1936. Roosevelt replied that she did not fully appreciate the situation. If he failed, there would be *no United States in 1936.*

The New Deal

As the nation's banking system collapsed in the spring of 1933, leading millions of Americans to lose their meager savings, Roosevelt knew that national finance had to be stabilized. Between 1933 and 1934, the White

House and the Democratic Congress undertook three major initiatives. The federal government, through the newly established Securities and Exchange Commission (SEC), policed Wall Street. Meanwhile, the Banking Act of 1933, also referred to as the Glass-Steagall Act, prohibited financial institutions from speculating on Wall Street. To protect citizens from the actions of speculating bankers, the U.S. government created the Federal Deposit Insurance Corporation (FDIC). Now, if a bank failed, smaller depositors had federal insurance and could feel secure in keeping their savings in some place other than a mattress. Although Roosevelt expressed concern that some bankers might be tempted to make bad loans knowing that taxpayers would bail out depositors, advisers reassured him that vigorous federal oversight would prevent such abuses.

Assisting the legion of unemployed required immediate attention. Roosevelt regarded welfare, or relief, as a "narcotic" that undermined citizens' self-respect—a stance that Hoover could have endorsed. Americans needed to work for their federal checks, preferably contributing to their communities, which, in turn, would instill in them a sense of pride.

Initiatives such as the Federal Emergency Relief Administration (FERA, 1933–1935), the Civil Works Administration (CWA, 1933–1934), the Works Progress Administration (WPA, 1933–1943), and the National Youth Administration (NYA, 1935–1939) addressed unemployment on an unprecedented scale. FERA funded 240,000 projects, including the construction of 200,000 miles of roads. The CWA built or improved 500,000 miles of roads, while the WPA built or renovated 2,500 hospitals and 13,000 playgrounds. Concerned that youths were dropping out of school and flooding a depressed labor market, the NYA provided jobs to 600,000 college students and 1.5 million high school students so that they would continue their education.

The 1935 Social Security Act mimicked some of the social-welfare features that many European governments had already adopted. Focusing on industrial workers—farm laborers and small business owners were excluded from coverage—Social Security provided pensions and unemployment insurance. Not wanting the public to regard Social Security as welfare, workers and employers would be required to pay into the system to fund pensions and short-term compensation for those thrown out of work through no fault of their own. Since the federal government set the retirement age at sixty-five, and the average life expectancy was sixty-two, there was little danger that the Social Security fund would become insolvent.

Democratic senator Robert Wagner of New York, the "father" of Social Security, pushed Roosevelt to support labor legislation which changed the relationship between the federal government and employers. The 1935 Wagner Act created the National Labor Relations Board (NLRB), empowering the federal government to mediate disputes between workers and management. Wagner guaranteed "collective bargaining rights," meaning that workers had the right to organize unions. The NLRB, with its representatives appointed by the president, would ensure that management did not interfere when workers voted on whether to have a union serve as their bargaining agent. Three years later, Wagner's Fair Labor Standards Act defined a work week as consisting of forty hours of labor, with any hours beyond that receiving overtime pay. The 1938 law also created a national minimum wage—25 cents an hour.

Roosevelt knew that he also had to salvage America's agricultural sector. Farmers would not produce until their markets received federal assistance. In 1933, the Democratic Congress approved the Agricultural Adjustment Act (AAA), which gave subsidies to farmers. The intention was to provide federal price support and to encourage farmers to take excess crop land out of production.

By 1936, when the Supreme Court declared that the AAA was an unconstitutional extension of federal power over the states, farmers had received $1.5 billion in subsidies (nearly $25 billion in today's currency). Subsidies continued under different programs. Meanwhile, workers, who were paying more for their food and clothing due to reduced agricultural production and higher crop prices still had money in their pockets because of other New Deal programs.

American farmers and ranchers, particularly in the South and West, benefited from other federal programs—most especially, access to affordable electrical power. Ninety percent of farms in 1936 had no electricity because power companies saw little profit in stringing lines through sparsely populated regions. The lack of electricity meant that dairy farmers could not refrigerate stored milk, while other farmers could not pump water to irrigate their fields. The Rural Electrification Administration (REA) spent $410 million ($6.7 billion in today's currency), and reduced the number of rural Americans without electrical power by more than half. For its part, the federally-supported Tennessee Valley Authority (TVA) provided flood control and electrical power to hundreds of thousands across several rural states.

Creating New Deal Democrats: The Southern Front

Democrats had been largely irrelevant to national politics since the 1896 presidential election when southern and western Protestants alienated eastern Irish and German Catholics. Calls for Prohibition, Catholic immigration restriction, and currency inflation which would have helped farmers pay off their debts with worthless money while destroying the value of urban workers' paychecks did not go over well in the Industrial Heartland. Giving Nebraska congressman William Jennings Bryan, the standard bearer of rural America's cultural and economic grievances, the presidential nomination three times (1896, 1900, 1908) proved the adage that the definition of insanity was doing the same thing over and over and expecting a different result.

Republican divisions in 1912 had given Democrats an opening to win Congress and the White House. Although Wilson had been president of Princeton and governor of New Jersey, his formative years had been spent in the post-Civil War South where racial antagonism flourished like kudzu. Wilson wished to increase the regulatory power of the federal government with the goal of improving working conditions for most Americans. Despite such liberal impulses, however, he never transcended his origins. As president, Wilson segregated federal facilities and hosted a viewing of a 1915 Hollywood extravaganza, *The Birth of a Nation*. Wilson praised the film's sympathetic depiction of the Ku Klux Klan as "writing history with lightning."

Convinced that only America's moral superiority could save the world, Wilson led the U.S. into war with Germany in 1917. He pledged to make "the world safe for democracy," at a cost of 116,000 American lives. The British and French made it clear to the U.S. that they wished to humiliate Germany and strip it of as much of its wealth and land as possible. They had no interest in promoting democracy in central Europe, let alone in their overseas colonies. Far from making the world safe for democracy, the European war made possible the subsequent political careers of Benito Mussolini, Adolf Hitler, and Joseph Stalin.

Disgusted voters repudiated Wilson's heirs in the 1920 election. Foreign policy, however, was not the only Democratic weakness. Cultural divisions continued to plague Democrats. By 1924, a second Ku Klux Klan, inspired by *The Birth of a Nation*, had sprung up in Texas, as well as the Midwest, Pennsylvania, and New York. While the second Klan, like its Reconstruction predecessor, continued its antagonism toward African-Americans, there were new enemies for rural Protestants to defeat: adulterers, alcoholics, Catholics, and Jews.

The second Klan had more adherents in the North than in the South, and, therefore, became more of a player in national Democratic politics than had been true of the first Klan. At the 1924 Democratic National Convention, the party deadlocked between its urban Catholic and rural Protestant factions. William Jennings Bryan, wanting his brother to be nominated for vice president on the Klan-backed ticket, snarled at Catholics, "You are not the future of our country." It took 103 ballots for the Democrats to select a sacrificial compromise candidate. Although the second Klan soon collapsed because of a sex scandal, most Protestant Democrats would not support their party's Catholic nominee, Al Smith, in 1928.

Southern Democrats understood that the Great Depression had brought their party to national power. Democrats gained control of the House after the 1930 midterm elections and captured the Senate two years later. Southern Democrats benefited enormously. Most obviously, southerners had successfully maneuvered to nominate Speaker of the House John Garner of Texas for vice president. Garner was a seasoned insider who viewed the New Deal as an opportunity to provide Dixie with the economic reconstruction it not had received after the Civil War. Southern Democrats counted on Garner to influence Roosevelt.

There was another reason southern Democrats were in such good spirits. In the years preceding World War I, southern Democrats had adopted poll taxes, all-white party primaries, and other means to eliminate 90 percent of the black electorate and 30 percent of the white electorate. (Most of the disenfranchised whites were impoverished Pentecostals who, to Southern Baptists, had a bad habit of worshipping with blacks and decrying greedy businessmen.) As voter turnout in the South plummeted, Democrats were reelected term after term with little opposition. In Congress, committee chairs directed what legislation would be written or voted upon. Seniority determined who became chairs. As the most senior Democrats in Congress, southerners chaired nearly every committee in the 1930s, even though they accounted for just one-third of the party's ranks.

Southern Democrats expected federal agricultural subsidies, flood control projects, electrification, and military bases. Roosevelt, however, understood that southern Democrats demanded more than funding in exchange for their allegiance. The federal government was not to attack racial segregation and voter disenfranchisement, and most certainly not support labor unions in the South. If Yankees in Chicago wanted to sit at the same lunch counter with African-Americans, or join a union, that was fine, so long as Roosevelt did not encourage such outrages in Birmingham.

Creating New Deal Democrats: The Northern Front

The million southern blacks who had migrated North during World War I were loyal Republicans through the 1932 election. Their turnout in Philadelphia had been strong enough to give Pennsylvania's electoral votes to Hoover. Once it became clear that federal jobs programs in the North would not discriminate in hiring, larger numbers of northern blacks concluded that Roosevelt deserved their support. Even if Roosevelt would not champion civil rights in the South, northern African-Americans needed jobs and the "Party of Lincoln" had none to offer. The year 1932 marked the last time a Republican presidential candidate carried the black vote.

Paradoxically, immigration restriction had unintended consequences for Republicans. Prior to World War I, immigrants had flooded into a handful of industrial states: Illinois, Michigan, New York, Ohio, and Pennsylvania. Immigrants swelled the population of those states, giving them more seats in the House of Representatives and thus more Electoral College votes to select the president. The constant turnover of transient immigrants had lessened the likelihood that southern and eastern European Catholics and Jews would assimilate. Republicans had written off the one-party Democratic South because they held the industrial North and appealed to the Protestant West. Their national political domination, however, had depended upon immigrant communities *not* learning English and *not* voting. Republicans had no interest in appealing to immigrants and their American-born children.

Republicans paid a steep price for their failure to appeal to Catholics and Jews. Between 1920 and 1936, the size of the American electorate increased 40 percent. Nearly all that electoral expansion was due to the American-born children of Catholic and Jewish immigrants. Most had no familiarity with politics, content to find a job at a steel mill or automobile plant, get married, and have children. The Great Depression, however, made their basic goals nearly impossible. Social and economic conservatives offered them nothing beside lectures on the evils of alcohol and exhortations to have patience, as the economy would improve without federal intervention. Roosevelt gave them action—and the reassurance that they were not to blame for their hardship. Northern Catholics and Jews responded by voting Democratic.

The northern Catholic, Jewish, and black vote was clustered in a dozen urban centers. For instance, 40 percent of all voters in Illinois in the 1930s lived in Cook County (Chicago), while 51 percent of New York voters resided in New York City. If Roosevelt could carry a dozen northern urban counties by a margin of 60 percent or higher, he would have been on his way to winning 220 electoral votes. (Picking up votes in smaller industrial cities often secured the remaining balance needed.) Adding those electoral votes to the South's 170 meant that a Democratic presidential candidate could expect to receive 390 electoral votes, with only 266 needed to win the White House.

Northern cities also became the launchpads for an energized union movement. In the mid-1930s, the Congress of Industrial Organizations (CIO) enlisted workers in the auto, electrical, mining, petroleum, and steel industries. Where union membership had stood at a low of 3 million in 1930, it grew to 9 million by 1940. Nearly all the CIO's loyalists were northern blacks, Catholics, and Jews who lived in urban counties. Seventy percent of CIO members in Michigan in the 1930s, for instance, lived in Wayne County (Detroit). Grateful for the 1935 Wagner Act, the CIO devoted its resources to championing Roosevelt. In some states, the CIO's largest affiliate unions became the state Democratic Party in all but name—notably the Steel Workers Organizing Committee (later the United Steel Workers of America) in Pennsylvania and the United Automobile Workers (UAW) in Michigan.

Beyond the economic crisis and the federal response, there were two other factors contributing to Democratic success. The first factor was the reform wing of the Catholic Church. As early as 1891, Pope Leo XIII had issued an encyclical, or papal letter, *Rerum Novarum* (*On the Condition of Labor*). Leo XIII recognized that Catholics might have to join unions to assure a decent standard of living. In 1931, Pope Pius XI followed up with another encyclical, *Quadragesimo anno* (*After Forty Years: Reconstructing the Social Order*). Pius XI championed a role for government and workers in regulating capitalism. American Catholic bishops in northern cities such as Buffalo, Chicago, Milwaukee, and

Pittsburgh embraced Leo XIII and Pius XI's social encyclicals. Priests joined union picket lines and provided meeting facilities. Church approval of unions meant much to the working-class laity.

The New Deal advanced in the face of a hostile news media. Republicans controlled 80 percent of the press. Newspaper publisher William Randolph Hearst was not atypical in 1936 when he accused Democrats of belonging to the "imported, autocratic, Asiatic socialist party of Karl Marx and Franklin Delano Roosevelt." *Chicago Tribune* publisher Robert McCormick argued that the New Deal cast the "shadow of Hitler on the government's walls" and in 1934 delivered an NBC radio broadcast warning of "the rising red tide in America."

Given press opposition, Roosevelt often bypassed the mainstream media to take advantage of the relatively new medium of radio. Roosevelt spoke to the American people in a warm, confident tone of voice. He never talked down to Americans and neither did he attempt to change his upper-class accent to sound like his lower-income supporters. While radio, as opposed to film, allowed Roosevelt to obscure the extent of his disability, he was obviously comfortable with who he was and felt no need to reinvent himself after every Gallup public opinion poll release.

Some Americans found Roosevelt reassuring; others considered him inspirational. In Dixon, Illinois, the Reagan family struggled during the early years of the Great Depression. Jack Reagan, an Irish Catholic, had married Nelle Wilson, a Christian Disciple. The tensions in such an interfaith marriage in the early twentieth century would have been bad enough, but were worsened by Jack Reagan's alcoholism. (Nelle Reagan was a local Prohibition activist, for understandable reasons.) His son, Ronald, once found his father passed out in a snow drift and had to drag him inside the house before he froze to death.

Ronald Reagan knew that his frequently unemployed father had a disease, not a sinful soul. Fortunately for the family, Jack Reagan found dignity and purpose in the WPA. Young Reagan was grateful to Roosevelt and hung on the president's every word—voting for him all four times. (Reagan's admiration for Roosevelt deepened after his death and the public revelation of his paralysis.) Roosevelt's can-do spirit inspired Reagan to seek a career first in radio broadcasting and then in Hollywood as an actor. Reagan credited Roosevelt with awakening in him a passion for politics, which led him to assume a leadership role in a union, the Screen Actors Guild (SAG). Without Roosevelt and the New Deal, it was improbable that the son of an alcoholic, Irish Catholic shoe salesman would have later become president of the United States.

Conservative Reaction: The Business Response

Fiscal conservatives reacted angrily as federal spending rose from $21 billion in 1930 to $40 billion—or 18 percent of America's gross national product

(GNP). To pay for New Deal programs, Democrats passed the Revenue Act of 1935—raising taxes and thus undoing the Mellon Plan. New Dealers also embraced deficit spending. In 1930, the federal government had a budget surplus of $7.7 billion. By 1940, the federal government's budget was $36 billion in the red. Most Americans had little problem with higher taxes and deficit spending. This was not surprising. Only 3 percent of citizens (4 million) in the 1930s were sufficiently well-off to be required to pay federal income taxes. Taking money from the few—and borrowing the rest—to benefit the many had little political downside. Such calculations would only begin changing when, due to the economic stimulus of World War II, the number of eligible income taxpayers rose to 32 percent of the population (43 million).

To conservatives' dismay, Myron Taylor of U.S. Steel and Gerard Swope of General Electric had no problem with rising corporation taxes and the imposition of higher labor costs due to unionization. Taylor and Swope figured that since their businesses took up such a large share of their respective markets, they could pass along their higher operating costs to the consumers by small per-unit price increases. Rival firms, with lower outputs, could also pass along higher costs to consumers but the per-unit increases would be greater. In that event, customers would likely abandon them in favor of less expensive suppliers. If smaller firms kept price increases low, they would not earn much profit—and possibly would operate at a loss until they went bankrupt.

There were a handful of wealthy families, as well as a legion of small businessmen, who battled (mostly politically, but sometimes literally) the New Deal. Pew (Sun Oil), DuPont (General Motors, DuPont Company), and Ford (Ford Motor Company) were among Roosevelt's most important conservative foes. No one in their ranks, however, loomed as large as **J. Howard Pew** of Sun Oil (later renamed Sunoco). From his Philadelphia offices, Pew coordinated efforts to undermine Roosevelt. Unlike some anti-New Deal industrialists who operated behind the scenes, Pew seldom passed up an opportunity to make speeches defending free enterprise, whether to a university audience or to members of the National Association of Manufacturers (NAM) and Congress [Document 2: p. 144].

In 1934, Pew persuaded the DuPonts, along with disaffected Democratic activist Jouett Shouse and National Steel leader Ernest Weir, to establish the Liberty League. They hoped to use the Liberty League to capture the national Republican Party and ensure that it did not compromise with Roosevelt [Document 3: p. 145]. Only then would the Liberty League provide the funds to guarantee Republican victory in the 1936 presidential election. The Pew family alone contributed $1.5 million to the cause. (In today's currency, that would be the equivalent of $26.5 million.) Their efforts were futile. Roosevelt won nearly 61 percent of the popular vote and carried all but two New England states.

Conservatives' problem was not lack of money. It was their image, their message, and their candidate. The Wall Street crash was too fresh in

Figure 1.2 J. Howard Pew (1882–1971), President of Sun Oil Company
Source: Courtesy of the Library of Congress Prints and Photographs Division

voters' memories for them to support the party of millionaires. Calling for reductions in federal spending while millions depended upon public works jobs and agricultural subsidies to survive was not bound to be popular either. Finally, there was the Republican nominee. Because of the 1934 midterm elections, there were only seven Republican governors left in the nation. Just *one incumbent Republican governor*, **Alf Landon** of Kansas, won reelection in 1934. Given massive Republican losses in Congress, the 1934 election made Landon the most senior Republican office holder in America and, consequently, the leader of the national party. Even if Landon had been an eloquent, passionate speaker—he was neither—parties usually choose their presidential nominees from states that were key to winning the Electoral College. Kansas was not one of those states.

Undaunted, Pew enlisted Weir and Lewis Brown (Johns Manville Corporation) to underwrite a different kind of anti-New Deal initiative. The outlines of their strategy emerged in 1938 and came to fruition with the launching of a conservative "think tank," the **American Enterprise Association** (AEA) in New York City. (The nation's first think tank, the liberal Brookings Institute, was born in 1916.) Seeking to avoid federal taxes by calling itself a non-profit educational organization, the AEA (later relocated to Washington and renamed the American Enterprise Institute) produced critiques of New Deal legislation for sympathetic newspapers and members of Congress. The AEA trained a generation of conservative activists. In 1945, twenty-one-year-old Phyllis Stewart joined the AEA as a researcher. She later became famous under her married name, **Phyllis Schlafly**.

Pew, along with Weir, Tom Girdler of Republic Steel, and the leadership of the National Association of Manufacturers, recognized that the union movement posed two threats. First, the CIO undercut their corporate profits. Second, unions were a significant source of Democrats' power. In 1937, the year the CIO launched organizing campaigns in the auto and steel industries, NAM spent $800,000 on anti-union literature. Girdler branded the CIO as a "racketeering, violent communist body" and stockpiled weapons. Private security and police forces killed eighteen CIO members and wounded 550 in clashes across the Industrial Heartland in 1937.

Conservatives understood that so long as Roosevelt supported the CIO, anti-labor violence alone could not ensure victory. Although New Deal Democrats were riding high in his native Pennsylvania, Pew had an ally he could call upon in Texas. Sun Oil exercised enormous influence along the Gulf Coast. Democratic House member **Martin Dies, Jr.**, never ignored an order from the Pew family to meet, whether in Washington, Philadelphia, or Texas. While Dies ardently pursued New Deal agricultural subsidies and public works projects for his district, he was outraged when northern liberals like Senator Robert Wagner denounced poll taxes and championed labor organizing. Only 8 percent of Dies' district could vote because of poll taxes. Oil refinery workers, a natural CIO constituency, were impoverished, disenfranchised, and divided into antagonistic white, black, and Mexican-American factions.

Pew encouraged Dies in 1938 to establish the House Committee on Un-American Activities. Vice President Garner, who had become disenchanted with the New Deal's support for labor unions, gave Dies his blessing. Although northern Democrats in Congress were suspicious of Dies' intentions, many did not want to go on record trying to explain why they opposed investigating un-American activities. After all, that would make them look un-American. Dies held well-publicized hearings in Washington, as well as Michigan, which had been a major battleground in the 1937 labor wars. He called anti-CIO witnesses who testified that various labor organizers were communists.

The 1938 midterm elections were disastrous for the New Deal, with Republicans picking up eighty-one seats in the House and eight in the Senate. Republicans also swept gubernatorial elections in Illinois, Michigan, Minnesota, New York, Ohio, Pennsylvania, and Wisconsin. Unions and management had battled in every one of those states. There was no precise way to assess the damage Dies and Pew had inflicted upon the New Deal. Conservatives, however, recognized that anti-communism had regained some of the electoral influence it had lost with the initial shock of the economic collapse in 1929.

Not all the businessmen opposing the New Deal had an affluent, northern, Protestant pedigree. In the late nineteenth century, the Goldwassers, a family of Eastern European Jewish peddlers, arrived in California. Over the next decades, the Goldwassers made their way to Phoenix, Arizona, opened a department store, anglicized their name to Goldwater, became Episcopalian, and joined the Republican Party.

Arizona benefited enormously from the New Deal. Washington spent $342 million in Arizona, funding programs to promote water conservation and flood control (when it did rain). In turn, Arizona's taxpayers sent back to the federal government $16 million—one of the best financial returns in the nation. The Goldwater heir was not impressed. Barry Goldwater denounced the New Deal for creating "dependency" on the government. In 1938, he blamed the CIO for "chaos," "riots," and "bloodshed," as well as for stoking the fires of class resentment. As was true of Ronald Reagan, Franklin Roosevelt inspired Barry Goldwater to enter politics.

Conservative Reaction: The Challenge from Within the Democratic Party

Given Democrats' advantage in the Electoral College, as well as the difficulty conservative businessmen had in moving the electorate in their direction, Republicans needed a better strategy. One way for Republicans to win was to emphasize the racial and foreign policy issues that divided Democratic voters. There was no shortage of divisive issues—"wedge" issues, as a later generation of political consultants would call them—in the 1930s. The economic crisis had masked Democrats' fracture points, but did not eliminate them.

Since the Civil War, southern Democrats' mental world had embraced several truths. First, the Republican Party had invaded the South, slaughtered her sons, and subjected the survivors to the rule of their former slaves. There was no honorable option for whites other than voting Democratic. Second, the white South believed in states' rights and limiting the power of the federal government—a conviction deepened by losing the Civil War. Third, a non-union, low-wage South lured businesses away from the North and provided Dixie with badly needed jobs. Fourth, the maintenance of poll taxes and segregation kept inferior people (black and poor white) from corrupting society. Fifth, the South desperately needed New Deal funds. Southern Democrats insisted that the fifth truth did not conflict with the second truth, so long as they quarantined the CIO and civil rights groups.

Representative **Hatton Sumners** of Dallas became a key southern Democratic critic of the New Deal. As chair of the House Judiciary Committee, Sumners bottled up civil rights proposals. Given that only

12 percent of his district could vote because of poll taxes, Sumners had a personal stake in disenfranchisement. His anti-civil rights stance, however, had racial and ideological components as well. In the 1920s, congressional liberals had sought to make the lynching of African-Americans a federal crime. Sumners argued that southern whites, to defend their daughters from rapists, had the right to take the law into their own hands.

By the 1930s, when Senator Wagner made a legislative run against lynching, Sumners shifted tactics. He argued that the federal government had no constitutional authority to exercise any law enforcement powers—whether in pursuit of southern mobs or Chicago gangsters. In effect, Sumners was calling for the abolition of the Federal Bureau of Investigation (FBI) and all other weapons-carrying civilian agencies in Washington. With this point, Sumners had expressed a strain of libertarian thought that regarded agents of federal law enforcement to be just as dangerous to individual liberty and states' rights as law breakers were to the social order.

In 1937, Roosevelt, upset with a Republican-dominated Supreme Court that thwarted his legislative agenda, proposed a judicial "reform." The president asked Congress for the authority to increase the number of justices on the Supreme Court. Regarding Roosevelt's ploy as a power grab, Sumners announced that he was breaking with the New Deal. Although Sumners, along with Garner, defeated Roosevelt's "court packing plan," it was a short-term victory. Resignations and deaths enabled Roosevelt to appoint a pro-New Deal Supreme Court. Garner chose not to run for reelection as vice president in 1940. Sumners later lamented that Roosevelt had made the states into "vassals" of the federal government [Document 4: p. 146].

While southern white Protestant Democrats were becoming disaffected over liberals' advocacy of civil rights and unions, some northern Catholics were experiencing their own unease with the New Deal. Not all Catholic clerics and laity embraced the social encyclicals of Leo XIII and Pius XI. In New York and Boston, middle-class Irish and German Catholics were entrenched in political and religious leadership roles. They did not relish the prospect of sharing power with southern and eastern European Catholics, let alone being part of an electoral coalition that included blacks and Jews.

Cardinal William O'Connell of Boston ordered priests not to read or teach Pius XI's social encyclicals and charged in 1934 that Roosevelt was an autocrat. New York Catholic Al Smith, the 1928 Democratic presidential nominee, joined the Liberty League and denounced New Deal socialism. Father Robert Gannon, the president of New York's Fordham University, warned that New Deal liberals, once they had seized control of America's educational institutions, intended "to eliminate all religion and all morality that does not conform to their peculiar ideology." For their part, Catholic newspapers outside the industrial Midwest praised Dies' investigation of communism in the CIO.

Among the Catholic critics of the New Deal none loomed larger than "radio priest" Charles Coughlin of suburban Detroit. Initially, Coughlin's nationwide radio broadcasts supported Roosevelt's programs. Up to 40 million Americans, mainly Catholic, listened to Coughlin. By the mid-1930s, however, Coughlin became convinced that the New Deal had made common cause with Soviet communism. He denounced the CIO and spoke of the "communistic Jews" who had taken over the U.S. government. Ninety percent of Coughlin's audience tuned him out. Eventually, a newly installed, pro-New Deal Detroit archbishop ordered Coughlin to cease broadcasting. Coughlin's loyalists were outraged.

Although most American Catholics were anti-communist, few would turn against unions or New Deal domestic programs. Foreign policy, however, was a different matter. The outbreak of the Spanish Civil War in 1936 brought the issue of international communism into the heart of American Catholic politics. Spanish general Francisco Franco, appalled by radical mobs which murdered thousands of priests and nuns, led a faction of the Army against the government. Nazi Germany and fascist Italy provided Franco with troops and weapons. Desperate, the government in Madrid looked for allies and the Soviet Union responded with troops and weapons. Thousands of communists in Europe, North America, and South America flocked to Spain to fight Franco.

Convinced that Franco was a Nazi puppet, many Jewish organizations supported the Madrid government. American Catholic clerical and lay leaders denounced the Madrid government as a tool of the Soviet Union. As the Spanish Civil War dragged on for three years, it became common for Jewish groups to call Franco's American Catholic supporters anti-Semites and Nazi sympathizers. In turn, American Catholic newspapers, clergy, and laity accused champions of the Madrid government of being atheistic communists. New Deal Democrats became aware that foreign policy, if entangled with international communism, had the potential to tear apart their party. For conservatives to take full advantage of this fracture, however, required that they emphasize anti-communism as a foreign, not necessarily a domestic, policy issue.

Foreign Policy Dissent

Roosevelt made the revival of the American economy his top priority. Most Americans likewise focused on economic issues. Few voters had any interest in foreign policy, and when they did look at the world they wanted nothing to do with it. Congressional Democrats, with the support of midwestern Republicans, passed two pieces of foreign policy legislation in the 1930s. The 1935 Neutrality Act barred American weapons manufacturers from selling arms to nations at war. Moreover, Americans traveling in war zones, if wounded or killed, were on their own. The U.S. government would neither protect them nor seek retaliation. Two years later, the 1937 Neutrality Act prohibited American ships from sailing into war zones and barred ships from nations at war from docking in U.S. ports. In 1941, two years after the outbreak of World War II in Europe, the Gallup Poll reported that 80 percent of Americans wanted to remain neutral.

While Americans desired to be left alone, Roosevelt knew it would be impossible. He believed that Nazi Germany, Fascist Italy, and Imperial Japan (the Axis Powers) were committed to waging another, far more destructive world war. Which side the Soviet Union chose was an open question. Advances in airplane and submarine technology since World War I, Roosevelt feared, meant that the Atlantic and Pacific oceans no longer provided America with the security that had once come with distance.

Faced with opposition from within his own party, Roosevelt proceeded cautiously. Southern Democrats would support military bases in their congressional districts because it brought in federal money. Of course, not expanding the size of the Army would mean that there would not be many troops stationed at those bases, but that was an issue for another day. Roosevelt could more easily increase the size of the U.S. Navy and its personnel. First, expanded naval construction facilities meant jobs. Roosevelt sold naval expansion to Congress and the public as an employment program, not as a defense initiative. Second, sailors were seldom in port, unlike Army troops stationed in the U.S., so out of sight was out of mind to most Americans.

When Germany conquered France in the spring of 1940 and drove British troops back to their island, Americans took notice. Roosevelt declared a state of emergency which permitted him to federalize state guard units—essentially drafting them into the U.S. Army. That action enlarged American military forces, with some of the federalized guard units destined to play major combat roles in World War II. Roosevelt also persuaded Congress to authorize the first peacetime military draft in American history. Congress, however, only agreed to the draft subject to an annual renewal vote. When conscription came up for reauthorization in 1941, it passed by one vote.

Of America's noninterventionists, the conservative faction of the Republican Party was the most determined. **Robert Taft** of Ohio, the son of President William Howard Taft, assumed congressional leadership of the noninterventionist faction. Elected to the Senate in the 1938 midterm elections, Taft became known as "Mr. Republican" for his untiring opposition to the New Deal. In 1941, when Roosevelt asked Congress to adopt "Lend Lease," an initiative to provide the British with destroyers to combat German submarines, Taft expressed himself in clear terms: "Hitler's defeat is not vital to us." Moreover, Taft continued, the "collapse of England is to be preferred to participation for the rest of our lives in European wars."

Conservatives had a mixture of motives for avoiding foreign entanglements. There were those like Taft who dreaded bloodshed and feared that U.S. intervention would further increase the power of the federal government and enable Roosevelt to impose the New Deal on a global scale. Other conservatives feared that U.S. military intervention, by destroying the Axis

Powers, would open the door to Soviet expansion in Europe and the victory of communist revolutionaries in China. (That prophesy came true.) Taft shared their dread for the future of postwar Europe and Asia. He did not, however, share the pro-German, and often anti-Semitic, sentiments of other antiwar conservatives.

Noninterventionist conservatives failed in their efforts to bring the Republican Party in line with their thinking. Corporate attorney Wendell Willkie secured the Republican presidential nomination in 1940. Not only did Willkie support Roosevelt's steps toward preparing America for war, he did not make opposition to the New Deal the centerpiece of his campaign. Willkie emphasized national unity, going only as far as to assert that Republicans were better managers of government programs than Democrats. For his part, Roosevelt invited Republicans to join his administration, placing them in defense-related positions. Henry Stimson, Hoover's Secretary of State, became Roosevelt's Secretary of War, and Frank Knox, the 1936 Republican vice-presidential nominee, became Secretary of the Navy.

Conservatives felt betrayed. In response, anti-New Deal conservatives, notably *Chicago Tribune* publisher Robert McCormick, salt magnate Sterling Morton, H. Smith Richardson (Vick Chemical Company), and Robert E. Wood (Sears-Roebuck), founded the **America First Committee** in the fall of 1940. While many partisans of the Liberty League, notably Ernest Weir, were among the 800,000 members of America First, J. Howard Pew took an uncharacteristically cautious approach to the organization.

Committed to preserving the neutrality acts and preventing Roosevelt from aiding Britain, America First became the place where opposition to Roosevelt's domestic and foreign policies merged. Textile heir **William Regnery** joined the America First board of directors for personal and ideological reasons. His German-immigrant father, Regnery believed, had suffered from government persecution during World War I. The Regnery heir also felt some sentimental attachment to Germany. He had spent the years between 1934 and 1936 studying in Nazi Germany.

What impressed Regnery most about Hitler was how much he reminded him of Roosevelt: "Both Hitler and Roosevelt—each in his own way—were masters of the art of manipulating the masses." Regnery blamed Roosevelt for antagonizing Germany and Japan, baiting them to declare war on the U.S. Pew sympathized with Regnery and gave him money to establish a conservative book publishing company and an opinion journal, *Human Events*.

America First's leaders were ecstatic when they recruited **Charles Lindbergh**. Lindbergh had become a national hero in 1927 when he made the first solo, nonstop flight across the Atlantic, as well as a national tragedy in 1932 when his young son was kidnapped and murdered. His isolationist roots were deep. During World War I his father, a Republican congressman from Minnesota, had lost his seat after opposing entrance into the conflict. Lindbergh's disgust with Roosevelt had equally strong roots. In 1934, Roosevelt had cancelled contracts with private carriers of airmail in favor

Figure 1.3 Aviator Charles Lindbergh (1902–1974)
Source: Photograph in the author's possession

of the U.S. Army Air Corps. Lindbergh, who had $250,000 invested in one of the private carriers, was livid. He warned, correctly as it turned out, that there would be numerous crashes, since private-sector pilots were superior to military fliers. Roosevelt reversed himself, but not soon enough to appease Lindbergh.

Lindbergh traveled to Nazi Germany in the 1930s and came away impressed. To Lindbergh, Nazi Germany was inspirational. He sympathized with Hitler's desire to solve Europe's "Jewish problem." No other political leader in Europe or the U.S., Lindbergh argued, tried to deal with Jewish rapists and communists. In 1938, Lindbergh received the Service Cross of the German Eagle, the greatest honor the Nazis could give to a foreigner.

America First's leaders, despite knowing Lindbergh's relationship with Nazi Germany, wanted to use his celebrity status to draw crowds. That fact, along with his anti-New Deal politics, was all America First needed to complete its vetting process. The problem was that Lindbergh had no appreciation for practicing politics in a democracy. He was prone to saying what he thought, rather than calculating how he could sugarcoat his caustic beliefs. In September 1941, at an America First rally in Des Moines,

Iowa, Lindbergh identified the culprits who were trying to manipulate the U.S. into participating in World War II: the British, Roosevelt, and the Jews [Document 5: p. 147].

America First board members were shocked that Lindbergh had said publicly what some of them were saying privately. Few in Congress, Democrat or Republican, came to Lindbergh's defense. Not everyone, however, disavowed Lindbergh. Regnery remained loyal, enlisting Lindbergh in the launching of *Human Events*. The conservative struggle against Roosevelt's foreign and domestic policies would continue, even if America First disbanded following the Japanese attack on the U.S. Pacific Fleet at Pearl Harbor and Germany's declaration of war in December 1941.

2 Conservatism Adrift, 1946–1960

Conservative Resurgence?

After World War II, Americans looked forward to purchasing automobiles and homes. The Depression had decimated their meager assets; then World War II raised their incomes. Defense needs, however, compelled the federal government to direct production away from consumer goods to military hardware. By 1945, there was sixteen years of pent-up consumer demand.

Many union members believed that their wages had not kept ahead of war-time inflation. They demanded raises. In addition, some CIO leaders wanted a seat at the boardroom table. General Motors, for one, was not about to share power with its employees, so strikes and production disruptions became inevitable.

Voters, even those who had supported Franklin Roosevelt, were in a foul temper because of the postwar strikes. Republicans won fifty-five House seats and twelve Senate seats in the 1946 midterm elections, giving them a congressional majority they had not enjoyed since Roosevelt's rise to power. Among the new Republican members of Congress were two who would provide hope to conservatives: Representative **Richard Nixon** of California and Senator **Joseph McCarthy** of Wisconsin.

Believing that the 1946 midterm elections were a referendum against the New Deal, Ohio senator Robert Taft drafted anti-CIO legislation. The 1947 Taft-Harley Act allowed employers to resist union organizing campaigns. Employers could hire anti-union speakers and distribute anti-union literature. Moreover, unions could no longer send contributions directly to individual candidates. (This was payback for the CIO Political Action Committee's intervention in the 1944 Texas Democratic primary which led Martin Dies to withdraw.) Taft-Hartley also required union leaders to sign affidavits that they were not members of the Communist Party USA.

In contrast to the late 1930s, the House Committee on Un-American Activities had a modest profile during World War II. Even if southern Democrats and northern Catholics disliked communists, so long as the Soviet Union was an ally against the Axis Powers they muted their criticism. Once the war-time alliance frayed and Republicans captured Congress,

Figure 2.1 Robert A. Taft (1889–1953), Republican Senator from Ohio, 1939–1953
Source: Courtesy of the Library of Congress Prints and Photographs Division

investigating un-American activities came back in fashion. Committee chair J. Parnell Thomas of New Jersey wanted to strike a blow against a major source of Democratic campaign funds and grab as much news media attention as possible. Thomas targeted Hollywood in 1947.

Screen Actors Guild president Ronald Reagan reassured Thomas that Hollywood was on the alert for communists. Reagan then observed that "democracy is strong enough to stand up and fight against the inroads of any ideology" without resorting to coercive federal action. Of course, Reagan continued, if the government proved that the Communist Party was an agent of the Soviet Union, then legislative action might be warranted. Reagan concluded that the committee should look elsewhere for communists.

Committee member Richard Nixon, who questioned Thomas's methods, kept a low profile during the "Hollywood Hearings." His service to the conservative cause came in 1948 during the presidential election. **Whittaker Chambers** appeared before the Committee on Un-American Activities with an explosive story. Soviet intelligence had recruited Chambers into its Washington spy apparatus. American counterintelligence operations, such as they were in the 1930s, did not take notice of Chambers because he did not fit their profile of a communist. He was Ivy League-educated and had a White Anglo-Saxon Protestant heritage that made him more likely to be a corporate board member than a Soviet spy. Of course, that was exactly why the Soviets recruited Chambers.

By the late 1930s, Chambers had turned against his Soviet superiors. He retained microfilm of the last batch of documents that he was supposed to deliver. This was part of his insurance policy against assassination. He also raised his public profile, becoming a foreign-affairs editor for *Time* magazine. The Russians were less likely to kill an American journalist on U.S. soil. Chambers was content with his new life until he saw the people he had known as Soviet operatives moving into politically important positions. He feared that he had left "the winning world," (communism) to join "the losing world" (democracy). However, as Chambers explained to his children, he had to bear witness against communism.

Chambers testified that he had moved classified information from operatives in the departments of Treasury and State to his Soviet handler. Among those he identified was **Alger Hiss**. Chambers did not identify Hiss as a Soviet agent, only calling him a communist. He hoped his one-time friend would come clean about his work. Hiss, however, had the opposite reaction, demanding to appear before the Un-American Activities Committee to rebut Chambers' charges.

Hiss was no ordinary federal bureaucrat. He had cultivated influential friends. Felix Frankfurter, his Harvard Law professor, had arranged for Hiss to obtain a job with the Agricultural Adjustment Agency in the early 1930s. Hiss soon came to the attention of the Secretary of Agriculture, Henry Wallace, who helped him get his dream job in the U.S. State Department. At the State Department, Hiss befriended Dean Acheson, who recommended him for better assignments. In 1945, Hiss accompanied Roosevelt to the Soviet Union as an adviser at the Yalta Conference. At Yalta, the U.S. essentially accepted Russian military domination of eastern Europe. Upon his return to America, Hiss joined Eleanor Roosevelt in San Francisco to establish the United Nations.

In 1948, when Chambers identified Hiss as a communist he was, in effect, calling into question the judgment of an incumbent Supreme Court Justice (Frankfurter), a former vice president (Wallace), a soon-to-be Secretary of State (Acheson), and the one-time First Lady (Roosevelt). Chambers had hit the heart of the New Deal Democratic establishment in Washington—and it hit back hard. President **Harry Truman**, who privately had reservations about Hiss, nonetheless felt he had no choice but to denounce the Un-American Activities Committee. Truman gambled that Chambers had no evidence to support his claims.

Republicans on the committee wilted—with one exception. Nixon found Hiss to be snotty and entitled. He disliked elites because of their unearned advantages in life. Nixon had come from a financially stressed family.

He could not afford to attend an Ivy League college and had to work to support his undergraduate and law school education. His best job, before being elected to Congress, was, arguably, serving as a naval supply officer in the malaria-infested Solomon Islands during World War II. Nixon also suspected that Chambers had not been entirely forthcoming. Chambers then admitted to Nixon that Hiss was a Soviet agent. Moreover, he had microfilm of documents from Hiss to prove his charges.

When Chambers appeared again before the Un-American Activities Committee, his revised testimony was devastating. Most of Hiss's allies deserted him. The federal government could not prosecute Hiss for espionage since the paper trail, the microfilmed documents, dated from the late 1930s. By 1948, the statute of limitations had expired. Hiss, however, had perjured himself before a congressional committee, which led to a short prison sentence.

The real winner in the Hiss-Chambers affair was Nixon. He had achieved what anti-New Deal conservatives had failed to accomplish for the past two decades: Nixon made key figures in the Democratic Party look foolish. Conservatives embraced Nixon. His triumph bolstered conservatives' belief that there was political profit to be made in the investigation of communist influence in Democratic circles.

Liberals never forgave Nixon for the embarrassment they suffered at his hands. They also resented his vivid partisan rhetoric. Calling Dean Acheson "the Red Dean of the Cowardly College of Communist Containment" played well with conservative audiences, but stoked liberals' desire for payback. In a paradoxical twist, conservatives would discover to their dismay that Nixon was not actually conservative.

The 1948 Election

To conservatives, the Hiss case was one more piece of evidence pointing to the impending collapse of the New Deal Democratic Party. Political insiders knew that Truman would not have even been on the 1944 Democratic ticket but for the big-city Catholic political bosses who disliked Vice President Wallace. The Catholic politicians believed that Wallace misunderstood the nature of the U.S. alliance with the Soviet Union. They viewed the alliance as a marriage of convenience while Wallace saw the Soviet Union as a postwar partner. To make matters worse, the urban bosses were convinced that Roosevelt would not survive a fourth term in office. That would make Wallace president.

Truman distrusted the Soviet Union, though he saw no way short of launching World War III to prevent its military occupation of eastern Europe. Given that one-quarter of Democratic voters were Catholic, with many claiming ancestry in eastern Europe, Truman could not risk losing their support. Truman would not stand by while the Soviets extended their influence (sometimes peacefully, sometimes violently) further into Europe.

Wallace, who had accepted the position of Secretary of Commerce as a consolation prize for being dumped from the ticket, became publicly critical of Truman's anti-communist advisers. Truman fired Wallace in 1946.

A year later, the "**Truman Doctrine**" became the cornerstone of U.S. foreign policy. Truman committed America to the containment of Soviet influence in Europe. The U.S. would offer economic and military assistance to non-communist nations resisting Soviet subversion. Truman believed that going back to a prewar noninterventionist foreign policy would only encourage Russian aggressors. Moreover, the Nazi extermination of 12 million Jews, Poles, Romani, and Russians had led many, though not all, Americans to conclude that the U.S. was indispensable to the global preservation of liberty.

In reaction to the Truman Doctrine, as well as to the Marshall Plan which pledged to rebuild the shattered economies of (western) Europe, Wallace decided to run for president on the leftist Progressive Party ticket. He attracted support in Chicago, Detroit, New York City, and Philadelphia. His voters tended to be Reform Jews, middle-class Protestants, and college-educated professionals. Wallace's partisans included George McGovern, a graduate history student at Northwestern University (and, years later, the Democratic Party's presidential nominee). McGovern identified with Wallace's opposition to what journalists were calling the "Cold War."

While Wallace could not expect to win, he could (and did) draw sufficient numbers of Democrats in Detroit and New York City to throw their states' electoral votes to the Republican presidential nominee, Thomas Dewey. Truman campaign workers lashed out at Wallace, charging that the Soviet Union was financing the Progressive Party while the American Communist Party provided its staff. There was no evidence to support such claims—at least not until the Soviet Union collapsed in the 1990s and some of its files on the Communist Party USA corroborated many of the accusations.

As if divisions over anti-communist foreign policy were not sufficiently damaging, the Democrats were seemingly breaking apart over civil rights. World War II had set the stage for a new way of thinking about race in the U.S. Nazi genocide appalled most Americans. When Nazi leaders stood trial for war crimes, they charged that the U.S. was hypocritical for tolerating segregation in the American South. The Soviet Union adopted the same rhetoric to discredit the U.S. in newly independent African and Asian nations. This was the context that led the White Anglo-Saxon Protestant leadership of America's elite universities to abolish anti-Jewish admissions quotas. Admissions should be based on merit, not family background.

World War II had another effect on race relations. African-Americans, like Catholics and Jews, had served honorably in the military. They expected to be treated as fully equal citizens. Additionally, the super-charged war economy led hundreds of thousands of southern blacks and whites to move North or to the West Coast in search of defense-related jobs. Between 1942 and

1960, 5 million African-Americans left the South. As the black populations of Buffalo, Chicago, Cleveland, Detroit, Milwaukee, and Pittsburgh grew, so did their political influence. Northern Democratic leaders were experiencing increased pressure to tackle civil rights in the South. Truman had reacted by issuing Executive Order 9981 to integrate the U.S. Armed Forces in 1948. He followed up by insisting that the Democratic Party platform embrace civil rights.

Although white southerners were angry, only a handful walked out of the 1948 Democratic Convention. South Carolina governor **Strom Thurmond** vowed to run against Truman on the states' rights ticket. Journalists, looking for a good catchphrase, called Thurmond's followers "**Dixiecrats**." On the campaign trail in Birmingham, Alabama, Thurmond made his stance clear: "there is not enough troops in the Army to force the southern people to break down segregation and admit the n----- race into our theaters, into our swimming pools, into our homes, and into our churches." As Thurmond perceived matters, northern liberals would not be satisfied until they had imposed race mixing and labor unions on the South. Inevitably, Thurmond predicted, violent crime in Dixie would spiral out of control as unions and blacks became empowered.

Thurmond's most important ally was William F. Buckley, Sr. The elder Buckley, who made his fortune in Mexican oil exploration, was a rare millionaire Catholic in the early twentieth century. He had mansions in Connecticut and South Carolina. Thurmond was a frequent visitor to the Buckley's South Carolina home, where he became well acquainted with William F. Buckley, Jr., who would become the godfather of the modern conservative intellectual movement.

In the political upset of the twentieth century, Truman won, despite Thurmond taking Alabama, Louisiana, Mississippi, and South Carolina, and Wallace throwing Michigan and New York to the Republicans. Democrats retook Congress, securing a fifty-four to forty-two majority in the Senate and a 263-to-171 majority in the House. Conservatives had gone into the 1948 election believing that Thurmond, Wallace, and Hiss had mortally wounded the New Deal Democrats. Instead, the Democrats triumphed, and the New Deal coalition, though strained, had held.

Truman's victory owed much to a political reality that conservatives did not want to accept. Millions of Americans had come of age during the Great Depression and World War II. Roosevelt had always been president, the New Deal had tried to improve peoples' lives, and the U.S. had defeated *right-wing* dictatorships in an alliance with a left-wing dictatorship. Media pundits would later call these men and women "the Greatest Generation," but the label they embraced had been the one stamped into the lining of their uniforms: "G.I." The initials stood for "Government Issued."

The **G.I. Generation** was the most Democratic-voting in American history. Two-thirds identified with the "Party of the New Deal." Although Truman may not have been a father-figure like Roosevelt, to many northern union

Figure 2.2 Strom Thurmond (1902–2003), Senator from South Carolina, 1956–2003
Source: Courtesy of Library of Congress Prints and Photographs Division

members and Catholics he was their kind of Southern Baptist: he drank liquor and cursed Wall Street. Truman vowed to carry on the New Deal, rebranding it as the "Fair Deal."

Hitting Back

After the 1948 election, conservatives alternated between disbelief and rage. Many conservatives blamed Dewey. Unlike Alf Landon in 1936, conservatives could not get Dewey to mount even a weak attack on the New Deal. This should not have been surprising. Dewey had risen in New York Republican ranks by prosecuting mobsters. A law-and-order, honest-government champion, Dewey had made a credible race against Roosevelt in 1944. He was a pragmatist with little interest in conservative policy issues.

By any measure, Truman seemed weaker than Roosevelt. To conservatives' dismay, Dewey chose not to indict the Democrats as the party of communist treason. From Dewey's perspective, America was locked in an ideological struggle against the Soviet Union. To win that life-and-death contest,

Republicans and Democrats had to put aside their partisan disagreements and unite against foreign enemies.

Beyond embracing a bipartisan foreign policy, Dewey and his supporters regarded the Republican Party as the historical home of African-Americans. They were not about to chase after the votes of disaffected southern Democrats by opposing Truman's civil rights initiatives. If anything, Dewey's partisans believed that Republicans should be more vigorous in their support of civil rights.

Dewey's defeat convinced Taft that it was time for him to assert conservative control of the Republican Party and bring it back to its isolationist, anti-New Deal principles. He had been displeased when Truman helped create the North Atlantic Treaty Organization (NATO) in 1949. The Democratic Senate ratified a treaty that embedded the U.S. into a collective security arrangement. If the Soviet Union attacked one of Europe's NATO members, it would be considered an attack on all, including the U.S. Taft regarded this as a constitutionally questionable surrender of congressional war powers to the president.

In 1950, communist North Korea invaded South Korea. Truman went to the United Nations, instead of Congress, and obtained authorization to defend South Korea. As Taft observed, Truman had not only bypassed Congress, the U.S. did not even have an alliance with South Korea. Indeed, Secretary of State Acheson had earlier gone on record stating that South Korea was not part of America's "defensive perimeter" in Asia. Acheson's statement may have encouraged the Soviet Union to believe that the U.S. would not intervene if its North Korean dependency attacked South Korea.

The Truman Doctrine of communist containment had shifted from Europe to Asia without a congressional debate, let alone congressional approval. Even Roosevelt, whom Taft thought had come close to being a dictator, had gone to Congress when he saw no other alternative. If constitutional government were to survive, Taft argued, the nation needed "a foreign policy for Americans" [Document 6: p. 149].

Taft recognized the potential payoff of making anti-communist attacks on New Deal Democrats. Americans had often discounted anti-communist rhetoric when it came from corporate executives. Congressional assaults, however, had more prospect for success. Of course, it helped if Republicans controlled Congress so that they could select the targets and stack the witness lists. It was also useful, as in the Hiss case, if the subject being investigated was guilty and if the inquisitor was a detail-oriented lawyer like Nixon. With the loss of Congress in 1948, what conservatives needed was a politician willing to stage a one-person show on the floor of Congress. More than a few conservatives had reached the point where careful investigation and guilt, or innocence, did not matter.

In 1950, Senator Joe McCarthy became the hero of his own drama. Randomly citing FBI files that director J. Edgar Hoover had leaked to him, McCarthy went on the floor of the Senate and identified various individuals as being communists or Soviet agents. Since McCarthy had senatorial privilege, the people he accused had no legal recourse to file slander suits. Taft egged McCarthy on, telling him, "If one case doesn't work, bring up another." The important thing, Taft knew, was to keep Democrats off balance. Voters would remember that a senator had accused a liberal journalist, college professor, or government employee of being a tool of the Soviet Union; their denials would be buried under the weight of new accusations.

There were ample reasons why McCarthy's name became associated in the public mind with slanderous red-baiting. The elements of "**McCarthyism**" included asserting that the federal government was filled with "card-carrying communists," ridiculing Acheson as a "pompous diplomat in striped pants, with a phony British accent," and charging that the Roosevelt-Truman presidencies represented "twenty years of treason."

McCarthy reserved his most vicious assault on Truman's former Secretary of State, George Marshall [Document 7: p. 150]. According to McCarthy, Marshall, as Army chief of staff during World War II, had timed American military operations to benefit the Soviet Union. Invading France in 1944, "the Second Front," weakened German defenses and enabled the Russians to roll over eastern Europe. Marshall, McCarthy argued, was the mastermind of "America's Retreat from Victory." Most Americans expressed shock that McCarthy had gone after a soldier of Marshall's stature.

Conservatives hoped that McCarthy, an Irish Catholic, would be their bridge to anti-communist Catholic Democrats. By depicting Democratic leaders as elitist and subversive, McCarthy adopted elements of leftist

Figure 2.3 Joseph R. McCarthy (1908–1957), Republican Senator from Wisconsin, 1947–1957
Source: Courtesy of Library of Congress Prints and Photographs Division

class-warfare rhetoric to advance a right-wing agenda. To McCarthy, the Democrats were the privileged plutocrats, while Republicans championed hard-working, humble people. It was a new tactic for conservatives.

While McCarthy earned the friendship of Boston's Joseph P. Kennedy, Sr., he did not make great inroads into Democratic Catholic ranks. Fundamentally, the majority of Catholics did not trust Republicans. Of the Catholics who endorsed McCarthy, most had been the lower-middle-class, ethnic Irish and German followers of Father Charles Coughlin. They had turned against the Democratic Party before World War II.

William F. Buckley, Jr., and his brother-in-law, **L. Brent Bozell, Jr.**, wanted to separate McCarthy's vices—especially his fondness for alcohol—from the anti-communist cause. In 1954, William Regnery published their defense of the Wisconsin senator: *McCarthy and His Enemies*. Buckley and Bozell expressed admiration for how "McCarthy, day in and day out, deals body blows to the soft underbelly of American Liberals, whose screams of anguish are so infrequent (by virtue of their entrenched power) that when they *are* made to scream, the occasion is ... newsworthy." Although McCarthy could have taken more care in making his charges, he was, Buckley and Bozell contended, serving his nation.

McCarthy's greatest political success came in 1952 when he set out to defeat Democratic senator Ernest McFarland of Arizona. Washington conservatives intervened in the Arizona election for two reasons. First, McFarland was a New Dealer who helped draft the Servicemen's Readjustment Act of 1944, also known as the G.I. Bill of Rights. This legislation provided World War II veterans with subsidized loans to buy homes and further their education by attending trade schools or colleges. Conservatives saw the G.I. Bill of Rights as a Democratic vote-buying ploy.

Second, the Republican senatorial nominee, Phoenix city council representative Barry Goldwater, was an ardent foe of the New Deal. He had drawn conservative praise by identifying McFarland as an ally of Truman, "that architect of socialism." Goldwater and McCarthy subsequently became staunch friends in the Senate. Indeed, Goldwater attacked his friend's enemies, arguing that "Those people who would like to do away with McCarthy are the type of people who would also like to coddle communists." To oppose McCarthy, Goldwater argued, was un-American.

Even as conservatives cheered McCarthy, Taft moved to secure the 1952 Republican presidential nomination. Taft calculated that the Democrats, reeling from McCarthy's verbal assaults and unable to win the stalemated war in Korea, were more vulnerable than they had been in 1948. "Mr. Republican," however, made a fatal miscalculation: he initially did not take General **Dwight Eisenhower** seriously as a rival for the presidential nomination. Eisenhower, allied with Dewey, routed Taft.

Conservatives characterized Eisenhower's supporters as "the East Coast Liberal Internationalist Republican Establishment." It was an accurate description but for the presence of Nixon as the vice-presidential candidate on the Eisenhower ticket. Nixon was a West Coast Internationalist Republican who forced his way into the establishment.

The Rise of Modern Republicans

Eisenhower not only won the presidency, he attracted enough voters (who did not split their tickets between the two major parties) to give the Republicans control once again of the House and Senate. Working-class Democrats, who would have never otherwise voted for a Republican, liked "Ike." Eisenhower, after all, was a war hero who projected warmth and reassured the public that he cared about his fellow Americans' wellbeing. Two years later, Republicans lost both the House and Senate. Eisenhower was far more popular than his party—let alone its conservative faction.

President Eisenhower lost no time in confirming why conservatives did not like Ike. While Taft, who died of cancer in 1953, had condemned U.S. intervention in the Korean War (1950–1953), other conservatives had called for military escalation. Their recommendations included bombing communist China which had intervened on North Korea's behalf. Truman had chosen to wage a limited war, largely because the Russians had acquired their own atomic bomb in 1949. While the Soviets could not yet attack the U.S., their atomic bombs held western Europe hostage. Americans did not like sacrificing 36,000 of their sons for half a peninsula, let alone taking on hundreds of thousands of Chinese troops with conventional weapons. Tellingly, Americans named two of the three most famous battlefields of the Korean War "Heartbreak Ridge" and "Pork Chop Hill."

Korea sank Truman's presidency. Eisenhower had no intention of becoming another victim. Although the Chinese had not figured out that Soviet dictator Joseph Stalin had been willing to fight to the last Chinese soldier, they were wearying of a war that may have cost 1 million of their men. Eisenhower knew that escalation or withdrawal were out of the question, while continuing the stalemate would doom his presidency. Luckily for Eisenhower, Stalin died in 1953, clearing the way for a truce.

Eisenhower accepted his break and when, a year later, congressional calls came for the U.S. to intervene on behalf of the French in their Indochinese colonial war, he rejected that option. Instead, Eisenhower created an independent, non-communist South Vietnam, hoping that Cambodia and Laos would remain neutral even as the Soviets and Chinese built North Vietnam in their image. Using NATO as his template, Eisenhower established the Southeast Asian Treaty Organization (SEATO) in 1954. In so doing, Eisenhower placed the Republican Party behind the principles of collective security and communist containment. There was no room in the Republican Party for American First isolationists or conservatives who advocated military escalation without considering the consequences.

On the domestic policy front, Eisenhower surrounded himself with so many businessmen that the joke went around Washington that his cabinet consisted of "nine millionaires and a plumber." (The Secretary of Labor was a leader in the plumbers' union and a Democrat.) His cabinet chiefs, however, were not of the J. Howard Pew ideological stripe. All were pragmatists who wanted to make peace with the New Deal and rally what Eisenhower called the "**Modern Republicans**." As Eisenhower candidly told friends, "Should any political party attempt to abolish Social Security and eliminate labor laws and farm programs, you would not hear of that party again in our political history."

Eisenhower worked with Democrats to extend Social Security to farm workers and self-employed professionals, adding more than 10 million people to the retirement program. He also championed the Federal Aid Highway Act of 1956 which funded the construction of roads and interstate highways. The federal government, working with the states, built 41,000 miles of roads at a cost of $26 billion (more than $300 billion in today's currency). In terms of the overall federal budget, Eisenhower cut defense spending by 27 percent and shifted money toward domestic programs. In 1953, 31 percent of the federal budget had gone to support domestic programs. By 1961, 49 percent of the federal budget went toward funding domestic programs.

The former general had resented McCarthy's attack on his mentor, George Marshall. He also did not appreciate it when McCarthy argued that "twenty years of treason" under Roosevelt and Truman, had become "twenty-one years of treason" after Eisenhower's election. Eisenhower quietly mobilized Modern Republicans to undermine McCarthy. In 1954, following the midterm elections, Republicans and Democrats censured McCarthy for abusing his power as a senator. The vote went against McCarthy sixty-five to twenty-two. While the censure did not remove McCarthy from the Senate, Eisenhower had rendered him powerless. Goldwater was among the few Republicans to stand by McCarthy.

Although Eisenhower did not believe racial equality was an achievable goal, he nonetheless moved forward on civil rights. In 1953, he appointed California governor Earl Warren as Chief Justice of the Supreme Court. A year later, the National Association for the Advancement of Colored People (NAACP) brought *Brown v. Board of Education* before the Court. The NAACP saw *Brown* as an opportunity to challenge the constitutionality of racial segregation in public schools. Warren drafted a sweeping ruling, arguing that segregation was not only unconstitutional, it limited the educational opportunities of minorities. The Warren Court overturned the Supreme Court's 1896 *Plessy v. Ferguson* ruling which had found segregation to be constitutional.

In 1957, Eisenhower took two civil rights initiatives—of which he did one reluctantly and the other more enthusiastically. Democratic governor Oval Faubus of Arkansas, in defiance of the *Brown* decision, mobilized the State Guard to prevent the racial integration of Little Rock's Central High School. Although Eisenhower thought the Warren Court had overreached in its assertion of federal power over the states, he could not allow governors to defy the Supreme Court. If he did so, then the federal courts would lose all authority. Unable to persuade Faubus to back down, Eisenhower felt he had no recourse but to federalize the Arkansas Guard, thus placing its troops under presidential command. He also deployed the 101st Airborne Division to Little Rock. The last time federal troops had occupied a southern city had been in the era of the Civil War and Reconstruction.

Eisenhower was firmer in his support of the 1957 Civil Rights Act. The legislation authorized the establishment of the U.S. Civil Rights Commission to investigate and publicize discrimination. There were no federal penalties for discrimination in hiring or access to lodging. While the 1957 legislation was limited in scope, the key point was that Congress had not passed a civil rights law since 1875.

Vice President Nixon mobilized Senate Republicans behind the 1957 Civil Rights Act. Democratic Senate majority leader **Lyndon Johnson** of Texas, who had presidential ambitions, knew he had to curry northern goodwill by embracing the act. Moreover, as the Texas director of the National Youth Administration (NYA) in the mid-1930s Johnson had insisted that there would be no discrimination in the hiring of Mexican-Americans and African-Americans. Given his history, and his ambition, Johnson worked with Nixon. However, the civil rights act passed with more Republican than Democratic support.

Conservatives Regroup

Truman's reelection in 1948, followed by Eisenhower's capture of the Republican Party, made conservatives question the value of electoral politicking. McCarthy's censure in 1954 brought down their hero, even as Nixon disappointed conservatives by embracing the Modern Republicans. Key conservatives sensed that before they could win at the ballot box, it would be necessary to mold public opinion by creating their own educational and news media organizations. J. Howard Pew understood this better than most of his contemporaries.

After World War II, Pew had doubled down on his investments in conservative publications, organizations, and individuals. Pew gave generously to Grove City College outside Pittsburgh. As a loyal alumnus and board member, Pew solidified Grove City College's role as a conservative Protestant alternative to Harvard. Unlike Harvard, Grove City College did not offer tenure to faculty and had little patience with pro-New Deal professors. Grove City also differed from nearly all institutions of higher education, private or public, by offering a curriculum emphasizing Christian and free-enterprise values. Some conservatives argued that their peers needed to send their children to colleges like Grove City. Most conservatives, however, would never consider enrolling their children at any school other than Harvard, Princeton, or Yale—regardless of the politics of the faculty.

On the publication front, Pew, in addition to providing funds to Regnery and *Human Events*, helped underwrite *Christianity Today*. Established in 1956 by Southern Baptist minister **Billy Graham** and his in-laws, the Bells, *Christianity Today* provided an intellectual home to evangelical Protestants. Its readership in the 1950s grew to 120,000, a remarkably high circulation for a religious magazine. Pew regarded *Christianity Today* as a rival to *The Christian Century* which catered to the well-educated, middle-class Protestants who voted for Eisenhower.

Graham's politics did not easily fit into a conservative box. On one hand, Graham was a devout anti-communist. As he argued in 1954, "Either communism must die, or Christianity must die, because it is actually a battle between Christ and anti-Christ." Graham preached at the massive rallies of the Christian Anti-Communist Crusade in the 1950s. Founded in 1953 by Australian immigrant Fred Schwarz, the Christian Anti-Communist Crusade warned that America was motoring down a dark road toward totalitarianism. Graham had no problem working with Schwarz and Pew to deliver his message of salvation to the several million people who attended his revivals in the 1950s.

On the other hand, Graham did not write off Eisenhower and he became close to Nixon. Moreover, Graham did not share his relatives' distaste for African-Americans. A native of North Carolina, Graham insisted that his revivals be racially integrated, whether in Chattanooga or Los Angeles. He also preached with a black Baptist minister, **Martin Luther King, Jr.**, of Montgomery, Alabama. Graham and King found common ground in their opposition to "immoral" rock and roll music.

Although Graham tried not to disparage other faiths, his financiers, family, and allies in the anti-communist cause were less restrained. J.B. Matthews, an aide to McCarthy and former researcher for Congressman Dies, published an article in 1953 arguing that liberal Protestant ministers were propagandists for the Soviet Union. To conservatives, Matthews was only stating the obvious. Eisenhower, who was not religious but thought going to church was a good idea, regarded Matthews' attack on clergy as "indecent."

Having pushed forward into the educational and religious arenas, Pew entered the field of radio and television broadcasting, hoping to reach a larger audience. What he needed to be successful was talent, which he found in **Clarence Manion**. The Irish Catholic dean of Notre Dame Law School, Manion had once been a Democrat. However, he became disenchanted with Roosevelt. By 1941, Manion had joined Regnery on the board of directors of America First. Although a Taft supporter, Manion briefly served in the Eisenhower Administration on a commission to investigate waste and fraud. Manion concluded that Modern Republicans were the real waste and fraud.

In 1954, with funding from Pew, Manion went on the radio over WGN, which was part of the conservative *Chicago Tribune* media empire. Eventually, 300 radio and television stations carried *The Manion Forum*. He hosted Goldwater and other conservatives, giving them a stage which they lacked in governmental and journalism circles. In terms of audience and potential influence, *The Manion Forum* was invaluable to conservatives. *Human Events*, which occupied the heights of conservative political magazine circulation in the 1950s, had 28,000 readers. Manion could reach that many people in a *single* media market.

While Pew, Schwarz, Graham, and Manion tried to influence American morality, education, and journalism, candy maker Robert Welch had other ideas. (The Welch Company made Junior Mints, among other products.) Like many conservatives, Welch had been led to question the value of electoral politics by Taft's defeat and McCarthy's disgrace. Most Americans, Welch feared, were irredeemable New Dealers on their way to becoming communists. What America needed was a righteous remnant of Americans who could form their own ideological community. In 1958, Welch founded the John Birch Society (JBS). He named the organization for an American soldier killed by Chinese communist guerrillas near the end of World War II.

The John Birch Society proved to be popular in southern California among Protestant Republicans employed in defense-related industries. Since most of the defense-related industries in the region were devoted to the technical fields of missiles and aircraft, their workers were highly skilled. Their spouses tended to have good educations, which often meant that they took great interest in national and international affairs. Although their comfortable lifestyles depended on federal spending, they believed that defense was the only constitutionally legitimate function of the federal government.

When Welch said that Eisenhower was a "conscious, articulate agent of the communist conspiracy," John Birch Society members agreed. Over morning cups of coffee, evening meetings, and weekend cocktail parties, JBS members discussed the dangers facing America and planned for the day when the Soviet Union officially took over the federal government. The JBS gave loyalists a community not infected by the New Deal and Modern Republican viruses.

Manion joined the John Birch Society, as did perhaps another 100,000 by the end of the 1950s. It was difficult to know precise JBS membership numbers since its followers feared federal surveillance and infiltration. Fred Koch, an oil-pipe supplier in Wichita, Kansas, provided funding to the JBS and inspired two of his four sons—**Charles** and **David**—to champion conservative causes. Pew also gave financial support to the JBS and served as an editorial adviser to the JBS's magazine, *American Opinion*. McCarthy's former researcher, J.B. Matthews, was the magazine's editorial adviser.

When Modern Republicans looked at the John Birch Society's ideology, financiers, and leaders, they were repulsed. They felt vindicated in their efforts to send conservatives to the margins of the Republican Party—though they would not remain marginalized for long.

Conservative Fusion

William F. Buckley, Jr., had been saddened by McCarthy's downfall. He was convinced that conservatism had to be about something beyond playing defense—and losing. Further, while Taft had been a politician of rare nobility, given the international communist threat, a noninterventionist foreign policy would doom America. Buckley had the inherited wealth, as well as exceptional writing and speaking skills, to be something more than a mere politician. He could be the John the Baptist of the American Right, preparing the way for the nation's political salvation.

In 1955, Buckley launched a new conservative magazine, the *National Review*, which would become one of the most influential political magazines in American history. He proclaimed that "The growth of government—the dominant social feature of this century—must be fought relentlessly." Moreover, working with liberals, whether Democratic or Republican, Buckley argued, was the road to totalitarian socialism. Conservatives must reject bipartisanship and stay true to their principles. Finally, conservatives should never forget, and Americans needed to learn, that "The century's most blatant force of satanic utopianism is communism." Both McCarthy and Whittaker Chambers received invitations to write for the *National Review*. Pew funded conservative student internships at the *National Review* and *Human Events*.

Figure 2.4 William F. Buckley (1925–2008)
Source: Photograph in the author's possession

From outsiders' perspective, the *National Review* was indistinguishable from *Human Events* and other conservative publications that attracted a few thousand true believers and avoided bankruptcy only because of the generosity of their wealthy sponsors. All this was true, but it missed the bigger picture.

Buckley envisioned the *National Review* as the intellectual heart of conservative "fusionism." There were many strands of conservative thought and politics: religious conservatives who emphasized moral issues and economic conservatives opposed to government regulation, unions, and social-welfare programs. On foreign policy, there were anti-communist interventionists, as well as noninterventionists.

The Great Depression had fractured the Republican Party, depriving conservatives of a reliable vehicle to promote their policies. Buckley saw a glimmer of hope. When one looked closely at the conflicting strands of conservatism, there was a common thread: fear of an expansive federal government that undermined business, morality, and national security. Orienting domestic and foreign policy around anti-communism and against big government would glue conservatives together; casting the U.S. government as a threat to freedom and morality would complete the cementing of the conservative coalition.

All conservative fusionists needed was a political party. The Democrats were hopeless, which meant that conservatives had to supplant the Modern Republicans. How to accomplish that goal was the question. Fusionists had an answer: break southern Democrats off from their party and funnel them into the Republican Party. Modern Republicans would be crushed under the weight of refugee southerners.

Converting the white South into a conservative ally was not far-fetched. Since the 1938 midterm elections, southern Democrats and conservative northern and western Republicans had forged an informal alliance to prevent the passage of additional labor legislation. The challenge for conservative Republicans was to expand that common ground with southern Democrats—most especially Thurmond's "Dixiecrats."

In 1956, ninety-nine southern Democratic members of Congress signed the "**Southern Manifesto**," also known as the "Declaration of Constitutional Principles," pledging to resist the *Brown* decision [Document 8: p. 151]. Strom Thurmond, who joined the Senate in 1954, helped draft the manifesto. Nearly all southern Democrats made the pledge to fight racial integration—except for Tennessee senators Estes Kefauver and Al Gore, Sr., and Texas senator Lyndon Johnson. Kefauver, Gore, and Johnson harbored muted sympathy for civil rights and went as far as they dared in the 1950s without being voted out of office.

Thurmond led the fight against the 1957 Civil Rights Act, staging a record-breaking twenty-four-hour, eighteen-minute filibuster to derail voting on the legislation. The *National Review* endorsed Thurmond's resistance and defended the racial basis for segregation and disenfranchisement, writing:

> The central question that emerges—and it is not a parliamentary question or a question that is answered by merely consulting a catalogue of the rights of American citizens, born Equal—is whether the White community in the South is entitled to take such measures as are necessary to prevail, politically and culturally, in areas in which it does not predominate numerically? The sobering answer is Yes—the White community is so entitled because, for the time being, it is the advanced race. It is not easy, and it is unpleasant, to adduce statistics evidencing the median cultural superiority of White over Negro: but it is a fact that obtrudes, one that cannot be hidden by ever-so-busy egalitarians and anthropologists.

Although grateful for Buckley's support, Thurmond was not ready to become a Republican. He was, however, prepared to assist Goldwater in becoming the 1960 Republican presidential nominee. Despite having voted for the 1957 Civil Rights Act, Thurmond respected Goldwater. After all, Goldwater had denounced Eisenhower's 1957 budget as "the siren call of socialism." Moreover, Goldwater's support for the 1957 Civil Rights Act was predicated on the fact that it had not given the Civil Rights Commission any enforcement powers. Goldwater might prove less supportive of civil rights legislation if it gave the federal government enforcement power over the South.

Thurmond, like other southern Democrats, was moving toward embracing the *National Review*'s conservative fusionism. The federal government that tried to destroy southern states' rights by imposing civil rights was the same government that wasted taxpayers' money on domestic programs and failed to spend enough money on national defense. Although Thurmond would not condemn cotton subsidies, he denounced federal programs that benefited the North.

Reagan's Journey

While conservatives looked to Thurmond and Goldwater as up-and-coming political leaders, they were missing a story taking place outside Washington. Their oversight was understandable, and not just because the one who ultimately brought them to power was a Hollywood actor. He was also a New Deal Democrat.

Prior to U.S. entry into World War II, Ronald Reagan had found success as a supporting actor. Reagan could do either drama or comedy, sometimes combining the two. Film critics, and later political reporters, dismissed Reagan as a man of little substance. They failed to look closely enough. In the 1942 war film *Desperate Journey*, Reagan stood up to the "A-list," scene-grabbing British actor Errol Flynn, and left a warm impression with audiences. It said a great deal about "B-List" Reagan's drive that he left any impression at all. Reagan knew how to make a connection with audiences—skills that professional politicians like Alf Landon, Thomas Dewey, and Robert Taft lacked.

Although Reagan wanted to follow Jimmy Stewart and other actors into combat, his poor eyesight kept him stateside during World War II. He had to content himself with serving with the Army Signal Corps making military training films. Reagan threw himself into the war effort and cut back his commercial projects.

While his patriotism was unassailable, Reagan's career path had to account for an unpleasant fact. To finance World War II, the federal government adopted a marginal tax rate of up to 94 percent for incomes above $200,000. That meant that for every dollar earned above $200,000, the federal government would take 94 cents. Reagan, who was making an average of $42,000 for each movie ($810,000 in today's currency), realized that acting in a lot of films made no sense financially.

Reagan had joined the Screen Actors Guild in 1938. His interest in union politics grew as he saw how badly the movie studios exploited lesser-known actors. Reagan also came to regard Hollywood's communist organizers as manipulative bullies. After World War II, Reagan and his friend, actor William Holden, tried to convince screen legend John Garfield that the Soviet Union was less than perfect. Garfield began to listen, until a communist actor dragged him away from the meeting and lectured him on associating with reactionaries. The incident left Reagan feeling sad—and angry.

In 1947, Reagan helped organize the **Americans for Democratic Action (ADA)** and became its California leader. The ADA, whose founders included Minneapolis, Minnesota, mayor Hubert Humphrey and CIO president Phillip Murray, wanted to save the New Deal's legacy from communists and conservatives. Its organizers expelled communists from unions and state Democratic Party organizations. The ADA also fought back against Taft on domestic and foreign policy issues.

Reagan went on the campaign trail in 1948 to help Truman defeat Wallace, Thurmond, and Dewey. He also recorded radio advertisements. Some were on behalf of Truman, with Reagan describing Dewey as the "banner carrier for Wall Street." Other radio spots supported Humphrey's race for the U.S. Senate. As Reagan said of Humphrey, he was "fighting for all the principles advocated by President Truman for adequate low-cost housing; for civil rights; for prices people can afford to pay."

While Reagan found purpose in union and electoral politics, his marriage to the twice-divorced actress Jane Wyman fell apart. The divorce was not amicable. When Reagan wanted to see his daughter and son, Wyman would put them out on the street curb so he would not go inside her house. He did not drown his sorrows in alcohol, since his father's example served as a painful warning, but hitting the night scene with Holden was another matter. Reagan admitted he had numerous affairs, mainly because he was depressed and working less as he aged out of roles.

His life turned around for two reasons. First, he met an ambitious young actress who asked him to reassure studio heads that she was not a communist. Nancy Davis married Reagan in 1952 and gave him the ultimate makeover. In contrast to Reagan, Davis came from a well-off Protestant Republican family. She led him away from the Christian Disciples and to the Episcopalians. Davis also insisted on changing the pronunciation of the Reagan name. The Irish Catholic pronunciation was "Ree-gan," which Davis thought was low-class. He became, instead, "Ray-gun," which had a more respectable Scottish Protestant ring to it. Davis also moved him toward the Republican Party.

Reagan's second life-changing event came in 1954. General Electric (GE) recruited him to host a television program, *GE Theater*. GE had moved on from the days of Gerard Swope and making peace with the New Deal. The corporation was looking for ways to influence the consumer public to buy their products while encouraging employees not to place the union above their loyalties to GE. Moreover, the show enabled GE to use the charismatic Reagan to advocate for its corporate positions. Reagan earned as much from GE as he had made at the height of his film career.

He became so popular on the new medium of television that GE sent him on tours of plants. In the beginning, Reagan was not political, but over time he began to share with workers (and management) some concerns he had about the growing social-welfare state. Taxes, while not at World War II levels, were still high in comparison with the 1930s and more people were being taxed—including the middle and working classes. Reagan wondered how much more Eisenhower was going to expand domestic programs and viewed with alarm his redirection of federal spending away from national defense.

Reagan was evolving into an anti-communist conservative. He did not, however, repudiate Roosevelt and the New Deal. Reagan believed that after Roosevelt's death, national leaders had lost sight of the dangers too much federal regulation and taxes posed to the American people. As a product of Hollywood, Reagan would never be a social conservative. He felt he should not condemn those who binged on alcohol and sex given his personal and family history. Reagan also knew many people in Hollywood who were hiding their sexual orientation. As far as Reagan was concerned, what people chose to do to entertain themselves in their private life should remain private.

The 1960 Election: Modern Republicans and Conservatives

After Roosevelt's death, Republicans had successfully pushed for a constitutional amendment (the Twenty-Second) to prevent subsequent presidents from serving more than two terms. Their timing could not have been worse. No sooner had the Twenty-Second Amendment been ratified than the

American people elected a president who could have easily won a third term in office. Then again, as far as conservatives were concerned, two terms for Eisenhower was two terms too many.

Both Thurmond and South Carolina textile operator Roger Milliken urged Goldwater to run for president in 1960. Milliken, who had once shut down one of his plants after it unionized, was close to Thurmond, Buckley, and other Goldwater boosters. To raise Goldwater's national profile, Brent Bozell wrote the senator's "autobiography," *The Conscience of a Conservative*, in 1960 [Document 9: p. 152]. Buckley's brother-in-law denounced agricultural subsidies, advocated privatizing Social Security, promised to reduce the federal budget by 10 percent annually, and championed states' rights.

Conservatives depicted Goldwater as a principled defender of states' rights in the manner of the framers of the Constitution, not the Ku Klux Klan. Lest anyone associate states' rights with the denial of African-American rights, **Karl Hess**, a researcher for the conservative think tank the American Enterprise Association, composed an essay for the mass circulation *Saturday Evening Post*. Writing under Goldwater's name, Hess insisted that the senator's southern appeal was based on economic, not racial, issues.

While conservative fusionists wanted to define states' rights as a matter of federal economic regulation and coercion, they were their own worst enemies. It was difficult to insist that Goldwater and his supporters were not bigots when the *National Review* came out with editorials that seemed to indicate otherwise. In 1960, the *National Review* argued that: "In the Deep South the Negroes are, by comparison with whites, retarded ('unadvanced,' the NAACP might put it). Any effort to ignore the fact is sentimentalism and demagoguery. Leadership in the South, then, quite properly, rests in white hands."

As Republicans and Democrats struggled to address civil rights in the 1950s, they had to grapple with a grass-roots campaign that had emerged in the South. In 1955, Rosa Parks, an African-American woman in Montgomery, Alabama, refused to give up her bus seat to a white rider and move to the back, as was the custom. Her refusal sparked a boycott of Montgomery's bus service that lasted into 1956. Looking for a spokesman, the boycott organizers chose a young black Baptist minister, Martin Luther King, Jr. Eloquent and inspirational, King became the face of the Montgomery Bus Boycott.

The resistance against segregation spread beyond Montgomery. By 1957, King joined other black clergy in founding the Southern Christian Leadership Conference (SCLC). King embraced non-violent civil disobedience to evoke sympathy and move public opinion against segregation and disenfranchisement. Billy Graham appreciated King's commitment to non-violent protest tactics and continued to share a pulpit with him at religious revivals. Others were not as broad-minded.

What irked southern white Democrats was that the SCLC expected segregationists to respond to non-violent protest with violence, thus arousing national revulsion against discrimination. The problem was that knowing that was the case, most segregationists still responded with violence. By 1960, the South had become America's leading news story and the unavoidable subject of political debate.

The 1960 Republican presidential nomination belonged to Nixon, as Eisenhower's vice president—at least that was what Modern Republicans believed. Goldwater's supporters thought otherwise, but they did not control the party's nomination machinery any more than Taft had in 1952. What they had in finance, conservatives lacked in organization. It did not help matters that Goldwater did not want to run for president. He may not have trusted Nixon, but Goldwater knew that Nixon was more knowledgeable on domestic and foreign policy issues than he was. Nixon had also cultivated allies in the Republican Party across the nation.

Modern Republicans remained convinced that their party could win back the black vote, especially as Democrats fought among themselves over civil rights. King's father, a prominent minister in Atlanta, was an outspoken Republican and had the means to pay his poll tax and vote. Jackie Robinson, who had integrated professional baseball in 1947, voted Republican and endorsed Nixon. If the face of the Democratic Party was Strom Thurmond, the Modern Republicans might recapture the black vote in the North.

The 1960 Election: Democrats

Even as Modern Republicans shoved aside conservatives, the Democrats were scrambling to hide their divisions and hold the New Deal coalition together. Given his legislative experience, political skills, and a reservoir of campaign cash from Texas oil men, Lyndon Johnson should have been the Democratic presidential nominee in 1960.

Johnson's disadvantages, however, outweighed his advantages. The last time a resident of a former Confederate state had won the White House was 1912—and Woodrow Wilson had buried his southern origins and accent. Johnson could do neither. At best, he could put on a Stetson and try to look like a cowboy, though Goldwater had trade-marked that fashion style. Ironically, southern Democrats did not trust Johnson because of his support for civil rights, while northern liberals did not trust Johnson to be more supportive of civil rights.

Senator **John F. Kennedy** of Massachusetts was an improbable Democratic presidential candidate. His father may have been an indispensable financial angel, but Joseph P. Kennedy's political baggage was considerable. He had been sympathetic to America First's agenda and had contributed money to Joseph McCarthy. Indeed, McCarthy had hired Joe Kennedy's son Robert to serve as his one of his legal advisers.

When John Kennedy wrote the Pulitzer Prize-winning biographical work *Profiles in Courage* in 1956, liberals and conservatives noted the irony. (Kennedy's speechwriter, Ted Sorenson, allegedly ghostwrote the book.)

After all, Kennedy had avoided the McCarthy censure vote. Critics, both New Deal Democrats and conservatives, observed that Kennedy might have benefited from showing less profile and more courage. It was a fair observation, underscored by Kennedy's efforts to leave as little of a legislative record as possible in the House and the Senate. It was difficult to attack presidential candidates on their domestic and foreign policy stances if there was little on record to criticize.

Kennedy's Catholicism might have been a liability—as it had been for Al Smith in the 1928 presidential election. Nixon and the Modern Republicans, however, knew that times had changed. Catholics had proven their loyalty to America over Rome during World War II. Kennedy had demonstrated his own bravery in the war. Nixon did not want to make Kennedy's religious faith a political issue, especially since the parallels to the 1928 election were discomforting. Nixon, like the 1928 Republican presidential nominee Herbert Hoover, was a Quaker.

When some Republican conservatives ignored Nixon's pleas, Buckley and the *National Review* criticized their religious (as opposed to racial) bigotry. More potentially troublesome to Kennedy were anti-Catholic Democrats who were clustered in the South. In 1960, 95 percent of southerners were Protestant, while the rest of the nation was two-thirds Protestant. Most southern white Protestants belonged to socially conservative fundamentalist and evangelical sects which disliked the Catholic faith.

Both the Southern Baptist Convention and the National Association of Evangelicals—the latter claiming a strong southern base—warned that Protestant America was on the verge of being destroyed by the Catholic Church. As Ramsey Pollard, the president of the Southern Baptist Convention, pleaded, "All we ask is that Roman Catholicism lift its bloody hand from the throats of those that want to worship in the church of their choice."

Given the prospect of southern white Democrats defecting from the party over religious and racial issues, Kennedy had to put Lyndon Johnson on the ticket as vice president. Northern Democrats hoped that southerners would rally behind one of their own, even if they did not trust him.

One of the key moments of the 1960 election took place in October 1960. King had joined students in Atlanta to compel restaurants to serve African-Americans. Arrested along with 280 students, King received a four-month prison sentence. His family had an understandable concern that he might not survive prison. Nixon's campaign hesitated to respond given that this was a local, not federal, law enforcement issue. Kennedy and his brother Robert had no such concerns. They called Georgia officials to arrange for his release. The northern black vote went decisively to Kennedy.

Kennedy defeated Nixon by 112,000 popular votes. The overall electoral vote could have easily gone to Nixon in several states where the popular vote was tight. Kennedy owed his election to holding the white South, mobilizing excited Catholics, and winning 68 percent of the black vote in the North.

Conservatives, looking at the election results, came to two conclusions. First, Modern Republicans deserved to become extinct. They had blown an opportunity to defeat what they believed to be a weak candidate. Second, chasing after black voters was a fool's errand. The key to success was to win over southern white Democrats. The next time around, conservatives would be ready to lead. Whether they could win the White House (let alone capture Congress) mattered less than purging the Republican Party of its Eisenhower faction and changing its stances on domestic and foreign policies.

3 Crisis and Opportunity, 1961–1972

Racial Issues, North and South, 1961–1963

President John F. Kennedy focused his 1961 inaugural address on foreign policy, vowing "that we shall pay any price, bear any burden, meet any hardship, support any friend, oppose any foe to assure the survival and the success of liberty." It quickly became clear that his assistance to Martin Luther King's family during the 1960 election had been a ploy to attract northern black voters, rather than an expression of support for civil rights. Kennedy's motivation had been to keep the majority of African-Americans in the Democratic Party while not alienating southern Democrats. Losing either group would have damaged the New Deal coalition.

Southern Democrats were relieved that Kennedy had little interest in presenting civil rights legislation to Congress. Their problem, however, was not the federal government—it was Dixie's restive black population. The scale of the civil rights demonstrations was unprecedented. Between 1961 and 1963, law enforcement arrested 20,000 demonstrators across the South. In 1962, an African-American student attempted to enroll at the University of Mississippi ("Ole Miss") Mississippi governor Ross Barnett incited protesters against the black student. As Barnett, a Democrat, declared, "God was the original segregationist," otherwise He would not have created different races. The violence at Ole Miss became so bad that Kennedy felt he had no alternative but to restore order with U.S. troops.

A year later, Birmingham, Alabama, became a center of resistance against segregation. King anticipated that Birmingham law enforcement would react badly, hoping that would increase public pressure on Kennedy to act on civil rights. Birmingham police followed the segregationists' script. They arrested hundreds of demonstrators while firefighters sprayed black children with high-powered hoses. The national news media broadcast film of the Birmingham protests, building sympathy in the North for civil rights and moving Kennedy toward embracing civil rights legislation. At the same time, however, resentment against the New York-based television networks increased across the white South.

Figure 3.1 University of Mississippi ("Ole Miss") Riot, 1962
Source: Courtesy of Library of Congress Prints and Photographs Division

While national attention focused on the South, a subtler development in race relations took place in the northern cities. Northern Catholics, empowered by New Deal labor legislation and the G.I. Bill of Rights, wanted to hold on to their improved social and economic status. Many had relocated to all-white suburbs. For those who remained in the cities, the church parish and home ownership defined their lives. Their house was often their only asset, while their neighborhoods were more than just a place to live. The neighborhood was where they attended Mass, worked at the mill, and bowled.

Urban ethnic neighborhoods were insular. In the Polish Hill neighborhood of Pittsburgh, for example, no one would rent or sell their home to an ethnic Italian, let alone an African-American. "White ethnics," as the media took to calling them, sat on their front porches in Baltimore, Chicago, Cleveland, Detroit, New York, and Pittsburgh. They talked with neighbors— and watched for people who did not belong. By the end of the 1950s, white ethnics noticed that there were more African-Americans overflowing from their crowded neighborhoods into working-class Catholic neighborhoods.

Southern migration increased the black population of Detroit from 140,000 (9 percent) in 1940 to 300,000 (16 percent) in 1950. By 1960, Detroit's black population was 482,000 (29 percent). According to public opinion surveys in 1950s Detroit, white members of the United Automobile

Workers (UAW) expressed great fear of black encroachment. This was a problem for Michigan Democrats since UAW members and Detroit's African-Americans were the backbone of the state party. The UAW rank-and-file blamed African-American poverty on bad lifestyle choices rather than on discrimination. Ironically, that is what middle-class Protestants had argued decades earlier when discussing Catholic immigrants from southern and eastern Europe.

Beyond identifying blacks with crime, white ethnics were also convinced that they were destroying the property values of their houses. In 1950s Baltimore, as was true in other northern cities, white real estate developers adopted a tactic known as "block-busting." Realtors would target the periphery of a working-class black or white ethnic neighborhood, and buy a house. They would then subdivide the house into rental units and find poor blacks to crowd into the units. The realtor-landlords would refuse to fix toilets or clear trash. Neighbors, fearing that their home values would plummet, began panic-selling to the realtors at cut-rates. Property values in 1950s Baltimore, for instance, fell 50 percent in block-busted neighborhoods, allowing realtors to purchase houses at a bargain.

Having seen their only major asset wiped out, and fearful of the crime that came with deteriorating neighborhoods, white ethnics blamed African-Americans for their misery. After several years, block-busting realtors could apply for federal grants and tax breaks to renovate historical neighborhoods. They would then evict low-income black renters and sell the homes at a profit to middle-class professionals.

Realtors claimed that they were promoting the racial integration of white neighborhoods. They also informed the news media that their white ethnic critics were racists. In turn, working-class Catholics called the block-busters predators who disguised themselves in the cloak of racial justice. Many politicians were tempted to exploit urban America's growing class and racial antagonisms. There was little upside, however, for northern Democrats, since it was their voters who were antagonistic toward each other.

Civil Rights Reaction, 1961–1964

In Alabama, **George Wallace** emerged as a national political figure. A member of the G.I. Generation, Wallace had remained loyal to Harry Truman in 1948. As a state legislator, Wallace supported a New Deal for Alabama, advocating the construction of better hospitals and schools—albeit segregated. By 1962, Wallace had recoiled from civil rights protest. Elected governor of Alabama, his 1963 gubernatorial inaugural address received national news media attention for one line: "Segregation today, segregation tomorrow, segregation forever" [Document 10: p. 153].

What the news media overlooked was Wallace's deliberate racial appeal to northern white ethnics. Wallace was looking beyond the Alabama governorship. He was putting forward a strategy to break up the Democratic electoral coalition by depicting blacks as agents of social disorder in both North and South. Uniting southern white Protestants and northern working-class Catholics was Wallace's ticket to the White House.

Conservative Republicans rejected Wallace as a leader, but did not necessarily repudiate his strategy. William F. Buckley, Jr., and the *National Review* had no use for either George Wallace or Ross Barnett. It was not that the *National Review* opposed segregation. Conservative "fusionists" believed that Alabama and Mississippi had the right to exclude black students from admission to "white" universities. This was a states' rights issue; the federal government had no constitutional authority to intervene in university admissions policies, or to compel businesses to serve African-Americans.

The problem with Barnett and Wallace, the *National Review* argued, was that they were alienating states' rights supporters in Congress and the news media. Moreover, Wallace remained at heart a New Dealer. He might maintain segregated universities and hospitals in Alabama, but Wallace was also inclined to raise taxes and spend money building new universities and hospitals. Wallace also had little use for the conservative movement's emerging icon, Arizona senator Barry Goldwater. At least Barnett was willing to pledge his support for the Arizona conservative's 1964 presidential campaign.

In 1962, Goldwater had received a heated lecture from former president Eisenhower, who had supported Kennedy's intervention at Ole Miss. Conservative newspaper publisher Eugene Pulliam reassured Goldwater that he was right to oppose Kennedy. Goldwater also consulted his friend, Phoenix attorney **William Rehnquist**, on the Ole Miss confrontation. Rehnquist informed Goldwater that Kennedy's decision to send federal troops to Mississippi and impose desegregation was unconstitutional. He was referring to the 1878 "*Posse Comitatus* Act" which limited the federal government's legal authority to use the military as an instrument of domestic law enforcement. Paradoxically, or not, the original legislation had been intended to prevent Republican presidents from sending federal troops to the South to protect blacks from violence.

Goldwater also drew upon the legal advice of **Robert Bork**, a Yale Law School professor. Bork argued that the legal issue was "not whether racial prejudice or preference is a good thing, but whether individual men ought to be free to deal and associate with whom they please for whatever reasons appeal to them." The law professor regarded individual rights as an absolute bulwark against government coercion. In 1963, Bork shared his legal insight with the politically centrist readers of *The New Republic* magazine. He later regretted expressing his thoughts outside conservative circles.

As a leader of the conservative faction in the Arizona Republican Party, Rehnquist's words carried weight with Goldwater. In 1962 and 1964, Rehnquist had organized attorneys to go to the polls and observe, photograph, and challenge black and Mexican-American voters. Rehnquist's

Figure 3.2 Barry Goldwater (1909–1998), Republican Senator from Arizona, 1953–1965, and 1969–1987
Source: Courtesy of the Library of Congress Prints and Photographs Division

actions were not just about the segregation and disenfranchisement of racial minorities. By the beginning of the 1960s, the Arizona Republican Party was the white party while the Democrats looked for electoral success by securing voting rights for African-Americans, Mexican-Americans, and Native Americans.

Both Clarence Manion and *National Review* writer William Rusher had been discussing the electoral advantages of appealing to western and southern white voters' opposition to civil rights. If successful, conservatives could lead southern whites away from the Democratic Party. Politicians and journalists began to call this the "**Southern Strategy**." Strom Thurmond had shown the way forward in 1948. The Modern Republican civil rights detour was over, at least as far as Goldwater's supporters were concerned.

Kennedy's assassination in 1963, and Vice President Lyndon Johnson's ascension to the White House, gave momentum to the passage of federal civil rights legislation. The 1964 Civil Rights Act made it a federal offense for businesses to discriminate in employment, housing, and providing service to lodgers and diners. It also established the Equal Employment Opportunity

Commission (EEOC) to investigate allegations of discrimination in employment. Johnson was lining up northern Republicans and Democrats and trying to peel a few southern Democrats away from the segregationist bloc.

Goldwater insisted that his opposition to the 1964 Civil Rights Act was not motivated by support for racial discrimination—although discrimination is what helped keep Arizona conservatives in power. Rather, Goldwater argued that Johnson's legislation was an unconstitutional assault on states' rights and an infringement on business owners' right to refuse service or employment to anyone they desired. Further, Goldwater asserted, the 1964 Civil Rights Act coerced people to comply with federal dictates, making America a police state just like the Soviet Union [Document 11: p. 154].

The 1964 Election

The American Enterprise Institute (AEI), which changed its name from the American Enterprise Association in 1962, wanted Goldwater in the White House. As a tax-exempt, non-profit educational organization, the AEI could not directly participate in the electoral process. Its researchers, past and present, however, could take a leave of absence from the AEI to work on a Goldwater campaign. If successful, AEI allies would take positions in the Goldwater White House. Failure meant returning to their jobs at the Washington-based think tank and feeding legislative resistance to President Johnson's domestic and foreign policy initiatives.

AEI researcher Karl Hess, and former think tank writer Phyllis (Stewart) Schlafly, made enormous contributions to the Goldwater campaign. Hess became Goldwater's speechwriter and helped draft the 1964 Republican Party platform. Racial hatred did not motivate his opposition to federal power. Indeed, Hess became an advocate of a libertarian alliance of Right and Left against American "militarism" at home and abroad.

Schlafly drew upon her own financial resources to self-publish a salute to Goldwater and conservatism, *A Choice, Not an Echo*. Her book became the go-to reference for Goldwater campaign volunteers and went on to sell 3 million copies. The popularity of Schlafly's book persuaded Goldwater that he had to lead a crusade against the ever-expanding New Deal State.

Goldwater's volunteers were well-financed, motivated, and linked through a national communication network. *The Manion Forum*, *Human Events*, and the *National Review* provided campaign news outside the national media and regular Republican Party circles. Many of the Goldwater volunteers, especially the John Birch Society contingent, had never been engaged in electoral politics. They were Goldwater conservatives, not Republicans.

Modern Republicans were not prepared for the conservative offensive. New York governor and Standard Oil heir Nelson Rockefeller pursued the Republican presidential nomination. Rockefeller had money, but few enthusiastic volunteers willing to turn out in primaries and state Republican Party meetings to show their support. When Rockefeller faltered, Pennsylvania governor and corporate heir William Scranton tried to rally the Republican Party against Goldwater. Scranton's effort came too late.

At the Republican National Convention, Goldwater gave an uncompromising acceptance speech. Normally, presidential candidates use their acceptance speech to introduce themselves to voters who had paid little attention to the primaries. Nominees usually reassured voters that they were pleasant people who wanted to be voters' friend. Goldwater, however, took the red-hot speech written for him and gave it even more passion. Two lines electrified the audience and appalled the nation: "I would remind you that extremism in the defense of liberty is no vice! And let me remind you also that moderation in the pursuit of justice is no virtue!" [Document 12: p. 155].

Journalists noted that Goldwater, rather than appealing to the ideological center in order to attract the largest number of voters possible, had kept to the Right. Eisenhower summoned Goldwater once again, but this time he did not meekly listen to the general's lecture. Instead, Goldwater told Eisenhower that extremism was not a bad thing. After all, it was extreme for Eisenhower to have invaded Europe during World War II.

The problem for Goldwater was his political tone-deafness. When Americans heard the word "extremism" in 1964, they were not thinking about defeating Hitler. Instead, Americans thought about the three civil rights workers reported missing in Philadelphia, Mississippi, or the bombing of black churches in Birmingham, Alabama. Rather than consider that most Americans did not share his understanding of extremism, Goldwater made matters worse for himself. He contended that the civil rights movement provoked a violent response through its non-violent tactics. Civil rights activists were radicals undermining the liberty of citizens who wanted to be free to serve or not serve whom they pleased. The more Goldwater talked, the more unhinged he appeared.

Buckley had distanced the conservative movement from the John Birch Society—and lost subscribers to the *National Review* in the process. Goldwater's rhetoric, however, undermined Buckley's efforts to police the conservative movement. The senator also left the Republican Party open to attack. One expected that California's Democratic governor, Pat Brown, would charge that all the Goldwater convention speech lacked was an ending salutation: "Heil Hitler!" For Governor Scranton to imply that Republicans should vote for Johnson, however, was noteworthy. The *Saint Louis Post-Dispatch* reflected the national news media assessment of Goldwater's supporters: "The Goldwater coalition is a coalition of southern racists, county-seat conservatives, desert-rightist radicals, and suburban backlashers."

Goldwater antagonized voters nearly everywhere he went. He advocated privatizing Social Security, which, in effect, would end the retirement system and most probably defund the federal unemployment compensation entitlement. Goldwater promised to abolish the Tennessee Valley

Authority and force farmers to pay more for electricity. He doubled down on his opposition to civil rights legislation and attacked labor unions—uniting bickering northern African-Americans and white ethnics against a common enemy.

It became obvious that Goldwater was not actually running against Johnson. Goldwater had two other enemies in mind. The first was Franklin Roosevelt. Goldwater wanted to dismantle the New Deal. His other target was the American people. Americans, Goldwater implied, had embraced federal subsidies and ripped up the Constitution. More than a few conservative intellectuals in the 1950s had concluded that the greatest threat to America was Americans who had grown accustomed to federal benefits. Goldwater appeared to be rendering the same judgment. Politicians typically flattered, not insulted, voters, but Goldwater was not a politician: he was a prophet calling for retribution against a sinful people.

All Johnson had to do was sit back and watch Goldwater implode. Johnson, however, could not resist setting off Goldwater. In what became known as the "Daisy Girl" television commercial, a young girl plucked the petals off a flower while an ominous voice in the background began the countdown for launching nuclear missiles. Then, an atomic mushroom cloud flashed across the screen as Johnson warned that people needed to get along with each other—and hinted that Goldwater would start World War III.

Goldwater cried that Johnson was depicting him as a nuclear bomber who wanted to slaughter children. The problem for Goldwater is that he did not know when to stop talking. Johnson only ran the "Daisy Girl" commercial once. Goldwater, however, kept bringing the commercial up at campaign stops. The three national television networks felt obliged to show "Daisy Girl" at no charge to Johnson so that viewers would know what Goldwater was attacking.

The 1964 election results were devastating for Republicans. Independents, who would normally split their ballots between the two parties, were so terrified of Goldwater that they voted Democratic all the way down the ticket. Dozens of Republican members of Congress lost their seats. The Republican share of the northern black vote fell from 24 percent in 1960 to 12 percent in 1964. Seven million Republicans who voted for Nixon in 1960 either chose Johnson or did not cast a presidential ballot. Johnson won 61 percent of the popular vote and carried forty-four states in the Electoral College.

There was some good news for conservatives. Goldwater had declared that he was going to "hunt where the ducks are." He campaigned vigorously in the Democratic South, where he waged a states' rights crusade. Goldwater managed to swing five southern states away from the Democrats: Alabama, Georgia, Louisiana, Mississippi, and South Carolina. Senator Thurmond, who worked tirelessly for Goldwater in South Carolina, switched his party affiliation to Republican. The "Southern Strategy" may not have resulted in a conservative victory in 1964, but its test run showed promise.

The Great Society

Johnson viewed his landslide reelection as a mandate for the expansion of federal social-welfare programs, as well as an endorsement of more legislation against racial discrimination. Having entered politics in the age of Roosevelt, Johnson believed that the U.S. government had the power (and obligation) to eradicate poverty, racism, and urban decay. As Johnson had announced in 1964, he was not seeking to build a better society. The Texan was going to build a *Great* Society.

The Great Society had many components. There would be a new federal agency, the Office of Economic Opportunity (OEO), to coordinate anti-poverty programs. Cities would build affordable housing and revitalize and integrate neighborhoods. A minimum Social Security payment, or floor, would be established so no matter how little money they paid into the system, retirees would be guaranteed a decent income. America, like its European counterparts, would have a national health insurance program with the creation of Medicare and Medicaid. Additionally, the federal government would provide subsidies for law students to go into low-income areas and provide free legal services to the poor.

Johnson's domestic programs failed for a variety of reasons. Social Security was already under financial stress by the 1960s as Americans lived longer and drew more on the system. By eliminating the relationship between what people paid in and what they collected, the minimal payment guaranteed fiscal insolvency. Social Security payroll taxes would have to be raised, but each increase meant that employers' labor costs also went up. Inevitably, employers would look at their rising labor costs and opt to relocate overseas or replace humans with robots.

Medicare, intended for retirees, required greater financial resources than Johnson had intended. Prolonged life expectancy meant escalating health care costs. As for Medicaid, which Johnson intended to provide health care to the poor, his advisers underestimated the cost. Johnson's policy experts had forecast that Medicaid would be a $2-billion-a-year program by 1990. The 1990 price tag was $90 billion. (Adjusted for inflation, $2 billion in 1965 would have been $15 billion in 1990.) Since the states shared in Medicaid costs, that meant their own budgets would come under pressure and force tax hikes or cuts in other services such as education and law enforcement.

Great Society programs also created unintended consequences. White ethnics resented block-busting realtors drawing War on Poverty funds to "revitalize" neighborhoods. Urban Democratic politicians despised federally subsidized legal aid workers who relished suing city governments for police brutality and inferior trash-collection services. The issue of policing became an increasingly sore point between legal aid advocates and law enforcement. In the decade of the 1960s, violent crime increased by over 100 percent. White ethnics blamed African-Americans for rising crime rates, citing drug addiction and out-of-wedlock births in slum neighborhoods. Civil rights activists argued that racism and poverty spawned crime.

Johnson's critical mistake on domestic policy was not understanding that the 1960s were not the 1930s. The 25 percent unemployment rate during the Great Depression had created the political environment to support the expansion of federal power. In contrast, the unemployment rate in the 1960s stood at 4 percent and the economy grew roughly 5 percent annually. Americans did not see widespread destitution. Instead, there were what sociologists were calling "pockets of poverty." Those pockets were far from the expanding suburbs, situated in places like the slums of North Philadelphia or in the Appalachian "hollers." Out of sight often proved to be out of mind.

Given America's booming economy, voters could not understand why social-welfare spending, adjusted for inflation, grew 322 percent in the 1960s. Many voters were also troubled by the Great Society's departure from the philosophy of the New Deal. In the 1930s, welfare programs required work in exchange for relief. The Great Society largely set aside work requirements. Moreover, the New Deal had made a distinction between the "deserving" and "undeserving" poor. The Great Society did not pass judgment on welfare recipients. Once the public became aware that it was possible to receive more money collecting welfare benefits than holding a minimum-wage-paying job, voter backlash against the Great Society became inevitable.

In contrast to social-welfare programs, most Americans, especially in the North, supported the 1964 Civil Rights Act and the 1965 Voting Rights Act. The right to dine at a restaurant or vote in an election were freedoms basic to citizenship in a democracy. Once Congress passed these laws, however, most Americans thought the issue of discrimination was solved. Johnson's policy advisers, however, had drawn a link between discrimination and poverty: both had to be solved or neither would be solved. The War on Poverty was central to securing civil rights for racial minorities.

Fundamentally, Johnson failed to persuade the public that the War on Poverty was necessary. When the era of urban riots dawned in 1965, it was too late for Johnson to win over the people. In 1965, in the Los Angeles neighborhood of Watts, a white police officer arrested an African-American for drunk driving. A rumor spread through Watts that white police officers had murdered the black driver. Rioting erupted, resulting in the deaths of thirty-four people and the torching of 977 buildings in a 150-block area.

In 1967, 100 cities experienced rioting. Detroit had the nation's worst riot following the actions of white police officers who tried to break up a homecoming party for two returning black Vietnam veterans. That city suffered $250 million in property damage. (Adjusted for inflation, that figure would be $1.7 billion today.) Many white Americans expressed impatience with African-Americans. They also faulted the War on Poverty for failing to make cities safer.

Vietnam

Unlike Kennedy, Johnson had placed a higher priority on domestic programs than foreign policy. Although an anti-communist, Johnson regarded foreign affairs as a distraction from domestic reforms. To his dismay, he had inherited from Kennedy a deteriorating military situation in South Vietnam. Kennedy had approved the removal of South Vietnamese president Ngo Diem in 1963, believing that his brutality fueled the communist insurgency. What got lost in translation was that when Kennedy agreed to Diem's ouster he thought South Vietnamese military officials meant that they would send him into exile—not assassinate him. With Diem gone, North Vietnamese communists accelerated terrorist attacks in South Vietnam. By 1964, North Vietnam was on the verge of conquering South Vietnam.

Johnson did not want to intervene militarily in South Vietnam for two reasons. First, anti-communist members of Congress, Democrat and Republican, would insist that the U.S. focus on winning the war in Vietnam. They would either scale back or block the implementation of the Great Society. Second, Johnson was depicting Goldwater as a crazed warmonger, which was not hard to do when he made jokes about lobbing hand grenades into the men's room of the Soviet Kremlin. In 1964, Johnson was the peace candidate who warned Americans that if they voted for Goldwater the nation would be at war within six months. As conservatives ironically observed, Johnson was correct. They voted for Goldwater and America was at war within six months.

The president's options were limited. Johnson could not allow the communists to conquer South Vietnam given that the specter of McCarthyism still loomed over Washington. Moreover, the Truman Doctrine remained a bipartisan rock of American foreign policy. When North Vietnamese patrol boats fired on an American destroyer in the Gulf of Tonkin in the summer of 1964, Johnson seized upon the opportunity to demonstrate strength—and restraint. Johnson went to Congress with the Gulf of Tonkin Resolution, requesting authorization to respond to the communist attack. He insisted it was a limited response, not a prelude to military escalation. Johnson's advisers observed that they were avoiding Harry Truman's mistake in Korea when he bypassed Congress in favor of seeking UN participation. Only two senators voted against the Gulf of Tonkin Resolution. Even Goldwater rallied behind Johnson.

After his inauguration in January 1965, the military situation in South Vietnam deteriorated further. Johnson commenced bombing North Vietnam in February 1965. The North Vietnamese responded by infiltrating more troops into South Vietnam along the Ho Chi Minh Trail, which ran through the "neutral" nations of Laos and Cambodia. By March 1965, Johnson introduced the first combat troops into South Vietnam. Three months later, Johnson had sent 125,000 troops to defend South Vietnam—a number which grew to 525,000 by 1968. All the while Johnson kept sending peace messages to North Vietnam. His diplomatic gestures convinced North Vietnamese leaders that Johnson did not want to fight and that they could wear down American resolve.

Johnson's failure in Vietnam had military as well as political roots. Countering an insurgency with conventional tactics proved ineffective. Artillery shells and bombs did not distinguish between friend and foe, unlike well-trained Special Forces. Moreover, Johnson believed that he had to be careful about bombing North Vietnam given the presence of 300,000 Chinese support troops. Johnson did not want another Korean War. Of course, if bombing North Vietnam was to be limited, and Cambodia and Laos continued to aid North Vietnam without fear of reprisal, then there was only one choice left: bomb South Vietnam. The U.S. dropped several times the number of bombs on South Vietnam than it had on Germany and Japan in World War II. Seldom has a major power chosen to destroy its ally rather than take the war to the enemy's homeland.

Political considerations trumped everything when it came to Vietnam. Johnson wanted to minimize the war for the American people. He would not raise taxes, preferring to borrow money and float deficits. Tax hikes would draw attention to the war and lead Congress to demand a choice: pay for the War in Vietnam or for the War on Poverty.

Johnson refused to call up the Guard and Reserves, as Wilson, Roosevelt, and Truman had done. National Guardsmen and Reservists tended to be in their late twenties or older and established in their communities. Sending them to Vietnam would create too much community disruption. In any event, it was not necessary to use Reserves or the Guard to fulfill manpower requirements. There were so many draft-eligible men in the 18–25-year-old cohort thanks to the post-World War II Baby Boom that the military did not need Guard or Reserves. Selective Service could also continue to exempt college students with the II-S draft deferment. Forcing young men to put off college to serve in the military would, like calling up the National Guard and Reserves, draw attention to the war.

The Baby Boom draft cohort was large enough that Selective Service could focus on drafting eighteen and nineteen-year-olds. Younger draftees were less likely to be married or set in a career. Consequently, the average age of American soldiers in Vietnam was nineteen, compared with twenty-six in World War II. What youths had in physical endurance, they often lacked in mature judgment. On the battlefield, that could be bad for soldiers and civilians alike.

Most fatefully, the Department of Defense developed a special troop rotation system for Vietnam. Rather than serve the full two years of their military obligation, or until the war was won, individuals who went into combat would be rotated out after one year. Johnson hoped that quick turnaround, also made possible by the enormous size of the draft cohort, would minimize the war's disruption of everyday life.

The economic, political, and social consequences of Johnson's Vietnam policy proved disastrous for the nation—and for the Democratic Party. Borrowing and deficit spending for the war began to overheat the American economy. By 1966, the inflation rate rose to 6 percent—eating away Americans' paychecks.

Rotating soldiers and Marines on a one-year basis undermined American combat effectiveness. In Korea and World War II, for instance, troops served for the duration—which meant until victory, death, or severe injury. If a soldier or Marine suffered death or injury, it would typically happen in the first three months of deployment. After that period, veteran troops learned to rely on each other and to anticipate each other's actions. Combat deaths and injuries declined because of the "seasoning" process. In Vietnam, the constant influx of new, inexperienced troops increased American casualties. The more youths who returned home missing limbs, or who died, the more Americans noticed the war that Johnson had hoped they would ignore.

College draft deferments also had unanticipated consequences. Between 1960 and 1970, college student enrollment grew from 3 million to 10 million. Avoidance of the draft fueled some of that increase among males, but the massive Baby Boom itself expanded the college student pool. As student enrollment swelled, the number of college professors grew from 111,000 in 1940 to 551,000 by 1970.

Over the course of the 1960s, larger numbers of students and faculty protested the war and, most especially, the draft—which affected youths if they flunked out of college. Since World War II, many colleges had been engaged in projects related to the Cold War, from Michigan State University building the governmental infrastructure of South Vietnam to Pennsylvania State University developing submarine-launched Polaris missiles. Such activities drew the attention of campus student and faculty protesters opposed to America's anti-communist foreign policy. Opponents of the Cold War came to regard college campuses as political organizing bases with which to capture the Democratic Party.

The expansion of American universities, as well as the provision of student draft deferments, helped feed into a class bias in terms of who went to Vietnam and who did not. Just 17 percent of college students in the 1960s came from working-class backgrounds while 80 percent of the soldiers who served in Vietnam had blue-collar origins. In World War II, soldiers came from all classes.

Public distrust of the political system grew as Johnson escalated the war. The sons of his Secretary of Defense, Secretary of the Army, and Attorney General claimed student draft deferments and participated in campus protests. Meanwhile, the children and grandchildren of influential Modern Republicans and conservatives found ways to avoid going to Vietnam. The grandson of Eisenhower's ally in the Senate, Prescott Bush of Connecticut, did not go to Vietnam. **George W. Bush** took a student draft deferment and then secured a prized slot in the Texas National Guard, which would not be deployed to Vietnam. Among conservatives, the grandson of publisher Eugene Pulliam, Dan Quayle, got into the Indiana National Guard. The son of William F. Buckley, Jr., Christopher Buckley, kept out of Vietnam by claiming health issues.

News media commentators and politicians in the 1960s took to calling supporters of the Vietnam War "**hawks**," and labeling the peace advocates "**doves**." Arizona congressman Mo Udall, a Democrat, coined a term for conservatives who supported the Vietnam War but preferred that working-class youths do the fighting: "**chicken hawks**."

The G.I. Generation expressed the greatest anger toward antiwar protesters and those who evaded the draft. Eventually, however, being a chicken hawk, or an antiwar protester, proved to be no barrier to political advancement. Vietnam became so unpopular among the post-G.I. generations that serving in the war seemed irrelevant to winning the White House. It may have even been an impediment. Only a minority of Baby Boomers served (41 percent) and the number of veterans declined after the elimination of compulsory military service in 1973. While eight presidents had worn the uniform in World War II, no Vietnam veteran (or Korean War veteran for that matter) advanced to the White House.

Youth Movement

In contrast to the majority-Democrat G.I. Generation, the Baby Boomers were ideologically divided. Two major political youth groups emerged in the early 1960s at opposite ends of the political spectrum. At one end of the spectrum were youths who identified themselves as "New Left," as opposed to the "Old Left." The chief organization of the New Left was Students for a Democratic Society (SDS). Founded in 1960, SDS grew to 100,000 members by 1969. SDS drew from the ranks of middle- and upper-middle-class white college students. Most had parents who were Franklin Roosevelt supporters in the 1930s—with a number voting for Henry Wallace in 1948. There were few Catholics, or children of Republicans, in New Left ranks.

While the Old Left of the 1930s looked to industrial unions and the working class as agents of social change, the New Left of the 1960s did not. Convinced that the white working class and the labor unions were irredeemably anti-communist and racist, partisans of the New Left wanted to organize racial minorities and enlightened middle-class college students. They rejected racial discrimination and America's Cold War foreign policy. Their political beliefs were a mixture of anti-authoritarian libertarianism and anti-anti-communism. Like their counterparts on the Right, the New Left identified their enemies as Roosevelt, Truman, Eisenhower, and Johnson.

The UAW, along with a handful of wealthy liberal donors, had helped fund SDS, believing it would become the youth arm of a revitalized

Democratic Party. They would regret their generosity. Not only did the New Left hold liberals in contempt and oppose the Vietnam War and the Great Society, SDS denounced the nation of Israel. Many liberal Jewish donors had celebrated the creation of Israel after World War II. In 1967, when Israel won a crushing military victory against its Arab neighbors, the New Left denounced Zionism—the belief in a Jewish State—as racism.

Some Jewish liberals, who had embraced Zionism and anti-communism, felt betrayed by SDS. Of greatest concern were the growing number of Democrats who saw Israel as just one more example of American-inspired imperialism. Israel's birth in 1948, after all, owed much to Truman's support—and his willingness to push back opposition from Great Britain, the Vatican, and nearly all the Arab nations.

While a labor union helped establish SDS, it was fitting that the "New Right" came into existence with the support of Buckley. In 1960, Buckley organized a meeting at the family estate in Sharon, Connecticut. The Young Americans for Freedom (YAF) subsequently issued its manifesto, the "Sharon Statement," underlining its departure from the "Old Right" of the 1930s. By 1969, YAF had grown to 50,000 members—half that of SDS.

YAF rejected Taft's **isolationism** and Eisenhower's embrace of communist containment in favor of a more confrontational foreign policy. The new conservative organization also avoided the Protestant moral sectarianism of the Old Right, which had often intertwined with anti-Catholicism and anti-Semitism. YAF embodied the fusionist conservatism the *National Review* had championed since 1955: anti-New Deal, anti-communist, and anti-Modern Republican.

There was a class and cultural divide in YAF from its very founding. The lower middle class, usually Irish and German, Catholic youths who joined YAF were often the first members of their families to go to college. Their parents might have voted for Roosevelt in 1932, but had turned against the New Deal and listened to the radio broadcasts of Father Charles Coughlin. By the early 1950s they were drawn to Joseph McCarthy. Such YAF partisans attended Catholic colleges, community colleges, or state universities. They were anti-communist, socially conservative, and fearful of an expansive federal government. Unlike other conservatives, they enlisted in the military. Clarence Manion's son, Daniel Manion, for instance, fought in the Vietnam War. In YAF ranks they became known as moral "traditionalists."

More affluent YAF members came from Republican Protestant families. (YAF had few Jewish members.) They followed their fathers' path to elite private colleges. Such YAF members were often libertarians who rejected government regulation of the boardroom and the bedroom. What drew them to YAF was the organization's opposition to growing federal power. They could work with their socially conservative counterparts so long as they did not try to use governmental power to impose their morality on others. YAF libertarians opposed stiff criminal penalties for narcotics possession, supported the legalization of prostitution, and denounced the Vietnam War.

68 *Analysis and Assessment*

Young libertarian males often avoided going to Vietnam. Some even followed the lead of Karl Hess, who went from the Goldwater presidential campaign to advocating an antiwar alliance with the New Left. Hillary Rodham, the daughter of affluent suburban Republicans, illustrated the trajectory from New Right to a reformed Democratic Party. Rodham campaigned as a "Goldwater Girl" in 1964 and then took her anti-authoritarian libertarianism to Wellesley and Yale Law School. Her college years saw her draw close to antiwar Democrats. Rodham completed her ideological journey by the time she married a charming law school classmate from Arkansas.

While YAF and SDS officially held contrasting views on the Vietnam War, unofficially, there were enough antiwar libertarians in the conservative youth movement to muddy that issue. The civil rights battle was another matter. To reform-minded Democrats and the New Left, the civil rights movement was central to their belief system. Birmingham, Alabama, and Philadelphia, Mississippi, were secular stations of the cross where the martyred endured pain in the hope of triumphant resurrection.

In contrast to SDS, most YAF members were indifferent to the civil rights struggle. Young conservatives focused on what they believed to be a far more important issue: communist expansion overseas—and in Washington. The New Left regarded YAF's priorities as more than wrong-headed—they were immoral. In 1961, SDS president Al Haber charged that YAF was allied with "racist, militarist, imperialist butchers" and did not deserve a presence on the nation's college campuses.

Ironically, the conservative and radical youth organizations were born and crashed in the same year. In 1969, SDS divided into factions which supported moving into a post-anti-communist Democratic Party and those advocating the bombing of buildings associated with law enforcement, the military, and Wall Street. Meanwhile YAF split between its libertarian and traditionalist factions. The traditionalists won the battle for control of YAF, but only after purging many libertarians. In the long term, casting out its elite-educated future high-income earners limited YAF's political influence—which, nonetheless, would still be considerable. That influence would be seen in Washington, though not on the college campus.

Reagan's Rise

Johnson's War on Poverty and the war in Vietnam sowed the seeds of political reaction. Ronald Reagan and Richard Nixon, both dismissed among political commentators as has-beens in the early 1960s, were the beneficiaries of the Great Society's implosion.

During the 1964 election, California conservatives, who had noticed Reagan's mounting dissatisfaction with the growth of government at the state and federal levels, approached him about making a televised fundraising appeal for Goldwater. Reagan agreed to do so, but not because he endorsed

Goldwater's assault on the New Deal. Rather, he believed that Johnson's domestic policy proposals represented a betrayal of Roosevelt.

Reagan's broadcast, "A Time for Choosing," was well-received, netting $8 million in donations to the Goldwater campaign [Document 13: p. 156]. (Adjusted for inflation, Reagan produced the equivalent of nearly $63 million today.) Tellingly, Reagan used a phrase that Roosevelt had made famous. Americans, Reagan argued, had a "rendezvous with destiny." In contrast to Goldwater, Reagan did not attack the New Deal, or rage against the American people for their addiction to government programs. There was also another difference. When Goldwater's lips were at rest he seemed to be sneering at voters. Reagan smiled as if in a pleasant conversation with friends.

After Goldwater's rout, California conservatives discussed running Reagan for governor in 1966. As Hollywood studio head Jack Warner said when he learned of the Reagan chatter: "Jimmy Stewart for governor. Ronald Reagan for his best friend." Warner was not entirely joking. California governor Pat Brown, having humiliated Richard Nixon in the 1962 gubernatorial election, appeared unbeatable. Events, however, intervened to change the political context.

Welfare spending in California, as a portion of the state budget, had grown from 2.5 percent in 1946 to 15 percent by 1966. Brown led the effort to increase welfare eligibility and eliminate work expectations. In 1963, 375,000 Californians received some form of state and federal welfare benefits. By 1966, that number had reached 1.5 million. Both working-class Democrats and middle-class Republicans began to charge that "Welfare Queens" refused to accept employment since they could collect generous welfare payments for having children out of wedlock. Although nationally just under half of the single mothers receiving welfare in 1966 were African-American, "Welfare Queen" became shorthand for black.

Complaints against "Welfare Queens" grew in the aftermath of the 1965 Watts riot. Governor Brown, like Johnson, cited inner-city poverty, discrimination, and bad policing as causes of urban unrest. Unfortunately for Brown and Johnson, larger numbers of voters interpreted their sociological analysis as little more than making excuses for criminal behavior. While working-class whites might have sympathized with those who disliked abusive police officers, it was politically foolish to appear to be explaining why some rioters felt compelled to shoot firefighters.

Beyond riots, crime, and welfare, one more element entered the California political mix: activist college students. An altercation in 1964 at the University of California at Berkeley between campus authorities and students distributing political literature evolved into full-blown demonstrations. Once the Vietnam War escalated in 1965, peaceful protests gave way to violent clashes between student activists and police. As the flagship public university in California, Berkeley was at once a source of civic pride and class resentment. To the working-class taxpayers who subsidized free educations for the middle class, the Berkeley protests were insulting. Additionally, the fact that the male protesters were avoiding the Vietnam War while working-class youths went in their place made Berkeley a liability to Brown.

Reagan's decisive win with 57 percent of the vote shocked Great Society liberals all the way to Washington. As California governor (1967–1975), Reagan's policy positions angered and delighted conservatives. He also frustrated liberals who never figured out how to cut into his voter appeal.

The former actor criticized the 1964 Civil Rights Act and the 1965 Voting Rights Act, leaving him open to charges of racism. While he had a blind spot when it came to civil rights, Reagan was reluctant to cede too much power to government. Reagan did not believe the state, or federal, government, had a constitutional right to order businesses to cater to African-Americans, empower a public school to check into a teacher's sexual preference, or prevent a woman from obtaining an abortion. As governor, Reagan opposed efforts by conservative California Republicans to ban gay and lesbian teachers from public schools and signed into law a measure to make abortion safer and more available.

Reagan condemned violent student and faculty activists. He had no problem urging the arrest and prosecution of campus radicals. Reagan, however, did not retaliate by slashing university appropriations. All he had to do was sit back and watch as the rising costs of expanded student enrollment and university administration stressed college budgets. California universities responded by imposing, and then escalating, tuition charges. This dynamic ultimately shifted the finance of California's universities away from the taxpayers to students and their parents—who then blamed faculty and administration for their growing financial burden.

The California governor made much of the fact that he reduced welfare rolls by 200,000. This represented a 13 percent cut to a program that Brown had increased by several hundred percent. Reagan also signed off on tax hikes. He replied to conservative critics that with Democratic control of the state assembly, he had no choice but to agree to tax hikes, limited cuts to welfare, and looser abortion restrictions. This was as true as it was politically convenient. Democrats' inadvertently gave Reagan political cover on his Right flank. Conservatives, in California and nationally, were willing to give Reagan a pass since he was their only political star. By 1968, conservatives were even urging Reagan to run for the Republican presidential nomination. Given an alternative which they found distasteful, conservatives' embrace of Reagan was not surprising.

Nixon

Americans' frustration with the political system boiled over by the end of the 1960s. Martin Luther King, Jr., was in an unenviable position. Young radicals were impatient with his non-violent philosophy, demanding change "by any means necessary." In 1967, King had allied with the antiwar movement, denouncing "the greatest purveyor of violence in the world today—my own government." A year later, King's assassination sparked riots in 100 cities, including Washington. Eighty Democratic mayors and their city police chiefs blamed the Great Society for the riot surges of 1967 and 1968.

At the beginning of 1968, the North Vietnamese launched the "Tet Offensive," targeting provincial capitals and the U.S. Embassy in Saigon. They timed their military operation with the commencement of the presidential primaries. Militarily, the Tet Offensive was an American victory which resulted in the deaths of 40,000 communist guerrillas. The U.S. news media, however, emphasized American casualties and the fact that Johnson had been claiming prior to the Tet Offensive that the North Vietnamese were at the verge of defeat. Demoralized, Johnson announced that he would negotiate an end to the war and that he would not run for reelection.

Given his experience as a member of Congress and as vice president, Nixon was the logical Republican presidential nominee. Democratic Party leaders continued to despise Nixon for the humiliation he had inflicted upon them during the Hiss affair twenty years earlier. Conservatives also had their grievances. First, Nixon had not rallied in defense of Joseph McCarthy. Instead, he worked with Eisenhower to isolate and diminish McCarthy. Second, Nixon had been an active Eisenhower lieutenant, advancing the expansion of the welfare state in the 1950s. Third, given his civil rights record, Nixon did not appear able to advance the "Southern Strategy." Not surprisingly, Nixon privately shared his negative assessment of Buckley and other conservatives, calling them "wing nuts."

Democratic presidential nominee Hubert Humphrey might have been able to defeat Nixon if not for two developments. First, antiwar radicals and Chicago police had clashed in front of television cameras at the 1968 national convention, embarrassing Vice President Humphrey. Second, former Alabama governor George Wallace sealed Humphrey's fate by running for president as an independent. While still a foe of the civil rights movement, Wallace shifted his rhetorical targets. Wallace decried radical antiwar demonstrators and championed the "average man in the street" who labored as a police officer, steel worker, or owner of a small business. He also tossed out some gems that resonated with working-class whites. Wallace observed that privileged activists may have used a lot of "four letter words," but they did not know two important ones: "W-O-R-K" and "S-O-A-P."

To Democratic Party leaders, Wallace's populist, anti-elite speeches were no laughing matter. Wallace drew support from pessimistic working-class white voters under the age of thirty. He was not only attracting southern white Protestant voters, Wallace was gaining among white union members in Illinois, Michigan, Ohio, Pennsylvania, and Wisconsin. Although he could not win those key industrial states, Wallace could siphon enough votes from Humphrey to throw those states to Nixon. Buckley expressed horror at Wallace, leading him reluctantly to support Nixon.

Wallace received just 13.5 percent of the popular vote. Looked at more closely, however, Democrats had cause for alarm. Wallace won five

Figure 3.3 George C. Wallace (1919–1998), Three-Time Governor of Alabama: From 1963 to 1967, 1971 to 1979, and 1983 to 1987
Source: Courtesy of the Library of Congress Prints and Photographs Division

southern Democratic states: Arkansas, Alabama, Georgia, Louisiana, and Mississippi—nearly replicating Goldwater's 1964 performance. He also took enough working-class white Democrats to throw Ohio, Illinois, and Wisconsin to Nixon. Overall, Humphrey received just 35 percent of the majority white vote—which doomed the Democrats.

Wallace's key fundraiser, Texas native and former national YAF officer **Richard Viguerie**, realized that his extensive list of donors could be the foundation upon which to build a grass-roots populist conservatism that could appeal to disaffected New Deal Democrats. Viguerie's strategy, however, was not without its threat to conservatives and the Republican Party. It would mean broadening the base of the conservative movement beyond intellectuals and corporate leaders. Every Southern Baptist let in meant another voice in favor of socially conservative domestic policies—which potentially meant the expansion of federal regulatory powers. Moreover, every northern working-class Catholic attracted to conservatism represented more, not less, New Deal influence inside the Republican Party. If successful, however, this could be the beginning of a powerful new Republican coalition.

Nixon was both shrewd and reckless. On Vietnam, he reduced troop levels, replacing Americans with South Vietnamese soldiers. He also escalated the bombing of North Vietnam. Nixon suspected that most students opposed the war because they did not want to be drafted. So, he established a draft lottery even as he eliminated the student draft deferment. Once students knew if they had a high draft number, and were thus unlikely to be forced into the military, nearly all campus antiwar protests ceased. Nixon also established relations with China and negotiated trade agreements with the Soviet Union. Subsequently, both the Russians and the Chinese began to back off in their support of North Vietnam.

His recklessness, however, destroyed his presidency. Nixon knew that for the U.S. to prevail in South Vietnam, he had to intercept North Vietnamese soldiers and supplies along the Ho Chi Minh Trail in Laos and Cambodia. He also knew that the Democratic Congress, divided over the war, would not authorize the bombing of Cambodia and Laos. Nixon went ahead without the approval of Congress. When government officials began secretly releasing information about that bombing to the news media, Nixon established a clandestine unit, the plumbers, to seal the leaks. Illegal wiretaps, break-ins, and surveillance followed.

Nixon appealed to the "**Silent Majority**" of Americans who hated the war and the antiwar movement in equal measure. He promised "law and order" in the nation's inner cities and on the college campuses. Working-class whites, southern whites, and Catholics, who had most often voted Democratic, saw Nixon offering them political shelter from campus and inner-city disorder. Wallace had given the "Silent Majority" a taste of rebellion against Democratic liberalism in 1968. Nixon wanted to turn that rebellion into an electoral realignment.

Nixon also established himself as a reformer, creating the Environmental Protection Agency (EPA) in 1970. The federal government now had the power to regulate businesses and protect America's water supply and quality of air. In 1971, Nixon established the Occupational Safety and Health Administration (OSHA) to regulate labor conditions in the workplace.

Conservatives cried foul as Nixon expanded the regulatory functions of the federal government. Nixon gave conservatives two prizes. First, he appointed Arizona conservative William Rehnquist to the Supreme Court. Senate Democrats, who could have blocked Rehnquist's confirmation, did not delve deeply into his political activities in Arizona. In 1972, however, it was rare for members of one party to block the Supreme Court nominations made by the president from another party. Second, in 1973 Nixon established the Drug Enforcement Agency (DEA). Social conservatives rejoiced in Nixon's "War on Drugs," though many libertarians regarded the DEA as just one more example of federal regulatory overreach.

Electoral Realignment. Again?

After the 1968 election, South Dakota senator George McGovern led a successful effort to reform the Democratic Party's nomination process.

Under the established system, members of Congress and state legislatures, big-city party bosses, and the presidents of union locals typically served as Democratic National Convention delegates. State primaries were often "beauty contests," designed to show off a candidate to the press and the public. The actual selection of presidential nominees and delegates took place in the classic "smoked-filled rooms" behind closed doors. It was a "good ole boy" process that worked as nearly often as it failed. Truman had received the vice-presidential nomination in this manner in 1944, while Roosevelt's team had massaged egos and made promises to secure the presidential nomination in 1932.

McGovern demanded that the primary voters choose convention delegates. The Democratic Party, demoralized by Vietnam, campus and urban unrest, and Nixon's victory, went along with McGovern's changes. What Democratic leaders did not anticipate, though, was that most voters ignore primaries. Only the motivated showed up to vote. The most motivated Democrats in 1972 (and largely afterward), opposed America's Cold War foreign policy, sought to overturn state-level restrictions on abortion, and emphasized rehabilitation, rather than incarceration, of criminal offenders. McGovern embodied the reform wing of the Democratic Party. He ran for the Democratic presidential nomination taking advantage of the changes he helped write.

Post-World War II America experienced a host of economic and cultural shifts that affected politics—most especially Democratic Party politics. In 1940, the U.S. employed 854,000 miners and 111,000 college professors. By 1970, the number of miners had fallen to 164,000 while college faculty ranks increased to 551,000. Just prior to America's entry into World War II, there were 4.2 million municipal, state, and federal government employees in the U.S. By the early 1970s, America had 15 million people working as city, state, or federal government employees. A shift away from manufacturing and private-sector employment toward public-sector employment and jobs requiring advanced education had occurred largely out of sight of the news media.

The cultural impact of America's employment shift could not be ignored. College faculty, public-sector employees, and those with advanced education tended to be more liberal on social issues, more inclined to support the expansion of government, and more willing to impose higher taxes and greater regulations on corporations. For example, public opinion polling data in the early 1970s revealed that 73 percent of white-collar professionals, typically employed in the public sector, supported abortion with few restrictions. Seventy-three percent expressed sympathy for gays and lesbians. In contrast, among high school-educated working-class whites, 68 percent criticized abortion and 89 percent did not support gay and lesbian civil rights.

McGovern drew upon socially liberal white-collar professionals, public-sector employees, and university students to win the Democratic Party's presidential nomination in 1972. Wallace, who had returned to the Democratic

Party to run in the primaries, gave McGovern a scare. The southerner drew upon disaffected working-class whites who opposed the bussing of their children to all-black inner-city public schools to win the Michigan primary. An unsuccessful assassination attempt, which left Wallace paralyzed, removed him from the race.

The senator's remaining problem, however, could not be resolved. As McGovern appealed to feminists, abortion-rights activists, and anti-Cold War partisans, he repelled socially conservative working-class whites, labor union members, white southerners, and northern Catholics. McGovern also lost the support of many liberal Jewish intellectuals, including **Irving Kristol** and Norman Podhoretz, who thought the senator's allies were hostile to Israel. Their complaints grew as they perceived McGovern's followers as anti-Semitic, too tolerant of urban crime, and naïve about the Soviet Union's intentions around the world. The media soon designated this group as **"neoconservatives."**

McGovern was the first Democrat since the age of Roosevelt to lose working-class whites, the South, Catholics, and labor union members. Nixon won nearly 61 percent of the popular vote and carried forty-nine states. McGovern took Massachusetts and Washington, D.C., although he often scored well in counties that housed a public flagship university.

While McGovern's epic defeat placed him in the company of Barry Goldwater and Alf Landon, Democrats maintained control of Congress and dominated state-level offices in the South. Talk among Nixon White House staffers of an electoral realignment was as premature as Senator Robert Taft's belief that the 1946 midterm elections had ushered in a conservative golden age.

Conservatives took little joy in Nixon's victory. Buckley did not trust Nixon and regarded him as a traitor. William Rusher, who had been the publisher of *National Review* since 1957, refused to endorse Nixon for reelection because of his treacherous overtures to China. Conservatives also remained ill at ease at the prospect of bringing unrepentant New Deal-"Silent Majority" voters into the Republican tent. It was also an open question as to whether Nixon so much won the election, as the Democrats self-destructed by changing their primary nomination process and elevating McGovern to the top of the ticket. The minute Nixon faltered, conservatives would openly repudiate him. Unbeknownst to conservatives, however, Nixon's victory foreshadowed the biggest political realignment since the creation of the New Deal coalition forty years earlier.

4 Conservative Advance, 1973–1980

Falling, 1973–1975

During Richard Nixon's 1972 reelection campaign several of his operatives had placed wiretaps in the offices of the Democratic National Committee located at Washington's Watergate Hotel. When one of the listening devices failed, the campaign workers returned to replace the bug and were caught. Nixon, who initially knew nothing about the Watergate wiretaps, sealed his fate when he decided to cover up the activities of his rogue operatives.

Nixon's decision proved to be his undoing. He had been secretly recording his conversations in the Oval Office. Consequently, Nixon's recommendation to cover up the Watergate break-in was on tape. Moreover, Nixon's staffers, either by a slip of the tongue or because they wanted to save themselves from charges of obstruction of justice, informed the Democratic Congress that Nixon had been recording his conversations. Democrats demanded that Nixon turn over the "Watergate tapes."

Conservative Republicans were reluctant to defend Nixon, while Modern Republicans did not want to be associated with political corruption. It had not helped Nixon's political position when his vice president, Spiro Agnew, stepped down in 1973 following revelations that he had taken bribes. Even Nixon's friend, Billy Graham, deplored the Watergate cover-up. Graham subsequently reduced his political activities. Abandoned by all, Nixon resigned as president in 1974 rather than face impeachment.

Gerald Ford, who had replaced Agnew as vice president, took possession of the Oval Office. A Republican congressman from Michigan, Ford identified with the Eisenhower, rather than the Goldwater, wing of his party. Lyndon Johnson had spent years ridiculing Ford's intelligence. To conservatives, Johnson's abuse of Ford was the only mark of distinction the Michigan congressman had achieved in Washington.

Ford's presidency witnessed the free-fall of the Republican Party. The 1974 midterm elections saw the Democrats gain forty-nine House seats, largely in northern, upper-middle-class suburban districts that had been represented by Modern Republicans. Ironically, Eisenhower Republicans were more likely to lose their House seats than were Goldwater conservatives. Congressional districts with a large proportion of college-educated, socially liberal voters turned against their Republican representatives. Conservative congressional districts, in contrast, had great numbers of working-class white voters who had not gone to college. These voters were often socially conservative and, though not willing to undo the New Deal order, were happy to bury the Great Society.

Conservatives wept few tears. Even though Republican ranks thinned in the House, those remaining were more ideologically conservative. There was also cause for celebration. Conservatives had rejoiced in the election of **Jesse Helms** to the Senate in 1972. Helms was a rising star who came from the all-important South, which conservatives hoped to capture from the Democrats. He served up red-hot rhetoric. The North Carolinian identified African-Americans with rising crime rates and denounced liberal college students as purveyors of "orgies and mayhem." Helms all but called the Democratic Congress treasonous for standing aside as North Vietnam conquered South Vietnam in 1975. Like Johnson, Helms held Ford in contempt.

Just as political set-backs in the 1930s had spurred conservatives to establish a public policy think tank, the American Enterprise Institute (AEI), the dispiriting 1970s led their successors to repeat history. Colorado beer baron **Joseph Coors**, joined by textile magnate and Goldwater champion Roger Milliken, founded the Washington-based **Heritage Foundation** in 1973. While the AEI had played a major, unofficial role in the 1964 Goldwater campaign, Coors and other conservatives viewed it as insufficiently action-oriented. Where the AEI produced lengthy policy studies, Heritage generated shorter position papers which were distributed to sympathetic office holders and news media outlets. The Heritage Foundation strained its non-partisan, non-profit tax exemption status—more so even than the AEI had in 1964.

In many ways Coors was an ideal replacement for J. Howard Pew, who had died in 1971. Coors detested labor unions, though he had to tolerate one at his company. Brewing, after all, was historically a bastion of unionism and workers were highly skilled and thus in demand by his competitors. As a member of the University of Colorado board of regents, Coors had spent the 1960s calling for the expulsion of student radicals and for the dismissal of their faculty allies. The other regents mostly ignored Coors, believing that it was their duty to protect the public reputation of the state's flagship university.

Coors campaigned for Goldwater but found a better presidential candidate in 1968: Ronald Reagan. He was willing to overlook Reagan's relatively liberal record as California governor, seeing in the former actor something Coors had never seen in Goldwater—a winner. The Heritage Foundation could supply Reagan with policy ideas and, if things went well, White House staffers. That did not mean, however, that conservatives abandoned the AEI. They made it possible for the AEI to increase its budget ten times over in the 1970s.

While conservative businessmen created a new think tank to advance their political agenda, others were contemplating the construction of an electoral majority. Former Nixon White House staffer **Patrick Buchanan** had been convinced that the 1972 election was the winning template for conservatives. Nixon's humiliation did not have to be the end of conservatives' efforts to build upon the "Silent Majority."

Having grown up in a lower-middle-class Catholic family which embraced Father Charles Coughlin's anti-New Deal radio broadcasts, and which revered Joseph McCarthy as a warrior-saint, Buchanan was destined to be blunt. In 1975, as a conservative newspaper columnist, Buchanan spelled out his vision: "If there is a role for the Republican Party, it is to be the party of the working class, not the welfare class." Buchanan later left no room for doubt about his meaning, arguing that Republicans needed to recruit working-class whites and forget about African-Americans, who were too attached to federal programs to break away from the Democrats.

The Republican Party may have been reeling from Nixon's downfall, but conservatives were regrouping for the next battle—just as they had after the disastrous 1936 Roosevelt landslide. Ford, who decided to run for reelection in 1976, did not appear aware that conservatives had identified *him*, and the Republican Party, as the enemy.

Fighting for Control, 1973–1976

In 1972, the Democratic Congress had approved a constitutional amendment to send to the state legislatures for ratification. The proposed Equal Rights Amendment (ERA) stated that: "Equality of rights under the law shall not be abridged by the United States or by any State on account of sex." Democrats and liberal Republicans did not think that the ERA was controversial. Indeed, Ford's wife, Betty, was a proud ERA supporter. Conservative activist Phyllis Schlafly, however, saw matters differently.

Having spent her political career as a foe of federal economic regulation and international communism, Schlafly introduced herself to the wider public in the early 1970s as a champion of morality and foe of feminism [Document 14: p. 158]. Schlafly launched a STOP ERA campaign through her newly christened Eagle Forum. Her undertaking appeared to be doomed. Thirty-five of the thirty-eight state legislatures needed to ratify the ERA had done so by 1973 and the national Republican Party had endorsed the ERA. Undeterred, Schlafly counterattacked. The ERA, Schlafly asserted, would eliminate child support for divorced women. Further, if the U.S. went to war again and reinstituted the draft, young women would be forced to fight. Worst of all, Schlafly claimed, gays and lesbians would be able to marry— thereby destroying the moral foundations of the family.

Her attacks took their toll on the ERA and she succeeded in preventing its ratification in the remaining states. Conservatives, however, were not of one mind when it came to Schlafly's moral warfare tactics. While social

Figure 4.1 Phyllis Schlafly (1925–2016)
Source: Courtesy of the Library of Congress Prints and Photographs Division

conservatives found the sexual liberation of the 1960s and 1970s repulsive, libertarians and economic conservatives were either appalled by Schlafly's moral crusade or indifferent.

Beyond ideology, the personal, as the New Left liked to say, was also political. There were gays in conservatives ranks. Close to home, Schlafly's son John was gay. Marvin Liebman, a founder of the Young Americans for Freedom and the American Conservative Union in 1964, was gay. The same was true of Terry Dolan, who helped found the National Conservative Political Action Committee (NCPAC) in 1975. Both the American Conservative Union and NCPAC raised campaign funds for conservatives—which, in practice, had meant *economic* and *anti-communist*, not social, conservatives.

While STOP ERA gathered momentum and threw Democratic and Republican liberals off balance, conservatives moved to wrest the Republican presidential nomination from Ford. Their preferred candidate was Reagan. Sixty-one former members of YAF either worked on Reagan's presidential primary campaign or served as delegates to the 1976 Republican National Convention. Helms mobilized North Carolina voters to support Reagan. Many voters in North Carolina were either anti-communist active-duty troops or Vietnam veterans who found Ford to be insufficiently anti-communist. Meanwhile, Richard Viguerie used his donor mailing lists

Figure 4.2 Jesse Helms (1921–2008), Senator from South Carolina, 1973–2003
Source: Photograph in the author's possession

from the 1964 Goldwater and 1968 Wallace campaigns to raise money for Reagan. NCPAC also collected funds for Reagan, as did the American Conservative Union.

At first, Ford did not take the conservatives' challenge seriously. He cruised from primary victory to victory. What Ford failed to consider, however, was that he carried primaries which were limited to registered Republicans. In states with "open primaries," meaning that voters could be independents or Democrats, Reagan shocked Ford. Tens of thousands of working-class whites, Catholic and Protestant, voted in the Republican, rather than the Democratic, primaries. Ford's advisers dismissed Reagan's voters as fake Republicans and, therefore, irrelevant. They overlooked two points. First, Ford barely won the presidential nomination. Second, many of Reagan's primary voters would likely not support Ford in the general election.

At the 1976 Republican National Convention, STOP ERA and Helms took on the party platform. Conservatives sought to recast the Republican Party as an anti-abortion, anti-feminist, and anti-ERA organization. Helms was successful in adding some anti-abortion language to the Republican Party platform. Schlafly, however, failed to get the Republican Party to repudiate its support for the ERA. Betty Ford could claim much credit for blocking Schlafly while Gerald Ford remained in the background. Nonetheless, moderate Republicans had made a significant concession to social conservatives.

Democrats should have easily won the White House in 1976. Constitutionally, Ford was legally the president. However, since Nixon had appointed him, his lack of an electoral mandate made him appear less than legitimate. Reagan had wounded Ford during the primaries and exposed his weakness with alienated Democrats who had given Nixon a landslide victory over McGovern in 1972. Although Ford was, literally, a Boy Scout, he had tainted himself by agreeing to serve as Nixon's vice president. Reagan, in contrast, was so far removed from Nixon that no one associated him with Watergate.

Unfortunately for Democrats, the party continued to be divided over the fallout from the Vietnam War. Democrats were also not of one mind when it came to the ERA and abortion rights—the latter becoming a hot issue when the U.S. Supreme Court, in *Roe v. Wade* (1973), set aside state-level restrictions on the termination of pregnancies. While most Democratic Party figures in the 1970s had turned against the Truman Doctrine of communist containment, there was no consensus when it came to social issues. Democrats needed a presidential candidate who could bridge the party's divisions, welding the New Deal and the Great Society together while not offending their bickering voters. It turned out there was a candidate none of the Democratic Party leaders had considered: a former one-term governor of Georgia.

Jimmy Carter advanced through the Democratic presidential primaries and caucuses being all things to all people. To southern white Protestants, Carter was one of their own—a socially conservative, patriotic Southern Baptist. To southern and northern blacks, Carter was a champion of civil rights. To northern Catholics, Carter was a foe of block-busting who wanted to preserve the "ethnic purity" of urban neighborhoods. To social liberals, Carter was a "with-it" politician who sat down for an interview with *Playboy*. In an era before cell phone recorders and the internet, Carter used his often contradictory statements to appeal to all the Democratic voting blocs without too much fear of a public backlash. When caught in an inconsistency, Carter responded that he was misquoted by an elitist news media that disapproved of regular Americans like him.

Carter insisted that his academic training at the U.S. Naval Academy had prepared him to be an engineer. He was also a businessman, having run the family's peanut farm. In sum, Carter would be an excellent manager of America, looking for efficiencies in government operations and reducing taxpayers' costs, while improving service to the public. Although Carter would not admit it, his emphasis on technical expertise and managerial experience was not without precedent for a presidential candidate. In 1928, Herbert Hoover had touted his engineering credentials and business competence. Carter won, but the election results were surprisingly close.

The Crisis of the 1970s: Domestic Policy

World War II had been kind to the American economy. Beyond ending the Great Depression, the war either destroyed America's key industrial rivals (Germany and Japan) or diminished their economic power (Great Britain and France). When the U.S. committed itself to the economic and political reconstruction of western Europe and Japan, it led to the restoration of the nation's overseas business competitors.

In 1957, just 207,000 foreign-made cars were imported into America, accounting for 3.5 percent of the market. Two years later, foreign car imports rose to 615,000 cars, or 10 percent of the market. By 1978, 9 million automobile imports arrived in the U.S. The Japanese share alone of U.S. automobile market was 18 percent. America's industrial centers staggered under the pressure of foreign competition. Between 1979 and 1982 Michigan lost 250,000 unionized, well-paying automobile jobs. Flint, Michigan, a major component of the General Motors corporate empire, had an unemployment rate of over 20 percent by the end of the 1970s—three times higher than the national average.

Other industries, especially those that provided products to the automobile industry, also struggled. In Youngstown, Ohio, Youngstown Sheet and Tube closed in 1977, followed in 1980 by U.S. Steel and Jones & Laughlin. Between 1977 and 1980, Youngstown lost 38 percent of its manufacturing jobs and its workforce declined from 40,000 to 25,000. Although U.S. Steel maintained its operations in Gary, Indiana, the corporation modernized its plant, relying more on technology and, consequently, employing fewer workers. From 1979 to 1982 steel employment in Gary fell from 30,000 to 10,000.

In 1947, Ohio had accounted for 43 percent of all tire workers employed in the U.S. By 1972, that share had fallen to 25 percent. Meanwhile such rubber makers as Goodyear and Goodrich shifted their operations to the South. They were looking for lower-cost non-union labor and lower taxes, both of which they found in Dixie. The South's share of rubber workers rose from 13 percent in 1947 to 33 percent in 1972. Akron, Ohio, which had been the founding center of American rubber production in the late nineteenth century, experienced massive job losses. The number of tire workers in Akron, which had amounted to 55,000 just after World War II, fell to 10,000 by 1982.

Urban employment prospects worsened as jobs followed people to the suburbs. In 1960, 36 percent of suburban dwellers in Cleveland, Ohio, worked in a suburb rather than commuting to the city. By 1980 that proportion had risen to 62 percent. In New York, by 1980, just 20 percent of the suburban workforce commuted to New York City. Nationally, 70 percent of suburban dwellers worked in the suburbs, not the city.

Many of those who remained behind in the northern cities were impoverished minorities. Detroit, which was 34 percent black in 1970, was nearly 63 percent black by 1980. The "Motor City," which had not recovered from the 1967 riot, became a majority African-American city less because of black population growth and more because of the 100,000 whites who had fled the city in the 1970s.

Every resident who migrated from the city or the region represented one less taxpayer. To make up for cities' accelerating loss of tax revenue President Johnson sent federal funds to supplement their operating budgets. By 1974, the Democratic Congress fully embraced "revenue sharing" with the Community Block Grant Act. In 1967, the federal government underwrote 1 percent of St. Louis's budget. By 1978, American taxpayers covered 55 percent of St. Louis's budget. The share for Buffalo in those years went from 2 percent to 69 percent, while the figures for Cleveland, Detroit, and Philadelphia ranged from 25 percent to 50 percent.

While the American economy faced challenges from foreign competition, it also had to contend with government-inflicted wounds. By 1979, federal business regulations, including those created by Nixon's EPA and OSHA, added $100 billion annually to corporate operation costs. (Adjusted for inflation, that amount would be $358 billion today.) In an echo of the New Deal era, large businesses passed higher operations costs to consumers while smaller businesses faced loss of profits or bankruptcy. One difference from the 1930s, however, was the option to move corporate operations overseas to evade federal regulations (and taxes). That option worsened unemployment, which in the 1970s was averaging around 7 percent—a level not seen for years.

Federal spending rose steadily in the 1970s. In 1970, adjusted for inflation, the federal government spent $207 billion. By 1980, Washington spent $615 billion. With the end of the Vietnam War, defense expenditures rose steadily, but not sufficiently, to drive overall federal spending increases. Between 1970 and 1980, military expenditures increased from $80 billion to $134 billion. It was social-welfare programs that drove federal spending. For example, in 1940 Social Security cost taxpayers $35 million and served 220,000 people. By 1977, Social Security was a $100 billion program covering 33 million Americans. (If 1940 Social Security costs had remained in line with inflation, by 1977 it would have been a $144 million program.)

The federal government chose to finance spending with debt and taxes. America's national debt went from $382 billion in 1970 to $914 billion by 1980. Going into debt, with the federal government essentially borrowing money from itself and printing more currency, had financial consequences. For citizens, the cost of borrowing money increased as the federal government scooped up available funds. By 1980, the prime interest rate, the rate banks imposed upon their best customers to take out loans, was 18 percent. At that rate, individuals and businesses avoided loans and cut back on their expenditures. As businesses contracted and consumers stepped away from the market, unemployment worsened.

Federal spending also accelerated inflation. For instance, the price of one pound of hamburger tripled between 1950 and 1980—with the greatest hike occurring in the 1970s. By 1980, Americans experienced a 12 percent inflation rate. Continuously climbing inflation had negative consequences. Wages did not keep up with inflation. In the 1950s, American hourly wages, adjusted for low inflation rates, rose 8 percent annually. The 1960s saw hourly wages increase up to 6 percent annually. By the 1970s, as inflation mounted, the purchasing power of Americans' hourly wages declined by 0.3 percent. Americans had not seen this sort of income contraction since the Great Depression. The combination of rising unemployment and inflation gave birth in the 1970s to a new economic term: **stagflation**.

Given the federal government's ever-expanding appetite for revenue, there was no incentive to tie tax rates to inflation rates. This led to "bracket creep." In the 1960s, just 5 percent of Americans were in the highest tax bracket. By 1980, half of all working Americans were in the top bracket, even though the actual value of their wages had been plummeting. In 1970, adjusted for inflation, Americans on average paid $1,415 of their income to the federal government. Ten years later, the average federal tax obligation was $3,387. Part of what made the New Deal politically successful in the 1930s was that the federal government taxed the few to benefit the many. By the 1970s, the U.S. government taxed the many to give to the many—which diminished the political payoff for the champions of larger government.

As wages declined in value, and taxes rose, more women sought jobs. In 1950, around 40 percent of the workforce was female. That figure grew to nearly 52 percent in 1980. By the 1970s, it took two incomes to support a family where only one had been needed just two decades earlier. Social conservatives expressed the fear that families would fall apart as more mothers entered the workforce and children were without parental supervision. They were also alarmed at rising divorce rates. In 1960, the American divorce rate was 2.2 per 1,000 people. Twenty years later, the divorce rate was 5.4 per 1,000 people.

Along with family economic and social strains, the American homicide rate rose dramatically. In 1960, the murder rate was 5.2 per 100,000 people. By 1980, the homicide rate had nearly doubled to 9.1 per 100,000 people. Most of America's violent crime took place in collapsing industrial communities and northern urban centers.

Drug abuse, which often drove up crime rates as addicts sought to pay for their narcotics, also grew in the 1970s. Half of America's high school students reported that they had tried illegal drugs. Up to 22 million people (10 percent of the U.S. population) snorted cocaine. It was little wonder that pollsters reported that 60 percent of Americans in the late 1970s expected that their children's lives would be worse than their own.

The Crisis of the 1970s: Foreign Policy

The humiliating, globally televised, end of the Vietnam War in 1975 demoralized Americans. To make matters worse, the Organization of

Petroleum Exporting Countries (OPEC), whose membership was heavily Middle Eastern, retaliated against the U.S. for its support of Israel. Oil embargoes and dramatic price hikes caused fuel shortages across the U.S. and emptied the pockets of financially stressed Americans. The Iranian revolution and the subsequent seizure of U.S. Embassy personnel in the late 1970s further poisoned Americans' attitudes toward the Middle East.

Neither Ford nor Carter offered popular, let alone workable, solutions. Energy conservation, and attempting to broker a peace between Arabs and Jews, would not put gasoline in Americans' automobiles or keep their homes warm in the winter. The option of expanding American oil and coal production was off the table for the pollution-conscious environmentalists in both parties—though not for conservatives.

For the Soviet Union, it was an opportune time to extend its influence. America's economy was reeling and many voters, especially Democrats, were leery of military intervention. Soviet leader Leonid Brezhnev had felt confident enough in America's decline to launch his own version of the Truman Doctrine in 1968. The Brezhnev Doctrine asserted that once a nation became a communist ally of the Soviet Union it could never change sides. Additionally, the Soviet Union, deploying soldiers from its Cuban client state, supported communist insurgencies in Central America, South America, Africa, and Asia. The Soviet Union also enlarged its conventional and nuclear arsenal to deter the U.S. from defending its allies or, if necessary, to defeat the U.S. in a third world war.

The Soviet Union established a naval base at Cam Ranh Bay, Vietnam, taking over harbor facilities which the U.S. had spent $2 billion building. Brezhnev also deployed Cuban troops, along with Soviet advisers, to Angola. Soviet weapons and advisers went to Somalia, Ethiopia, and South Yemen, as well as to Nicaragua, El Salvador, and Guatemala. Never in its history had the Soviet Union been involved in so many simultaneous insurgencies across the globe. Best of all, Soviet intervention was low risk. The Cubans and the insurgents did the fighting; the Russians supplied weapons and advisers.

Fatally, the Soviet Union backed a revolutionary government in Afghanistan. When that government fell to counterrevolutionary forces in 1979, the Soviet Union sent in its own troops. From the Soviet point of view, turning neighboring Afghanistan into a puppet state was unavoidable. First, Afghanistan was a major supplier of opium which, once refined, became the heroin which flooded the world market—including the Soviet Union. Second, the Iranian revolution had sparked an Islamic awakening across the region. With a population of 40 million Muslims in the Soviet Union, the last thing Brezhnev wanted was for the Iranian revolution to spread into Afghanistan and then to the homeland.

Even if Americans were inclined to intervene militarily against Soviet-backed insurgencies—and they were not—U.S. armed forces were in little condition to fight. Having gone to an all-volunteer military in 1973, recruiters found fewer youths willing to serve. The Army, for example, fell

32 percent below its enlistment quotas in the 1970s even as the size of the military shrank. America's military branches lowered enlistment standards to the point where 28 percent of Marines lacked a high school education.

In previous eras, when unemployment rose, youths had enlisted in the military. The 1970s were different. Young Americans wanted little to do with the military. The American military in the 1970s had a problem with crime and drugs—as was true of American society at large. There was, however, a more important reason for rejecting military service—low pay. It was not unusual for the spouses of enlisted soldiers to go on welfare to support their families. To many Americans, the military was no longer an escape route from poverty and crime—it was a pathway to both.

The Vietnam War had created a host of problems for the American military that lasted into peacetime. While most soldiers in Vietnam had not "fragged," or killed their officers, and only a minority became addicted to heroin, the public perception was very different. Hollywood and the television broadcast networks contributed to the negative image of the U.S. military. Television shows and films depicted Vietnam soldiers either as psychotic killers and war criminals, or as emotionally damaged victims and the unwilling tools of drug-smuggling CIA operatives and defense contractors.

Although Vietnam faded into memory, the fictional veteran template remained—with the name of each subsequent war substituted into the plot line. Between Hollywood fiction and bleak reality, it was little wonder that the American military declined in quality and morale in the 1970s.

Conservatives' Response: Foreign Policy in the 1970s

In 1972 a few Democrats had embarked on an ideological journey to the right. Some were journalists, including *Public Interest* editor Irving Kristol, and others were academics, notably Georgetown University's **Jeane Kirkpatrick**. These were the neoconservatives who chose Nixon over McGovern. Their emphasis was on foreign policy, not social issues. Indeed, Kristol had written to a friend in the Ford Administration that social conservatives' efforts to restrict abortion were politically counterproductive. As Kristol argued, "In a heterogeneous society such as ours, it's folly to try to dictate to the citizenry a national policy on such a controversial moral issue."

The neoconservatives disliked Carter as much as they had McGovern. They objected when Carter's ambassador to the United Nations, Andrew Young, opened lines of communication with the Palestinian Liberation Organization (PLO). The PLO had been waging an insurgency against Israel since 1964. Members of the Congressional Black Caucus, outraged by neoconservative attacks on a prominent African-American civil rights leader, argued that it was time for America to issue a "declaration of independence" from Israel. Other civil rights organizations denounced Israel as a racist society which discriminated against nonwhites.

Neoconservatives countered that opposition to Israel's right to exist was anti-Semitism disguised as anti-racism. Some Jewish Democrats, as well as white evangelical Christians who saw the creation of Israel as a fulfillment of biblical prophecy, concurred with the neoconservatives. Carter, wilting under attacks from some of his most important voters, "encouraged" Young to resign in 1979. Civil rights groups, which were allied with the Democratic Party, believed that Carter had betrayed their trust.

Carter's antagonistic relationship with neoconservatives had begun early in his presidency. In 1977, at the University of Notre Dame, Carter repudiated the Truman Doctrine, announcing that "We are now free of that inordinate fear of communism which once led us to embrace any dictator who joined us in our fear." UN Ambassador Young underscored America's new direction in foreign affairs, asserting that: "I don't believe that Cuba is in Africa because it was ordered there by the Russians. I believe Cuba is in Africa because it really has a shared sense of colonial oppression and domination."

The key principle of the Carter Doctrine was human rights. America, Carter believed, should base its relationship with other nations on how well they treated their citizens, not on whether they would ally with the U.S. against communism.

Jeane Kirkpatrick was appalled. She believed that the U.S. had national security interests that outweighed concerns about how well or badly America's allies behaved with their own people. Moreover, Kirkpatrick argued, the U.S. had to distinguish between "totalitarians" and "authoritarians." Totalitarians, like the Soviet Union and China, invaded their neighbors or undermined them by supporting bloody insurgencies. Authoritarians abused a few of their people, but did not seek to subjugate their neighbors. Moreover, Kirkpatrick contended, authoritarian regimes were capable of "liberalization and democratization" in the long run. Totalitarian regimes, on the other hand, would never be capable of anything other than exercising "tyranny" over their people. Kirkpatrick's arguments became the cornerstone of conservatives' foreign policy—which was essentially a reassertion of the Truman Doctrine.

Unfortunately for Carter, his desire to reorient American foreign policy wilted in the face of the Soviet invasion of Afghanistan. Carter announced a boycott of the 1980 Moscow Olympics and required males, when they turned eighteen, to register for a nonexistent military draft. Neoconservatives were not alone on the Right in believing that Carter's response to the Soviet invasion of Afghanistan was laughable. The Heritage Foundation issued a paper in 1980 contending that Carter's actions were merely "symbolic in nature." What Carter needed to do, the conservative think tank argued, was to provide military support to the 400,000 ethnic Pashtuns who had fled to Pakistan. Under the protection of Pakistan, the Pashtuns were establishing guerrilla bases.

Conservatives' Response: Economic Policy in the 1970s

In 1977, Wichita, Kansas, corporate heirs Charles and David Koch helped establish the **CATO Institute**, a libertarian think tank in Washington. (They ultimately gave $30 million to CATO.) The Koch brothers believed that both the Heritage Foundation and the AEI looked to the federal government to regulate the marketplace on behalf of their allies.

Roger Milliken, a founder of the Heritage Foundation, for example, may have been anti-union, but he also felt threatened by the flood of textile imports. Rather than relocate his operations overseas, which would have been in line with CATO's free-market libertarian philosophy, Milliken refused to abandon his employees and their communities. Milliken wanted the U.S. government to impose tariff barriers on overseas competitors who paid workers little, had no environmental or safety regulation costs imposed upon them, and received subsidies from their governments. To libertarian purists, Milliken was advocating for political, or crony, capitalism—by which they meant using the federal government to restrict market competition.

Political capitalism was not new to the American experience. In 1906, America's largest meat packers, who exported to European nations with high-quality standards, faced intense competition in the domestic market from regional, low-standard butchering firms. The giant packers demanded federal regulation—the 1906 Pure Food and Drug Act—to drive out their domestic competition, which they knew could not afford to comply with improved standards. Similarly, in 1935, Texas senator Tom Connally, acting on behalf of the oil companies, drafted legislation to limit petroleum production. The 1935 Connally Hot Oil Act undermined the small wildcatters dependent upon unrestricted production. Limiting oil production also raised the overall price of crude, to the benefit of the remaining producers' profit margins.

The Connally Hot Oil Act and the Pure Food and Drug Act were tiny steps toward industries using the federal government to destroy market competition. By the 1970s, tiny steps had become great strides. Thousands of lobbyists in Washington served the cause of political capitalism, influencing legislation on behalf of their clients. Retired members of Congress made the trek to "K Street" in Washington to join the lobbyist ranks. In turn, lobbyists acquired administrative jobs in numerous federal departments, implementing regulations they had earlier helped draft, either as elected officials or as corporate representatives. Denouncing "influence peddling," but opposing efforts to curb lobbying, became a bipartisan sport in Washington.

While economic conservatives drew battle lines over political capitalism and protectionism, others were seeking a different sort of policy change. **Arthur Laffer**, who earned his doctorate in economics from Stanford University, had taught at the University of Chicago. The University of Chicago was a rare academic sanctuary for free-market economics faculty. Not content with teaching, Laffer wanted to influence public policy. That desire led him to take the position of chief economist in Nixon's Office of Management and Budget. Laffer followed the path blazed by economics professors at Columbia University who answered Roosevelt's call to create a New Deal for America. Like his liberal predecessors, Laffer came away from his Washington experience convinced that nearly everyone in government was wrong about everything.

Laffer argued against the conventional wisdom that raising federal taxes generated greater revenue [Document 15: p. 159]. In fact, Laffer contended, there was a point at which taxes became so high that businesses opted to cut back on production or relocate outside the U.S. to reduce or eliminate their burden. Ultimately, high tax rates generated *less* federal revenue and led to higher unemployment. Laffer's solution was simple: cut tax rates. With lower tax rates, businesses would have an incentive to remain in the U.S., expand production, and hire more workers—all of which would generate more federal tax revenue.

Long-term American economic growth, Laffer believed, would "pay" for the short-term loss of tax revenues caused by initial rate reductions. Tax cuts and subsequent economic growth might even "pay" for federal entitlement programs and possibly eliminate the government's deficit. However, without any reforms to entitlement programs, Laffer realized, such outcomes were unlikely.

Laffer insisted that there were at least two political payoffs for conservatives if they listened to him. First, cutting tax rates would take care of tax bracket creep, which not only hurt Republican corporate executives, but also sliced into the incomes of Democratic blue-collar workers. That might give working-class Democrats an incentive to vote for conservative Republicans. Second, since the New Deal, conservatives had fixated on federal deficits. Laffer's proposal encouraged conservatives to focus less on deficits and more on promoting economic growth. To Democratic voters, deficit reduction had always seemed to be Republican code words for eliminating entitlement programs. Economic growth, on the other hand, appeared friendlier to Democrats looking for work and posed no threat to entitlements. Grateful working-class Democrats might even vote for Republicans.

In many ways Laffer had updated the 1920s Mellon Plan for the 1970s. Laffer's prospect for long-term economic and political success, however, was better than Mellon's had been. The limitations of the Mellon Plan were mainly due to the small percentage of Americans who paid federal taxes, as well as its emphasis on expanding plants and production but not on placing more money into the hands of consumers. Laffer's idea, which became known as supply-side economics, benefited from the great number of Americans who paid federal taxes in the 1970s. Tax cuts put more money directly into millions of Americans' pockets, upper class, middle class, and working class. They could afford to spend, further stimulating economic growth. The more Americans had to spend, and the more the economy grew, the more likely they were to vote for Republicans.

Conservatives' Response: Social Policy in the 1970s

Carter had made a great effort during the 1976 election to cultivate two prominent southern white Protestant ministers: **Pat Robertson** and Jerry Falwell. Robertson's father, A. Willis Robertson of Virginia, had served in the Senate and was one of the signers of the Southern Manifesto pledging massive resistance to racial integration. A product of a well-off Episcopalian family, Pat Robertson had fought in the Korean War and then gone to Yale Law School. Robertson felt the draw of evangelical religion which led him to "missionary work" in New York's low-income Bedford-Stuyvesant neighborhood. He then founded the Pentecostal-inclined Christian Broadcasting Network (CBN) in 1960. When his father, fearful of facing black voters for the first time in 1966, begged his son to save his Senate seat, Pat Robertson refused. CBN, after all, had a racially integrated staff and audience. Carter, who saw in Pat Robertson a kindred spirit and useful ally, solicited his support.

Jerry Falwell, the pastor of the large, and growing, Thomas Road Baptist Church in Virginia, had drawn attention in southern white religious circles for his condemnation of Martin Luther King, Jr., in 1965. In a much-reprinted sermon, "Ministers and Marchers," Falwell argued that fighting alcoholism was a more appropriate cause for clergy than battling "the alleged discrimination against Negroes in the South." While blind to racial injustice, Falwell's concern for alcohol abuse was sincere. His father, Carey, and his uncle, Garland, trafficked in illegal alcohol in the 1920s. During a drunken fight, Carey Falwell shot Garland Falwell to death. By the 1970s,

Figure 4.3 Jerry Falwell (1933–2007)
Source: Photograph in the author's possession

Falwell had reassessed his opposition to civil rights and saw value in King's fusion of pulpit and politics. He viewed Carter, a fellow Southern Baptist, as a champion of morality.

In 1976, Carter had received less than a majority of the southern white vote—46 percent. Southern black voters had kept Dixie from going Republican. Still, if Carter had won less than 46 percent of the southern white vote he would have lost the region and the presidency. That made the support of Falwell and Robertson especially important to Democrats' control of the South. Unfortunately for Carter, his administration soon drove both religious leaders, and their followers, into the Republican camp.

Carter's Internal Revenue Service (IRS) and the Justice Department launched a review of private religious schools, or academies, in the South. It was true that southern segregationists had abandoned integrated public schools in favor of private, Church-affiliated academies. Since such schools were clearly violating federal civil rights laws, their tax-exempt status as educational and religious institutions could be revoked. Where Carter made his mistake was in not insisting that the federal employees operating in his name investigate religious academies more closely. The desire to preserve racial segregation did not spark the creation of all southern religious schools. Many such academies sought to be separated out from a public-school system that they believed to be immoral. When the federal government failed to make careful distinctions among Dixie's religious schools, southern white Protestants condemned Carter.

Socially conservative southern Democrats had expected Carter to reverse the party's liberal direction. The Democrats' 1976 platform, with its embrace of abortion rights, had dismayed the party's social conservatives but was not sufficient to drive them away. As for the ERA, Democrats could not be faulted for supporting a constitutional amendment that Republicans also endorsed. Helms and Schlafly were not the leaders of the Republican Party, while Carter, a devout Southern Baptist, was the head of the Democratic Party. Once it became clear by his public statements and actions that Carter was a rare social liberal in Southern Baptist ranks, moral conservatives revolted.

In 1979, Falwell founded the Moral Majority and placed its headquarters in Washington. While not officially endorsing any party or candidate, the better to maintain its non-profit tax-exempt status, the Moral Majority "educated" voters about social issues. Clergy, largely evangelical Protestants, distributed "score cards" laying out various candidates' positions on moral, economic, and national security matters. Falwell, in his 1980 manifesto, *Listen, America!*, championed free enterprise, condemned Democrats and Republicans who wanted to negotiate with the Soviet Union as living in "spiritual darkness," and looked forward to "America's Moral Rebirth" [Document 16: p. 160].

Carter did not necessarily have to fear retribution from the Moral Majority in the 1980 election. All he had to do was reassure social conservatives of his friendship and hope that Republicans remained the party of Ford and Eisenhower. Nothing went Carter's way.

In 1976, while enlisting the support of socially conservative Protestant Democrats, Carter had promised to host a national conference on family issues. It took four years for Carter to make good on that pledge. Carter had envisioned the White House Conference on the Family as a forum to discuss the economic difficulties facing Americans and what the federal government could do to help. This was standard-issue liberal Democratic politics: focus on the economy and chastise uncaring, Republican-led corporations. Then, Washington Democrats, working with moderate Republicans, would offer the usual solutions: raise the minimum wage, expand Medicare and Medicaid coverage, and levy higher corporate taxes.

Carter did not understand how much the base of the Democratic Party was changing in the 1970s. Of the 1,500 delegates to the Conference on the Family, only 250 were moral conservatives and few had ties to working-class constituencies. Most delegates, who often came from white-collar backgrounds, emphasized social, not economic, issues. They championed abortion on demand, gay rights, and expanded welfare funding, while insisting that the definition of the family had to be broadened to include nontraditional living arrangements.

Connie Marshner, a former University of South Carolina YAF leader and conference delegate, led a well-publicized walkout. Marshner argued that "Families consist of people related by heterosexual marriage, blood, and adoption." Further, Marshner continued, "Families are not religious cults, families are not Manson [mass murderers] families, families are not heterosexual or homosexual liaisons outside of marriage." The collapse of the conference gave the Moral Majority the incentive to defeat Carter. Republicans, however, still needed to give the Moral Majority a reason to support them.

The 1980 Election: The Battle

Carter had difficulty focusing on his Right flank in the lead up to the 1980 election given the challenge he faced from his Left flank. George McGovern criticized Carter for demonizing Soviet leaders, instead of trying to understand their national security interests. Carter, McGovern believed, had reverted to the false principles of the Truman Doctrine.

While McGovern had become an oracle of Democratic liberalism, Massachusetts senator Edward "Teddy" Kennedy, the younger brother of President Kennedy, was its warrior. Teddy Kennedy contended that Carter was too conservative for the Democratic Party. He wanted Carter to distance himself from social conservatives, raise federal taxes, hike the minimum wage, expand federal health care programs, and be less confrontational with the Soviet Union. These points became the basis for Teddy Kennedy to seek the Democratic presidential nomination in 1980.

Fortunately for Carter, Teddy Kennedy never recovered from a 1969 incident in which a young woman drowned in a car which he drove off a bridge. Teddy Kennedy was allegedly drunk, but there was no blood test performed since he waited ten hours to report the accident. Some Kennedy family allies in higher education and the news media tried to argue that Kennedy's near-death experience had matured him just like polio had matured Franklin Roosevelt. Democratic primary voters did not buy that argument, especially since Teddy Kennedy proved to be inarticulate, confused, and meandering on the campaign trail. Although Carter won the nomination, liberal northern Democrats were disgusted with their southern wing.

Meanwhile on the other side of the aisle, the battle for the Republican presidential nomination became heated. Political pundits, as well as liberal Democratic and Republican politicians, kept repeating the same litany: Ronald Reagan's time had passed, he was too old to run for president. (He was sixty-nine years old in 1980.) Former CIA director **George Herbert Walker Bush**, who had entered the 1980 Republican presidential primaries, not only recited the line privately, in public he made a point of jogging in front of television camera crews to emphasize his youthful vigor.

Illinois congressman **John B. Anderson**, who had also decided to run in the Republican primaries, dismissed Reagan as a relic of a faraway past. Contrary to the impression Anderson and Bush attempted to make, all three shared the same formative historical experiences of the Great Depression and World War II.

Both Anderson and Bush were less concerned with Reagan's age than with his conservative beliefs. Politicians, Democrat and Republican, boasted of their journal subscriptions, especially when soliciting editorial support. Reagan not only read the journals he subscribed to, he was a fan of such conservative publications as *Human Events*, the *Public Interest*, and the *National Review*. It was in conservative journals that Reagan read about Laffer's theory of tax cuts and economic growth. The neoconservative magazine *Commentary* gave Reagan a road map for reorienting American foreign policy.

Reagan believed in the political fusionism that the *National Review* had been championing since the 1950s. Social and economic conservatives could find common ground in their resentment of an increasingly intrusive, and costly, federal government. Both "Main Street" moralists and "Wall Street" free-marketers also shared a loathing for communism—the third component of the *National Review*'s fusionist framework.

Where Reagan differed from most economic conservatives (and liberal Democrats) is that he regarded the Great Society as a perversion, rather than the logical extension, of the New Deal. This meant that while every potential conservative constituency would get something from Reagan, they were not going to get everything. Reagan would not abolish Social Security or attack private-sector unions. Unions in the public sector, however, were fair game. As Reagan saw it, if government workers went on strike they were depriving taxpayers of the services for which they had already been paid. Moreover, President Kennedy, not Roosevelt, had given government workers the right to unionize and had done so through an executive order, not by legislation.

Reagan also believed that there were constitutional limits on federal power. Therefore, if social conservatives truly believed in states' rights over Washington dictates, then the voters in every state had to right to restrict, outlaw, or embrace abortion without congressional or judicial intervention. The same was potentially true for gay rights and a host of other social issues. Roosevelt had done just fine avoiding debates over moral issues and Reagan was content to follow his role model's example.

Reagan's core beliefs were visible in his 1980 Neshoba County, Mississippi, campaign speech [Document 17: p. 161]. The first clue was in Reagan's smiling yet jagged-edged quip that "We've had the New Deal, then Harry Truman gave us the Fair Deal, and now we have a misdeal." Many Democratic liberals, however, missed Reagan's identification with Roosevelt and Truman. Instead, they emphasized the fact that Philadelphia, Mississippi, where three civil rights workers were murdered by segregationists in 1964, was in Neshoba County. By speaking at the Neshoba County Fair, which was a major political venue for Mississippi political events, and by using the term "states' rights," Reagan, liberals asserted, had identified himself with racists. Carter, who in 1976 had campaigned in Mississippi alongside segregationist Democrats (and had carried the state), accused Reagan of allying with white supremacists.

Like Democratic liberals, libertarians and Republican liberals had little use for Reagan. CATO funder David Koch, who viewed Reagan as an unreconstructed New Deal Democrat, ran for vice president on the Libertarian Party ticket. Having ran its first presidential campaign in 1972 to defeat Nixon, the Libertarian Party was committed to downsizing the federal government.

Although Ed Clark, a corporate attorney, was the presidential nominee, Koch was the dominant figure on the Libertarian ticket. Koch, who provided a great amount of money to the Libertarian Party in 1980, championed the abolition of the minimum wage, corporate taxes, Social Security, the Securities and Exchange Commission, the FBI, and the CIA. Libertarians supported abortion rights, gay rights, and the legalization of narcotics. As for Reagan, the Libertarian Party argued that there would be "no change whatsoever from Jimmy Carter and the Democrats" if he were elected.

As a liberal Republican, Bush had no more use for Reagan than David Koch. Like his father, Senator Prescott Bush, he embraced Planned Parenthood. (After the *Roe v. Wade* decision, Planned Parenthood became a significant provider of abortion services.) Bush had also embraced the ERA. On the tax front, Bush dismissed Laffer's (and Reagan's) ideas as "voodoo economics," unworthy of consideration by serious people.

Illinois congressman John Anderson similarly heaped ridicule on Reagan throughout the Republican primaries. Anderson vowed to continue his opposition to the conservative takeover of the Republican Party, running

Figure 4.4 David Koch (1940–)
Source: Photograph in the author's possession

as an independent presidential candidate. In contrast, Bush repudiated all his core economic and moral beliefs to run as Reagan's vice president. Bush calculated that by serving Reagan he would be able to claim the presidential nomination in 1988. Conservatives calculated that after Bush held moderates to the Republican Party in 1980, they would then toss him off the ticket in 1984.

The 1980 Election: The Judgment

Opinion polls and news media pundits predicted that the 1980 election would be close, with Carter possibly winning given the potential for Anderson to siphon liberal Republican votes away from Reagan. Carter's increasingly shrill tone, however, indicated that he knew he was losing. According to Carter, Reagan was either a calculating, racist, war-mongering champion of the rich, or an idiotic, poorly educated, mediocre film actor. Rather than respond to Carter with anger, Reagan smiled and said "There you go again." Those were code words voters could understand: there you go again—telling lies, acting unhinged.

The 1980 election results had both immediate and long-term consequences for national politics. Far from being a close election, Reagan swept up 489 electoral votes to Carter's forty-nine. He also won 43 million popular votes, 8 million more than Carter. Seventy percent of southern whites, the great majority still registered as Democrats, voted for Reagan. Northern Catholics and working-class white Democrats in the North also voted for Reagan, swinging key states such as Michigan into the Republican column.

In contrast, Carter saw his core constituency of Southern Baptists defect to Reagan. In 1976, Carter had received 56 percent of the Southern Baptist vote. Four years later, he won only 34 percent. There were not enough black voters in the South to help Carter win, nor were their numbers sufficient in the North to counteract the newly emergent "**Reagan Democrats.**"

Voters not only ejected Carter from the White House, they elected thirteen new Republican senators. Republicans claimed a majority in the Senate for the first time since 1954. Senator Helms rejoiced that Americans had finally repudiated "statist liberalism." The New Deal order was dead—or so conservatives mistakenly believed.

Republicans also picked up thirty-three seats in the House, but remained short of a majority. The new House members elected in 1980 included a rising generation of combative, conservative Baby Boomers. Their leader was Georgia's Newt Gingrich, a college history professor who had only won election to the House in 1978.

While post-election pundits focused on Carter and Reagan, both Anderson and Koch merited more attention. Anderson's meager 7 percent of the popular vote, and lack of wins in the Electoral College, masked a telling development. Upper-middle-class, highly educated professionals, especially in the emerging technology center of Silicon Valley, voted for Anderson. He drew votes equally from liberal Republicans and Democrats who regarded Carter and Reagan as too socially conservative. If Reagan had not acquired such great support from northern and southern white Democrats, the liberal Republicans who defected to Anderson would have cost him the election. Conservative electoral victory could only be realized by bringing in working-class voters and religious activists—but at the cost of repelling college-educated, white-collar liberal Republicans.

As for Koch and the libertarians, their 921,000 votes underlined a stark reality. Americans had little use for libertarians. Koch and his brother Charles recognized in the aftermath of the 1980 election that running candidates and composing party platforms would only result in defeat. A better solution was to pump funds into the CATO Institute to influence federal regulations and laws out of the glare of electoral politics.

It was also important to establish organizations to work at the state level to change laws and subtly shape public opinion. Conservatives, including Jesse Helms and leaders of the American Conservative Union, had aided in the founding of the American Legislative Exchange Council (ALEC) in 1973. Representing a partnership between business and state legislators, ALEC's mission was to draft model legislation and combat public-sector unions at the local level. Unless conservatives "devolved" power from Washington to the states, however, initiatives like ALEC were not going to be successful. Reagan may have talked about changing state–federal relations, but he never repudiated the New Deal.

5 The Reagan Revolution and Its Discontents, 1981–1992

Reagan the Underestimated

In his 1981 Inaugural Address Reagan followed Franklin Roosevelt's 1933 template [Document 18: p. 162]. Like Roosevelt, Reagan spelled out America's enormous economic challenges, but remained hopeful:

> The economic ills we suffer have come upon us over several decades. They will not go away in days, weeks, or months, but they will go away. They will go away because we as Americans have the capacity now, as we've had in the past, to do whatever needs to be done to preserve this last and greatest bastion of freedom.

There was one major difference between Reagan and Roosevelt: their prescriptions for how to fix America's problems. Roosevelt advocated federal intervention in the economy to clean up the mess that he believed corporations had made. Reagan argued that the federal government itself had created the economic disaster which threatened the nation.

Washington Democrats were unimpressed with Reagan. Clark Clifford, President Harry Truman's Secretary of Defense, and now a fixture on the Washington cocktail circuit, dismissed Reagan as "an amiable dunce." Clifford predicted that Reagan would be "a hopeless failure" as president. Boston's **Thomas "Tip" O'Neill**, the Democratic Speaker of the House, met with Reagan and delivered a stern lecture. O'Neill informed Reagan that he would not get legislation through Congress. His opposition to Reagan went well beyond partisan politics, assuming an almost religious form. O'Neill believed that it was "sinful that Ronald Reagan ever became president." The sin, in O'Neill's mind, was Reagan's criticism of government regulation and taxation.

O'Neill and Clifford misread the political context as badly as they underestimated Reagan. In 1980, most American voters believed that the nation was mired in its worst economic crisis since the Great Depression. They also viewed America's loss of power overseas as an invitation to foreign aggression—much in the same way American isolationism in the 1930s

Figure 5.1 Ronald W. Reagan (1911–2004), President of the United States 1981–1989
Source: Courtesy of Library of Congress Prints and Photographs Division

had paved the road to World War II. Democratic leaders, most particularly those from the North, failed to appreciate the sense of urgency that drove over half of the electorate. Reagan understood that O'Neill was unwittingly playing the part of Herbert Hoover—out of touch, self-righteous, and an impediment to change.

Complacent Democrats also failed to recognize how rattled their southern colleagues were following the 1980 election. Southern whites had split their ballots, voting for Reagan but still supporting Democrats further down the ticket. The question for southern Democrats was how much longer white voters would split their presidential and congressional votes. If white voters saw their Democratic representatives opposing Reagan, would they turn against them? On the other hand, if southern white politicians supported Reagan openly, they risked losing black voters, who were increasingly dominating Dixie's Democratic Party. It was a dilemma, but not one which concerned northern liberals.

Most Democratic leaders also failed to appreciate how skilled Reagan was as a political leader. Critical journalists and politicians dismissed

Reagan's years as president of the Screen Actors Guild as little more than Hollywood glitz mixed in with some anti-communist posturing. Studio head Jack Warner, who had quipped that Reagan was fit to be a supporting character, but not governor of California, knew differently. As a union leader, Reagan had been a tough, persistent negotiator who had looked out for the financial wellbeing of the legion of actors and actresses who never received top billing. Once Reagan got it into his head that his was the right position to take, and that he had the facts to support his case, he might have compromised, but he never surrendered.

Reagan revealed how firm of a negotiator he was at the outset of his presidency. When the Professional Air Traffic Controllers Organization (PATCO) went on strike in 1981, resulting in the cancellation of thousands of flights, Reagan did not bend. He informed PATCO that it was illegal for federal workers to go on strike. After 11,359 of its 13,000 members refused to return to work, Reagan fired them. He also had PATCO decertified as a collective bargaining agent. When he had the law on his side, Reagan would not yield.

The former actor was an accomplished communicator, dedicated to perfecting his performance. Campaign aides marveled when they watched Reagan, whose poor eyesight had kept him out of combat in World War II, execute a special trick with his contact lens. Leaving one lens in, Reagan removed the other one so that he could read the notes he kept close to him, but still appear as if he was maintaining full eye contact with his audience. Incredibly, he suffered no headaches as a result.

He also came to Washington with a team. His media staff, which would ultimately include conservative writer Patrick Buchanan, knew that Reagan was the star performer. "Let Reagan be Reagan," as his advisers put it, and he would deliver. Reagan followed Roosevelt's example by going around Congress and the national news media to address Americans directly.

Both Reagan and Roosevelt understood the importance of leaving Washington to speak to Americans across the country. Local news media outlets, if given a chance to interview the President of the United States, would jump at the opportunity—leaving reporters from the prestige press and networks fuming at their exclusion. Their anger, however, usually did not last long, as Roosevelt and Reagan would invite them into the Oval Office for an off-the-record chat and ply them with cocktails.

On the domestic and foreign policy fronts, Reagan had "farm teams" from which he could draw: the Heritage Foundation and the American Enterprise Institute. Heritage Foundation staffers had drafted a plan of action prior to the 1980 election. While the American Enterprise Institute's Jeane Kirkpatrick received the modest posting as the U.S. representative to the United Nations, it was her ideas that helped shape Reagan's foreign policy. The Democratic leadership in Washington was not prepared for a Reagan White House that, as the old political adage went, "hit the ground running."

Reagan and the Economy, 1981–1988

Two pieces of legislation formed the core of the "Reagan Revolution." In the Economic Recovery Tax Act of 1981 Reagan proposed cutting federal taxes by 25 percent over three years, reducing capital gains tax (the tax on business profits) by 40 percent, and ending bracket creep by indexing federal taxes to the inflation rate. Meanwhile, the Omnibus Budget Reconciliation Act of 1981 trimmed federal discretionary spending by $35 billion and boosted defense outlays by 43 percent over six years.

Democratic opposition to Reagan's legislative agenda collapsed. Some critics credited Reagan's political success to the outpouring of sympathy following his near-death at the hands of an assassin in March 1981. While the public did rally behind Reagan and cheer his recovery, there was a more important development assuring his success. To House Speaker O'Neill's shock, forty southern Democrats defied him to support Reagan. Their ringleader was **Phil Gramm,** a former Texas A&M economics professor who was elected to the House in 1978.

Hostile Democrats and reporters called Gramm and his allies "**boll weevils.**" O'Neill vowed to punish Gramm, first by denying him important committee assignments and second by supporting Democratic primary challengers in Fort Worth. O'Neill's tactics, however, backfired. Gramm's profile rose across Texas. Inadvertently, O'Neill paved the way for Gramm's election to the Senate in 1984 *as a Republican*.

America's economic recovery was not immediate and not everyone enjoyed its fruits. In 1982, the U.S. experienced a recession which drove the unemployment rate to nearly 11 percent—four points higher than it had been in the last year of Jimmy Carter's presidency. The 1982 recession was not a product of Reagan's legislative initiatives. Rather, it stemmed from Reagan carrying on a Carter policy.

In 1979, Federal Reserve chair Paul Volcker, with Carter's support, hiked the prime interest rate to squeeze out inflation. Tight fiscal policy gave American corporations three options: first, reduce the payroll by embracing automation; second, declare bankruptcy and close; or third, relocate operations overseas. Each option had the same result: skyrocketing unemployment. Reagan, like Roosevelt, took to the radio to reassure Americans that his program for economic recovery would work—if given time [Document 19, p: 163].

American corporations, or at least the ones that did not close or move overseas, turned to automation—eliminating 2 million industrial jobs in the 1980s. Employment in steel, for example, fell 50 percent between 1980 and 1988. Steel production, however, did not decline in the long term. A similar development occurred in the American automobile industry. General Motors, which employed 600,000 in 1979, eventually shrank to 125,000 workers. Meanwhile, the number of GM automobiles sold doubled between 1979 and 2016.

Both steel and automobile producers demanded, and received from the White House, import quotas and higher tariffs imposed upon their overseas competitors. In response, foreign corporations, especially those from Japan and (West) Germany, located some of their operations to the U.S. Assembling Japanese and German cars in America bypassed import quotas and tariffs. Foreign-owned companies stemmed some of the American employment losses in the auto and steel sectors. Still, German and Japanese corporations were just as reliant on automation as American manufacturers.

In the mid-1950s, one-third of workers belonged to unions. By the mid-1980s that figure had been reduced by more than half. As private-sector union membership declined, more federal, state, and municipal workers joined the ranks of organized labor. Union demographics shifted from high school-educated, often socially conservative blue-collar workers, to college-educated, often socially liberal, public-sector professionals. Democrats had been dependent upon union members for campaign volunteers and funds since the New Deal. What Democrats lost in support from private-sector unions, they partially recovered with the growth of unionized government employees. Meanwhile, the influence of anti-communist, socially conservative workers diminished within the Democratic Party.

The collapse of "smoke-stack" labor unions in the 1980s underscored how much the times had changed. During the Great Depression, a large element of the Catholic Church supported workers' rights and offered whatever assistance it could. The Catholic Church of the 1980s did not repeat its earlier performance.

In the 1930s, most American Catholics were working class and shared a common desire for the federal government to improve their economic situation. By the 1980s, there were many well-educated, middle-class Catholics opposed to unions, higher taxes, and costly federal regulation. Complicating matters, the Catholic Church leadership of the 1960s had condemned many of its working-class white parishioners as racists. In the 1980s, many Catholic priests and bishops washed their hands of their white, working-class faithful, closing parishes in struggling mill towns and moving to the prospering suburbs.

While unionized smoke-stack jobs disappeared, well-paid jobs in technology-intensive fields, which required training in mathematics and the sciences, grew in the 1980s. Americans in the top 20 percent of income earners, most of them in technical fields, saw their wages and benefits increase steadily. For the other 80 percent, who were employed largely in blue-collar, retail, and service jobs, their wages grew at a lower rate. This is not to say that there was no improvement. Middle- and working-class Americans, on average, had seen the value of their wages in the 1970s fall by 0.3 percent. In the 1980s, Reagan's economic reforms helped turn that situation around. Middle- and working-class wages rose 0.9 percent—better than in the previous decade, but nowhere near the rising level of prosperity enjoyed by Americans in the 1950s and 1960s.

Analysis and Assessment

As the U.S. economy shifted away from employment in unskilled industrial fields, Americans increasingly viewed college degrees as a must-have commodity. In 1980, 49 percent of high school graduates went to college. By 1989, that proportion had grown to 60 percent. The problem was that unless students went into science- and mathematics-intensive areas of study, their post-graduate employment prospects were dim. Larger numbers of college graduates in the 1980s moved into low-paying service and retail jobs, forcing out high school graduates who had not gone to college. This worsened the standard of living for high school graduates, especially as their displacement from the retail and service sectors coincided with the disappearance of factory jobs.

The 1982 recession proved more severe than conservatives had anticipated. Continuously increasing social-welfare and defense spending also added to the national debt, as did the crash of short-term tax receipts due to the severity of the 1982 recession. Rising unemployment created political problems for Republicans. They lost twenty-six seats in the House in the 1982 midterm elections. Reagan's public approval rating fell to 42 percent, a level so low that pollsters saw little prospect for his reelection in 1984.

Reagan felt that he had to raise taxes in 1982. The Tax Equity and Fiscal Responsibility Act levied $98 billion in tax hikes over three years. (This would be equivalent to $254 billion in new taxes today.) In 1983, Reagan, agreeing that Social Security was on a financially unsustainable path, supported increasing the payroll tax, yielding $70 billion in additional revenue. Democrats protested, correctly, that Social Security payroll taxes were regressive, falling heavily on lower-income Americans. However, they often missed the other half of the equation. Since employers paid workers' wages, Social Security payroll tax hikes added to their labor costs. For many employers, it was less expensive to pay workers overtime (or automate) than to hire new employees, further worsening the job market.

Conservatives had followed Arthur Laffer's advice about de-emphasizing federal spending and deficits to focus on tax rates. The national debt in 1980 had been $900 billion. It rose to $1.5 trillion in 1984 and reached $3.2 trillion by 1990. Federal spending, adjusted for inflation, went from $615 billion in 1980 to $1.275 trillion in 1990. The federal deficit went from $165 billion in 1981 to $336 billion in 1984. However, federal tax receipts did increase, thanks to the 1982 tax hikes and the 1981 targeted tax cuts, reducing the federal deficit to $251 billion by 1987. Reagan *slowed* the rate of growth in government spending, but did not align spending with the tax receipts coming into Washington. Deficits and debts were inevitable.

Fiscal conservatives should not have been surprised that Reagan was committed to New Deal-era programs, even if his commitment resulted in deficits. In 1982, William F. Buckley, Jr., and the *National Review* mocked nostalgic Democrats who were celebrating the 100th anniversary of Franklin Roosevelt's birth. Reagan responded by hosting a birthday party for Roosevelt. Addressing critics on the Right who believed he was too willing to compromise, Reagan delivered a cutting rebuke: "Die-hard conservatives thought that if I couldn't get everything I asked for, I should jump off the cliff with the flag flying—go down in flames." Reagan cared about results, not ideological purity.

Reagan and National Security, 1981–1988

The national security side of the "Reagan Revolution" represented a departure from the foreign policies of Carter and Ford. At the heart of the "Reagan Doctrine" was a reaffirmation, as well as a revision, of the Truman Doctrine. Since the early 1960s, the U.S. had embraced the concept of "mutual assured destruction" (MAD). The idea was that America and the Soviet Union had built up their atomic arsenals to the point where neither would survive a nuclear war. In theory, mutual annihilation would ensure that neither side used their nuclear weapons. Arguably, the build-up of U.S. and Soviet nuclear arsenals made both nations less safe. If history demonstrated anything, it was that people with weapons used them. Desperate people were especially prone to resort to desperate measures.

Reagan's solution was simple: he rejected MAD. Instead, Reagan proposed developing anti-missile technologies, creating a defensive shield over the U.S. In a 1983 address to the nation, Reagan referred to what would become known as the "Strategic Defense Initiative" (SDI) [Document 20: p. 164]. Democratic critics in the news media and in Congress mocked SDI, calling it "Star Wars," after the science fiction film series.

Beyond SDI, the U.S. would increase defense spending, giving the Soviet Union the choice of bankrupting itself to keep up, or negotiating arms reductions. Reagan also wanted America to have sufficient conventional forces to win wars without resorting to nuclear weapons. He encouraged field commanders to take initiative and pledged that politicians would not place restrictions on their operations. Reagan would not be like President Johnson, who personally choose bombing targets. As Reagan promised in 1988, "young Americans must never again be sent to fight and die unless we are prepared to let them win" [Document 21: p. 165]. Finally, the U.S. would support anti-communist insurgencies in countries either allied with, or invaded by, the Soviet Union.

Annual defense spending went from $165 billion in 1981 to $336 billion by 1984. The Navy added forty-six ships to its combat fleet, while new and improved tanks, particularly the Abrams, could accurately shoot while moving at a rapid clip. Stealth technology protected military aircraft from radar detection. American armed forces added nearly 100,000 personnel. Military pay increased, lifting service personnel out of poverty.

Recruitment standards also increased. Given the rising level of technological sophistication of American weapons systems, enlisting high school dropouts was not a desirable option. If anything, the great amount of technical training the military had to provide to many of its recruits transformed the armed forces into a community, or two-year, college. This was an important development since high schools in the 1980s were abandoning vocational education in favor of a college preparation curriculum.

Reagan's defense policy sparked criticism across the ideological spectrum. On the Right, the Heritage Foundation argued in 1982 that Reagan's defense budget was insufficient to counter the Soviet threat. Norman Podhoretz, a major force behind the neoconservative journal *Commentary*, complained that Reagan was only hitting at the periphery of Soviet power. The 1983 U.S. invasion of the Soviet-allied Caribbean nation of Grenada, Podhoretz fumed, was a sideshow. North Carolina senator Jesse Helms, while supportive of efforts to arm anti-communist forces in Central America, chided Reagan for insisting that America's allies promote economic reform. Helms regarded anti-communist reformers in Latin America as New Deal socialists.

Georgia congressman Newt Gingrich expressed concerns about the direction of American foreign policy. While he could agree with Kirkpatrick's point that some dictators were useful allies in the fight against communism, still, the U.S. had to maintain moral standards or the nation would lose its soul. Gingrich was especially concerned with conservatives who gave full-throated support to the white-minority South African government. While South Africa was assisting the U.S. in supporting anti-Soviet insurgencies in its region, the government embraced apartheid, or racial segregation. Gingrich urged Congress to impose economic sanctions on South Africa to compel its government to embrace racial equality. His lack of success led Gingrich to complain that conservatives were in danger of becoming "the stupid party."

At the other end of the political spectrum, Democratic and Republican liberals raised numerous objections to Reagan's defense policy. Many insisted that Reagan was provoking the Soviet Union into a nuclear war. Moreover, by deploying additional nuclear and conventional weapons in western Europe, Reagan was destabilizing allies and boosting anti-American sentiment overseas. Liberals also argued that domestic social-welfare programs did not receive sufficient funding because of the money diverted to defense. In addition, Reagan's military build-up piled on debt. This last argument amused Reagan, as few Democrats had ever expressed concern about deficits and debts.

Lester Thurow, an esteemed liberal economist at the Massachusetts Institute of Technology (MIT), offered up another damning criticism. Defense spending diverted technological research and development resources away from business and, consequently, undermined the domestic economy. In the short term, Thurow had raised a valid point. It was difficult from the perspective of the 1980s to see what possible civilian economic application could be found in such military research as the development of cross-computer communication (electronic mail) and the networking of multiple computers into what would become known as the "internet."

Liberals and conservatives found one area of agreement when it came to foreign policy: providing military assistance to the Afghanis fighting their Soviet invaders. Numerous resistance groups sprang up in Afghanistan as the call went out to wage a holy war, or *jihad*, against the Russians. Among the anti-Soviet warriors who came to Afghanistan was the son of a wealthy Saudi contractor—Osama Bin Laden. As the Soviets staggered under the pressure of advanced American weapons technology, Bin Laden looked forward to the day when Afghanistan would enjoy a spiritual reconstruction.

Reagan and Social Policy, 1981–1988

During the 1980 election, Reagan had told Moral Majority leaders that while, as members of a tax-exempt, non-partisan religious organization, they might not be able to "endorse" him for president, he was endorsing their work. Reagan's banter gave Moral Majority leader Jerry Falwell a great ego boost. Connie Marshner, who had staged a well-publicized walkout from Carter's White House Conference on Families, joined the Reagan Administration as an adviser on family policy. Especially gratifying to social conservatives was the fact that the 1984 Republican Party Platform rejected abortion: "the unborn child has a fundamental individual right to life which cannot be infringed."

The 1984 Republican Party platform also denounced racial hiring quotas, or affirmative action. Reagan criticized affirmative action, arguing that "If you happen to belong to an ethnic group not recognized by the federal government as entitled to social treatment, you are the victim of reverse discrimination." While this was a presidential slight directed toward African-Americans, Reagan's phrasing was important. He attacked the federal government for championing affirmative action, without acknowledging that as president he had the power to undercut affirmative action policies. Reagan, in reality, had no intention of abolishing affirmative action.

It did not take long for social conservatives to realize that Reagan had given them rhetoric, not action. Marshner left the Reagan Administration and Falwell speculated that Reagan's advisers "probably couldn't spell abortion." The same Reagan staffers that disgusted Falwell also intercepted the president's issues of *Human Events*. Such staffers regarded the conservative publication as little better than a supermarket tabloid.

Among the most prominent of the frustrated social conservatives was Phyllis Schlafly. Having prevented the Equal Rights Amendment from becoming part of the Constitution, and having moved the Republican Party toward opposition to abortion, Schlafly expected recognition. Joseph Coors repeatedly requested Reagan to honor Schlafly with a federal office, perhaps as Secretary of Education. Schlafly indicated that she would accept a seat on the Supreme Court. Unwilling to give her either high-profile appointment, Reagan appointed her to serve as a member of the Commission on the Bicentennial of the U.S. Constitution. Reagan sidelined Schlafly and her

Eagle Forum—keeping them far from power, but close enough to retain them as allies.

Many liberals believed that Reagan had only weakly addressed the public-health crisis surrounding the outbreak of Acquired Immunodeficiency Syndrome (AIDS). At the same time, some social conservatives proclaimed that the disease was God's retribution against gays. Falwell at least included heterosexuals in his broader crusade against sexual immorality, arguing that "AIDS and syphilis and all sexually transmitted diseases are God's judgment upon the total society for embracing what God has condemned: sex outside of marriage." For his part, while Reagan may not have reacted quickly to the AIDS epidemic, he was not inclined to bash gays—especially since one of his Hollywood friends, Rock Hudson, died of AIDS in 1985. A year later, embarrassed conservatives had to tone down their anti-gay rhetoric when Terry Dolan, the chair of the National Conservative Political Action Committee, died of AIDS.

Social conservatives were alarmed by Americans' declining religiosity. The 1950s had proven to be the golden years of American religion. Billy Graham's crusades attracted millions and, according to various surveys of public opinion, 49 percent of Americans regularly attended church services. In 1952, 75 percent of Americans stated that religious faith was of great importance to their lives. By the end of the 1980s, just 38 percent of Americans attended church regularly and the number reporting that religion was important to them had fallen to 58 percent.

From the 1960s through the 1980s, more citizens, especially the college educated and the upper middle class, embraced a secular spirit. Affluent Protestant faiths, notably the Episcopalians and Presbyterians, lost anywhere from 20 to 33 percent of their flocks. The Episcopalians alone shed 1.5 million people in that period.

It was not just the old-line Protestant churches that lost members. A few million largely white, working-class Catholics either abandoned religious faith altogether or moved into evangelical Protestant pews. Such ex-Catholics never forgave the clergy for denouncing their opposition to block-busting. They were further aroused against the Church by its decision to close their parishes and abandon them to a wrenching post-industrial economy. The number of ex-Catholics went from 7.5 million in 1975 to 10.3 million by 1990. Only immigration from Mexico, Central America, and Latin America kept overall Catholic membership numbers relatively stable.

Social conservatives could at least boast that their denominations were growing. The more reflective among them, however, understood that in the larger picture the number of religious faithful was not increasing. Southern Baptists and Pentecostals gained at the expense of other denominations, not by winning converts from the secular camp.

There was one political development that cheered social conservatives. Reagan pushed for greater law enforcement power. Roosevelt had authorized the FBI to wiretap citizens and Nixon established the paramilitary Drug

Enforcement Agency. Reagan built upon his predecessors' initiatives to make Washington the national center of law enforcement. Decades earlier, Texas congressman Hatton Sumners had warned that Democratic liberals were taking over state and local law enforcement functions. Little could he have known that a conservative Republican would complete what Roosevelt had started.

Conservatives in the 1980s federalized crime, most especially narcotics trafficking. Far more drug offenders, subject to racketeering laws and mandatory sentencing policies, ended up in federal, rather than state, prisons. The rate of federal narcotics incarceration escalated. In 1980, there were just under 5,000 drug offenders in federal prisons. By 1990, that figure was over 24,000. A decade after that, more than 74,000 drug offenders were in federal prisons. Civil rights groups expressed concern that law enforcement targeted African-Americans. Although accounting for 10 percent of the U.S. population, African-Americans in the 1980s represented just over 40 percent of the inmates at federal and state prisons. Many were in prison on drug-related charges.

Violent crime, which had helped fuel Alabama governor George Wallace's law-and-order presidential campaign in 1968, continued to rise though the 1980s. Assaults went from 672,650 in 1980 to a little over 1 million in 1990. By 1990, New York City's annual number of homicides stood at 2,245. Los Angeles trended toward 2,500 homicides annually. Combined, the two cities, with 4 percent of America's population, accounted for nearly 21 percent of the nation's murders.

The federal government's response to soaring crime was mass incarceration. In 1980, federal, state, and county prisons had 540,000 people behind bars. That number grew to 1 million by 1989. The number of people in prison or released on parole or probation went from 1.8 million in 1980 to 4.4 million by 1990. Low-income African-Americans, especially those living in cities such as New York or Los Angeles, were six times more likely than whites to be homicide victims in the 1980s. Federal and local policing policies were keen on reacting to crime, but not very good at preventing crime. The proliferation of private security companies, gates, and steel bars over windows in 1980s urban America testified to deteriorating public safety.

Culture and Politics in the Reagan Era, 1981–1988

Most American voters did not blame Reagan for soaring crime rates and widening economic disparities. Reagan was, as his liberal critics put it, "the Teflon President"—like the specially coated fry pans, nothing stuck to him. At the 1984 Republican National Convention, Reagan praised Roosevelt and Truman—privately noting that most Republicans were not worth quoting. He went on to win reelection in a landslide greater than the one he received in 1980. Reagan collected nearly 59 percent of the popular vote and carried forty-nine states. Democratic presidential nominee Walter Mondale, who had served as Carter's vice president, carried his home state of Minnesota by less than 4,000 votes.

One element of Reagan's success was his ability to encourage Americans to be hopeful about the future. Reagan's optimistic spirit worked its way through American popular culture to the point where the public regained its faith in the federal government—or at least its faith in the White House and the military. Although Hollywood continued to produce dark films about the Vietnam War and corporate corruption, most Americans were flocking to movies with very different messages. Israelis Yorum Globus and Menahem Golan cranked out what Reagan's generation would have called B-list movies. Martial arts instructor-turned-actor Chuck Norris refought the Vietnam War (and won), defeated a multicultural cast of Soviet agents who invaded America, and wiped out Arab terrorists.

While respectable Hollywood scoffed at Globus and Golan's cut-rate "Cannon Group" action films, their profits were too great to ignore. Soon, big budget action films appeared, most with A-list actors, or those who would soon be A-list. Film critics dismissed Tom Cruise's film *Top Gun* as little more than an extended recruiting advertisement for the U.S. Navy. *Top Gun* grossed $176 million in American ticket sales in 1986. (That would be $393 million today.) Sylvester Stallone, as alienated Vietnam veteran John Rambo, not only redeemed his country by going back to Vietnam, he later battled Soviet troops alongside the Islamic resistance in Afghanistan. As the boxer "Rocky," Stallone beat up a steroid-enhanced, robotic Russian, and in the process helped the communists realize that they were on the losing side of history.

Not since World War II had Hollywood produced so many patriotic action films. Some prominent celebrities, reacting against Hollywood's liberal political landscape, revealed that they were conservative. Television star Tom Selleck, who had a popular series about a Vietnam veteran-turned private detective, went as far as to film a commercial for the *National Review*. Selleck stated that, just like Reagan, he not only subscribed to the flagship magazine of the conservative movement, he read it. Meanwhile, media celebrity and Dallas Cowboys football coach Tom Landry campaigned with Reagan and made a commercial discussing his personal relationship with God.

Liberals dismissed the conservative capture of popular culture as little more than a revival of Ancient Rome's "bread and circuses." The American gladiators of the 1980s may have fought on film rather than in the arena, but their function, according to Reagan's critics, remained the same as it had been centuries earlier: to distract the populace from fundamental economic and social problems. Few listened to liberals' lamentations and even fewer regarded Reagan as a reincarnated Nero.

Across the nation's universities, students joined their campus Reserve Officers' Training Corps (ROTC) with the intention of pursuing a military career. In 1974, the Army ROTC had 33,200 cadets. By 1983, there were 73,800 Army ROTC cadets on the nation's college campuses.

Other students flocked to majors in business and finance, leaving the liberal arts as receding islands. Milton Friedman, a free-market economist at the University of Chicago, became a youth oracle. His 1980 book, *Free to Choose*, enjoyed enormous sales and Friedman became a media celebrity. Overall, the cohort of Americans born in the early 1960s, and who entered their adult years in the 1980s, embraced Reagan. Just 20 percent voted Democratic—while 40 percent were Republican and the remaining 40 percent were independent but leaned center-right.

Conservatives in the 1980s felt empowered. The Heritage Foundation expanded its staff and drew more funds from such donors as Dow Chemical and Gulf Oil. In 1981, Heritage had a $5.3 million budget. By 1989, Heritage operated on $16.3 million. Both the Heritage Foundation and the American Enterprise Institute moved from the periphery of Washington politics to become the heart of the Republican establishment.

For liberals, the 1980s were disheartening. Mondale, in his 1984 presidential campaign, had pledged to raise taxes and terminate the Reagan Revolution. To liberals' dismay, not only did conservatives reject Mondale, a full quarter of registered Democrats—mostly working-class whites—voted for Reagan. Democrats, who still controlled the House, promoted numerous legislative and legal investigations of Reagan officials. At one point over 100 Reagan officials were under investigation for various corruption charges. Of the few investigations that resulted in a trial, nearly all defendants were found innocent.

The political dynamic in Washington changed because of the 1986 midterm elections. Republicans lost eight Senate seats, surrendering control of that chamber to Democrats. Campaigning in Alabama, Florida, Georgia, North Dakota, South Dakota, and Virginia, Democratic senatorial candidates persuaded voters that they were moderates seeking to reform, not undo, the Reagan Revolution.

In the South, Democrats successfully mobilized greater numbers of black voters and reassured white voters of their continued friendship. Southern Democrats emphasized their plans to improve the economy and largely avoided discussing abortion, affirmative action, crime, and foreign policy. If it proved impossible to avoid social issues, then Democratic Senate candidates copied the Carter tactic of separately telling whites and blacks what they wanted to hear—hoping that no one was recording their words.

Liberals, including a few *New York Times* columnists, celebrated the Democratic recapture of the Senate. With both legislative branches in the hands of Reagan's opponents, surely the conservative movement had been dealt a death blow.

The Conservative Retreat, 1986–1988

Democratic control of the Senate had immediate consequences for Reagan. Robert Bork, a Yale Law professor and U.S. Court of Appeals Judge for the District of Columbia Circuit, expected the Senate to confirm his nomination for a seat on the Supreme Court. His extensive criticism of federal civil rights legislation, which went back to the early 1960s, haunted Bork during his Senate hearings. Bork did not help his cause by seemingly calling into question the intelligence of the chair of the Senate Judiciary Committee, Joe Biden of Delaware. Liberal advocacy groups raised millions of dollars in an unprecedented, and successful, campaign to prevent Bork's elevation to the Supreme Court. Newly elected southern Democrats proclaimed their opposition to Bork.

Just as dismaying to conservatives was congressional Democrats' highly publicized hearings into what became known as the Iran-Contra scandal. The scandal had its origins in the early 1980s. Tip O'Neill despised the anti-communist guerrillas, the "contras," that Reagan supported in Nicaragua. To O'Neill, the contras were "murderers, marauders, and rapists." Liberals feared that Nicaragua would become another Vietnam. To prevent that from happening, House Democrats sponsored three measures between 1982 and 1984 to limit military aid to the contras. Although Republicans controlled the Senate, a handful of Republican liberals, also fearful of another Vietnam War, deserted Reagan, allowing the Democratic restrictions to pass. Reagan bided his time until after his reelection, when he believed that he could convince Congress to change its mind.

Unwilling to tolerate congressional interference with the conduct of foreign policy, national security adviser Robert McFarlane, and National Security Council deputy director **Oliver North**, took the initiative. Their plan was to violate the U.S. arms embargo against Iran, which was engaged in a merciless war with America's Iraqi ally. The proceeds from the illegal

Figure 5.2 Oliver North (1943–)
Source: Photograph in the author's possession

weapons sales would then be used to purchase weapons and generate funds for the contras. The principle actors behind the Iran-Contra operation were Vietnam War veterans who regarded congressional Democrats as either naïve liberals or allies of communism.

Ironically, Reagan persuaded Congress in 1985 to loosen restrictions on American support for the contras, but by then members of Reagan's team had already committed a host of illegal acts. After the news media exposed the conspiracy, the Democratic Senate grilled North and others in 1987. A growing number of liberals demanded Reagan's impeachment, even though there was no evidence of his knowledge or participation in the Iran-Contra affair. Most Democratic leaders knew that there was no public support for removing Reagan in the last year of his presidency. They were using the scandal as the basis for an anti-corruption-themed presidential campaign in 1988.

To make matters worse, America experienced a cascading failure of savings and loan institutions beginning in 1985. Over the next few years, more than a thousand such banks (one third of the total number) collapsed. Taxpayers ultimately paid out $124 billion in federal deposit insurance.

The roots of the savings and loan crises were bipartisan. In 1980, a Democratic Congress and president had pushed legislation to allow savings and loans to make more of their assets available for investment. Two years later, a Democratic House, a Republican Senate, and a Republican president pulled back on regulatory oversight of the savings and loans and allowed them to move into a wider array of investment activities. As Roosevelt had feared in 1933, without sufficient federal oversight of banking, the taxpayers would be left holding the bill for the incompetent, and sometimes fraudulent, practices of banking directors. Americans were shocked and angered by the number of politically connected people in both parties who had financially benefited from their ties to failed savings and loan institutions.

Conservatives' political challenges going into the 1988 election went far beyond the fallout from the savings and loan crisis and Iran-Contra affair. Reagan, like Roosevelt, had been the star attraction. When charismatic politicians enter a room, they suck up all the oxygen, leaving everyone else gasping for air. There were few viable successors to Reagan—just as there had been few capable of replacing Roosevelt. Both the Republican and Democratic parties had, respectively, lost their "player bench" because of disastrous midterm elections in 1986 and 1938. For Democrats to maintain control of the White House in 1940, they had to nominate Roosevelt for a third term. In 1988, the Constitution did not permit Reagan to run for a third term.

The Triumph of George H.W. Bush, 1988

Pat Robertson, the head of the Virginia-based Christian Broadcast Network, had supported Reagan despite his fear that the president had failed to reverse

America's moral decline. He also believed that focusing on economic policy without attending to the peoples' spiritual needs was unwise. Robertson, whose followers were mainly lower-income Pentecostals, argued that while "free enterprise" allowed for more individual freedom, "communism and capitalism in their most extreme, secular manifestations are equally doomed to failure."

Two considerations led Robertson to enter the 1988 Republican presidential primaries. First, he believed that Reagan's heir apparent, George H.W. Bush, was a social liberal in conservative clothing. Second, Christian conservatism had suffered a major public relations scandal. In 1987, the news media revealed that Jim and Tammy Faye Bakker, the leaders of Praise the Lord (PTL) ministries and the founders of a Christian amusement park, Heritage USA, were tied up in sexual and financial scandals. Public revulsion for the Bakkers extended to all religious conservatives. Jerry Falwell saw contributions to the Moral Majority decline by $2 million annually, while Robertson's television network lost $16 million.

Robertson spent $26 million to win a few dozen Republican Convention delegates. Not only did he fall far short of the presidential nomination, Robertson was unable to turn around the negative public perception of the Religious Right. More troubling, corporate donors who had given generously to conservative think tanks in Washington began to back away from anyone associated with Robertson and Falwell. The rising generation of high-tech entrepreneurs in California's Silicon Valley did not think that the federal government belonged in the bedroom any more than in the boardroom. Moreover, their customers included those who had abortions and who were in same-sex relationships. Why, they asked, should they alienate

Figure 5.3 Pat Robertson (1930–)
Source: Photograph in the author's possession

customers by funding think tanks like the Heritage Foundation which had welcomed Falwell and Robertson into their fold?

Conservatives grudgingly accepted Vice President Bush as their presidential nominee. They disliked his father, Prescott Bush, for the role he had played as Eisenhower's lieutenant in bringing about Joseph McCarthy's downfall. Their distaste for Bush was even greater. His contemptuous dismissal of Reagan's economic plan during the 1980 presidential primaries as "voodoo" still angered conservatives. Then Bush's complete reversal, embracing every Reagan policy, made conservatives wonder if he was an opportunistic social climber without any political convictions.

Bush's choice of Republican campaign operative Lee Atwater was not reassuring. Atwater had, like Connie Marshner, gone to the University of South Carolina in the 1960s. But while Marshner was allied with the social conservatives in the campus Young Americans for Freedom chapter, Atwater had shown pornographic movies to raise money for the campus Young Republicans. It surprised no one who knew Atwater that he would find a way to depict the Democratic presidential nominee, Massachusetts governor Michael Dukakis, as a clueless liberal who let black prisoners out on furlough to rape white women.

During the 1988 election, Bush pledged to continue Reagan's economic policies. As he chanted to crowds, "Read my lips ... No new taxes!" He vowed to stand up to the Soviet Union and keep America safe. Most importantly, Bush promised that he would be the equivalent of Reagan's third term as president. Bush got his victory, receiving 53 percent of the popular vote, and winning 426 electoral votes. He carried California, the South, and the battered industrial states of Illinois, Michigan, Ohio, and Pennsylvania. Democrats had little hope of capturing the White House if they could not win California and be competitive in what was becoming known as "the **Rustbelt.**"

The Agonies of George H.W. Bush, 1989–1992

As president, Bush showed conservatives that he was no friend. Faced with a Democratic Congress critical of escalating Reagan-era deficits and debt, Bush agreed to budget negotiations. Bypassing congressional conservatives, Bush raised federal taxes while Democrats promised that they would reduce spending on entitlement programs. Confronted by journalists who asked Bush about his pledge not to increase taxes, an irritated Bush responded with "Read my hips!" Jesse Helms and Newt Gingrich predicted that Democrats would never deliver on their pledge to reduce domestic spending.

Bush had made his national security credentials the centerpiece of his presidency. He had vowed during the 1988 campaign to fight the Cold War just as vigorously as Reagan. Soviet leader **Mikhail Gorbachev**, however, had other ideas. Gorbachev understood that the Soviet Union could not afford to keep pace with Reagan's military build-up and lacked the financial resources to sustain communist insurgencies in Africa and Central America. Fundamentally, the Soviet economy suffered from a lack of innovation and had no potential for growth. Both factors proved disastrous for Soviet foreign policy.

Gorbachev began a drawdown of Soviet troops in Afghanistan in 1988 and completed their withdrawal by 1989. That same year, protests erupted across Soviet-dominated eastern Europe. Most of the protests were peaceful, with a few exceptions. Rather than respond with force, as his predecessors had done in Hungary in 1956 and Czechoslovakia in 1968, Gorbachev opted to let the nations of eastern Europe have their freedom. West German leaders moved quickly to reunite their nation. In 1987, Reagan had gone to West Berlin and demanded that Gorbachev tear down the wall (built in 1961) that divided the city [Document 22: p. 166]. Just two years later, the Germans tore it down themselves.

German reunification in 1990 alarmed British and French leaders. Bush was somewhat more supportive, but insisted that Germany remain part of the North Atlantic Treaty Organization. While many Americans wondered what the point of NATO would be now that the Soviet empire appeared to be coming apart, the military pact had always served another purpose: to keep the (West) Germans under control. A reunified Germany would inevitably be the most militarily and economically powerful nation in Europe. That meant NATO had the potential to be an instrument of German power, rather than the means to restrain German power. The decline of American military and political influence in Europe commenced with German reunification in 1990.

Gorbachev had warned Americans leaders that he was going to do something to the U.S. far worse than go to war: he was going "to deprive them of an enemy." For forty-five years the Cold War had shaped American foreign policy. The Cold War had, despite the poorly conceived and executed Vietnam War, bound most Americans together in a common cause. For conservatives, the Cold War had been the glue that united their factions. Moral and economic conservatives shared a loathing of international communism. With the Soviet threat gone, not only would American foreign policy lose its guiding star, conservatives no longer had the common enemy that had drawn them together. It took no time for conservative disunity to appear.

Between 1980 and 1988, Iraq and Iran had waged a savage war. Iran, with a population nearly three times larger than Iraq's, still lost four times the number of soldiers—an estimated 1 million. The Reagan Administration armed Iraq, even though the U.S.-allied Israelis had bombed Iraqi nuclear reactors in 1981. In 1990, Iraqi dictator Saddam Hussein moved troops toward Iraq's border with Kuwait. The U.S. ambassador to Iraq, April Glaspie, assured Hussein that America had no interest in intra-Arab conflicts. Further, the U.S. had no military defense treaty with oil-rich Kuwait.

As Secretary of State Dean Acheson had done in 1950, Glaspie declared a country outside the American security perimeter—which then appeared to give a dictator the confidence to launch an invasion. To Hussein's surprise, Bush responded by deploying troops to Saudi Arabia in preparation for war with Iraq. Drawing upon the resources Reagan had built to challenge Soviet power, Bush sent 540,000 troops—with Britain and a few other nations contributing smaller numbers.

Meanwhile, neoconservatives went into action. **Bill Kristol**, as Vice President Dan Quayle's chief of staff, encouraged conservative media outlets to compare Hussein to Hitler. The son of neoconservative editor Irving Kristol, Bill Kristol had supported the Vietnam War while enrolled at Harvard, but avoided serving in the military. Kristol's efforts to rally public opinion behind a war with Iraq was not a one-person operation. Bush's Secretary of Defense, Dick Cheney, who, like Kristol, as well as Vice President Quayle, had avoided the Vietnam War, made the case for military intervention in the Persian Gulf.

Some on the Right saw no justification for going to war. Reagan's former Secretary of the Navy James Webb was a vocal critic of President Bush. A Marine veteran of Vietnam and recipient of the Navy Cross for valor, Webb had no use for "chicken hawks"—the pro-war conservatives who let others fight in their place. Webb argued that Bush's dependence on Texas oil men for campaign funding and advice pushed him toward a Middle Eastern war. Intervention in Iraq, Webb warned, would "galvanize the Arab world" against the U.S. and result in terrorist attacks against Americans. He also argued that with the economy slipping into recession, it was reasonable to suspect that Bush wanted to divert Americans' attention from his failing domestic policies.

Former Reagan and Nixon speechwriter Pat Buchanan also weighed into Bush's preparations for war in the Persian Gulf. Buchanan argued that "There are only two groups that are beating the drums for war in the Middle East—the Israeli Defense Ministry and its amen corner in the United States." The neoconservative *New York Post* and *Commentary*, as well as the *National Review*, accused Buchanan of being anti-Semitic. Neoconservatives observed that Buchanan's father had been a supporter of America First and had listened to Charles Lindbergh's antiwar broadcasts. The Buchanan family, therefore, was anti-Semitic and possessed Nazi sympathies spanning two generations. Antiwar Democratic liberals came to Buchanan's defense, arguing that opposition to Israel, let alone to President Bush, did not make a person a Nazi anti-Semite.

The Conservative Break-Up, 1992

Although the Persian Gulf War proved to be a U.S. military victory, Americans' celebration proved to be short-lived. Going into the 1992 election, American voters were concerned with the recession and began to question what the point was of the Persian Gulf War. Hussein remained in power, despite the Iraqi dictator being, as neoconservatives argued, the moral equivalent of Hitler. Moreover, the Bush Administration had also justified intervention because an Iraqi-occupied Kuwait would lead to higher oil prices. The Iraqis were gone from Kuwait, but oil prices remained high.

Buchanan entered the 1992 Republican presidential primaries to challenge Bush. Although Buchanan lacked the numbers to win the nomination, he collected enough votes to reveal the widening fractures between the interventionist neoconservatives and the Robert Taft isolationist faction that had been rejuvenated with the end of the Cold War. The Bush campaign went on the offense, arguing that "If he [Buchanan] doesn't think America should lead the world, how can we trust him to lead America?" As Buchanan's defenders retorted: who elected America to lead the world and why should foreign policy be prioritized over domestic policy?

Bush faced a more serious threat from a well-financed independent, Texas billionaire **Ross Perot**. Given that Perot was a graduate of the U.S. Naval Academy, Bush found it difficult to question his patriotism or have his operatives brand him as a Nazi sympathizer. Perot was a nationalist who believed that Bush had failed to protect American jobs from unfair overseas competition. He also faulted Bush for deploying troops into situations where American national security was not clearly involved. Perot's contempt for Bush was clear, as was his implicit rebuke of Reagan:

> Our president was sending delegations over to burp and diaper and pamper Saddam Hussein and tell him how nice he was. That's all public record. Then … our manhood was questioned and off we go into the wild blue yonder with the lives of our servicemen at risk because of 10 years of stupid mistakes and billions of dollars of taxpayer money.

Mounting discontent with Bush, which spanned the ideological spectrum, went beyond foreign and economic policy considerations. On the Christian Right, all was not well. Falwell had disbanded the Moral Majority in 1989, asserting that "our mission is accomplished." He admitted, however, that religious conservatives "have not solved the problems" which had inspired them to mobilize a few years earlier. Reagan had not eradicated abortion or narcotics. Bush was unlikely to do better.

In 1989, as Falwell closed the Moral Majority, Robertson launched the Christian Coalition. The Christian Coalition would look beyond presidential and congressional elections, to "educate" voters in legislative and state races. If social conservatives could not rely on the White House, then it was necessary to work at the grass-roots level outside Washington. As for supporting Bush's reelection, the Christian Coalition did so, but without evangelical fervor.

The Democrats, demoralized by losing three presidential elections in a row, listened to the advice of former Arkansas governor **William Jefferson "Bill" Clinton**. In 1985, a group of moderates, largely southerners, founded the Democratic Leadership Council (DLC). Clinton and his fellow DLC members urged their party to regain southern white and northern Catholic support by emphasizing economic, rather than social, issues. To convince "Reagan Democrats" of their sincerity, Clinton argued, the party had to nominate a moderate southerner with a command of rhetoric and media presentation. It just so happened that Clinton not only met all his requirements, he was available.

Bill Clinton focused on the economy, urged Americans to move on from the Cold War, and charmed his way across late-night television talk shows. When he could not avoid social issues, Clinton managed to denounce abortion while pledging to keep it legal. Reagan and Roosevelt had the ability to take both sides of an issue, and Clinton proved worthy of their company.

The electorate handed Bush a humiliating loss. He won just 168 electoral votes and received 37 percent of the popular vote. Bush reduced Reagan's popular vote share by 20 percentage points. Perot may not have won any electoral votes, but his proportion of the popular vote, nearly 20 percent, was record-breaking for a post-World War II independent candidate. While some Republicans blamed Perot for taking votes from Bush, most of his support came from independents.

Clinton's 43 percent share of the popular vote may have shown that he lacked a majority, but he had four years to build one before the 1996 election. His challenge would be to govern as a moderate while contending with Democrats who were moving to the left and conservative Republicans who regarded political compromise as a betrayal of principles. The paradox was that on many economic issues, as well as on the appropriate role of the federal government in the economy, Clinton was more conservative than Bush. Some Democratic liberals understood that and despised Clinton. Many Republicans chose to ignore that reality since they had already ruled out negotiation and bipartisanship.

6 The Politics of Division, 1993–2016

Bill Clinton's Successes and Set-Backs, 1993–1994

Bill Clinton had several "firsts" when he took office in 1993. He was the first "Baby Boomer" president, born a year after Franklin Roosevelt's death. Clinton was also the first president since 1945 not to have been in the military. Most significantly, he was America's first post-Cold War president—both by timing and by sentiment. If the Cold War was history to Clinton, then the New Deal was prehistoric. It was appropriate that the Clinton campaign theme song had been Fleetwood Mac's "Don't Stop"—as the lyrics urged, "Don't stop thinking about tomorrow … yesterday's gone, yesterday's gone."

With the end of the Cold War, Clinton saw a "peace dividend" ahead. Reducing the size of the military, Clinton believed, was not only a recognition of new realities, it could lead to good outcomes. First, as the only remaining "superpower" in the world, there was no threat to national security requiring the maintenance of a large military. Second, reductions in military spending could be redirected toward social programs and help lower, or eliminate, the federal deficit. Third, downsizing the military would make future adventures like the Persian Gulf War difficult—and perhaps unlikely.

Between 1993 and 2000, U.S. armed forces went from 1.8 million to 1.4 million personnel. Clinton cut the number of civilian employees in defense-related jobs nearly in half. The Navy reduced its fleet by 213 ships. In Clinton's first term, he sliced defense spending by $50 billion annually. By 1998, thanks in part to defense cuts, Clinton balanced the federal budget and avoided deficits for the next three years.

Outside the Heritage Foundation and the American Enterprise Institute, the public supported Clinton's defense adjustments. Anti-interventionist libertarians and Pat Buchanan-style isolationists welcomed the reductions, as did nearly all Democrats. Some conservatives took solace in the fact that Clinton's defense cuts were not a repudiation of Reagan, but, rather, a recognition that Reagan had won the Cold War.

Clinton experienced two set-backs in the first year and a half in office that gave an opening to conservatives. Having been elected with 43 percent of the popular vote, there were over 100 Democratic House and Senate members who had received a higher share of the vote in their districts and states than Clinton. Tip O'Neill's heirs had little loyalty to Clinton; most resented his eagerness to run away from post-1960s liberalism.

His other problem hit closer to home. **Hillary Rodham Clinton** was a liberal idealist, while Bill Clinton was a moderate pragmatist. In 1993, Hillary Clinton took the lead on devising a national health insurance program. Her efforts culminated in proposals that confused friend and foe alike. Even sympathetic media outlets stumbled trying to explain the health care program's goals, regulatory oversight, and funding. Health care reform collapsed.

In 1994, Republican congressman Newt Gingrich saw an opening. He wanted to "nationalize" House and Senate races, orienting them around several conservative policy initiatives. Gingrich who, like Bill Clinton, was a master of media staging, announced the ten-point "Contract with America" from the steps of the Capitol Building [Document 23: p. 167]. Conservatives pledged to lower taxes, reduce regulations, and overhaul welfare programs.

Not only did Gingrich want the House, which Republicans had not controlled since 1954, he set his sights on the Senate. Most grandly, Gingrich believed that conservatives could set the policy agenda from Congress, and not worry about expending time and resources trying to capture the White House.

Republicans picked up eight Senate and fifty-four House seats to give them control of both chambers. They also gained ten governors, including George W. Bush in Texas. Pat Robertson's Christian Coalition took credit for mobilizing religious conservatives—who accounted for 27 percent of the electorate in 1994. Most importantly, the South went Republican from top to bottom. Since 1972, southern whites had split their ballots. They voted Republican at the presidential level and Democratic down-ticket. That practice largely ended in 1994 as conservative Democrats completed their evolution into Republicans. Recognizing that conservatives would have gone nowhere without Gingrich as their architect of victory, they elected him Speaker of the House.

Conservative Bipartisanship, 1995–1998

Gingrich's friends observed that he produced a hundred ideas daily, of which five might be good. As Gingrich took command of the House in 1995, he reminded fellow representatives that he was a historian who shared Reagan's perspective about the past:

> If you truly believe in representative self-government, you can never study Franklin Delano Roosevelt too much. He did bring us out of the Depression. He did lead the Allied movement in World War II. In many ways, he created the modern world. He was clearly, I think, as a political leader the greatest figure of the twentieth century. And I think his

concept that we have nothing to fear but fear itself, that we'll take an experiment, and if it fails, we'll do another one—and if you go back and read the New Deal, they tried again and again. They didn't always get it right, and we would have voted against much of it, but the truth is we would have voted for much of it.

The House Speaker and the president worked well together, despite the bouts of bickering that came with their outsized egos. Liberals complained when Clinton fulfilled his 1992 campaign pledge "to end welfare as we know it." Joining forces with Gingrich, Clinton overhauled welfare with the Personal Responsibility and Work Opportunity Reconciliation Act of 1996. This legislation limited lifetime welfare eligibility to five years, required recipients to seek employment, and provided block grants to states to help them fund education and job training programs as well as child care for the working poor. In 1995, there were 13 million Americans on welfare. By 2016, the number of welfare recipients had fallen to 3 million.

Clinton and Gingrich succeeded where Reagan had failed. They had rolled back a major Great Society program while leaving the New Deal's legacy entitlements unscathed. Of course, it was easier to reduce federal spending on

Figure 6.1 Left: Newt Gingrich (1943–), Speaker of the House, 1995–1999; Right: Bill Clinton (1946–), President of the United States, 1993–2001, during the 1995 State of the Union Address

Source: Courtesy of the Library of Congress Prints and Photographs Division

the poor than it was to cut programs which the upper middle class supported. Voter turnout, after all, rose with income and education levels. National Public Radio (NPR) was safe from conservative budget cutters.

Crime rates began to fall by the late 1990s, though there was no consensus as to why. Clinton claimed that the $10 billion in federal funds he sent to cities to help them hire 100,000 new police officers lowered the crime rate. Conservatives argued that throwing more people in prison, as well as a new policy of policing, "fixing broken windows," did the trick. "Fixing broken windows" focused on the prevention of crime, showed citizens that their city cared about their safety, and lowered the level of violence. In practice, "fixing broken windows" meant catching litter bugs, arresting people who urinated in alleys, and stopping others from jumping subway turnstiles to avoid paying their fares. While these were minor crimes, it often happened that the people caught littering, urinating, and dodging subway fares had outstanding felony warrants. New York City's Republican mayor, Rudy Giuliani, embraced the new policing methods. Violent crime rates plummeted.

Liberals responded that violent crime fell in New York City because it fell nationally. Conservatives argued that the reverse was true: New York City's homicide rate was so high that when it fell it drove down the national violent crime rate. Regardless of who was correct, crime declined, major cities became safer, and many previously marginal neighborhoods attracted new businesses and residents.

The economy bounced back from recession. In 1993, Clinton, a champion of free trade—chiefly the removal of tariff barriers—pushed for passage of the North American Free Trade Agreement (NAFTA). More congressional Republicans than Democrats voted for NAFTA. American investment in Mexico subsequently rose from $2.3 billion to $7.9 billion between 1994 and 2002—a 244 percent increase.

While easing the movement of goods across the Canadian border did not raise alarm, there was less public enthusiasm for working closely with Mexico. Union organizers, most of whom were Democrats, feared that NAFTA would accelerate the relocation of American jobs to low-wage Mexico. Cheaply produced goods from Mexico would then flood the American market, destroying small businesses which had higher labor costs.

Nativists were also concerned that NAFTA might encourage greater Mexican immigration. Thanks to Johnson's push for immigration reform in the 1960s, 24 million immigrants had settled in the U.S. by the 1990s. Five million of these immigrants came from Mexico. Anti-immigrant voices warned that Hispanic immigrants represented a Spanish-speaking bloc that would never assimilate. As had been true before World War I, the most vocal advocates of immigration were corporations that wanted inexpensive, non-union workers.

There was another reason as to why some conservatives supported immigration restriction. They pointed out that the millions of Catholics who came to America in the early twentieth century sired children who became the backbone of the New Deal Democratic Party. Such conservatives worried that history might repeat itself, with working-class Hispanic Catholics laying the electoral foundation for a twenty-first-century New Deal.

Beyond divisive debates over NAFTA and immigration, there was an economic reality that remained unchanged from the 1980s. American wages continued to stagnate. Economists observed that consumer purchasing power increased in the 1990s, but not because of rising wages. The answer was that Walmart, given its enormous size and cut-rate pricing practices, lowered what Americans paid for food and clothing.

Walmart prices were low for two reasons. First, the wages Walmart paid to its employees were 20 to 25 percent lower than those paid by its competitors. As Walmart emerged as a national corporate giant, employing 1.4 million people in the U.S. by 2010, its wage scale had an enormous economic impact on communities. Indeed, Walmart was the largest employer in many towns. Second, Walmart imported goods from low-wage China, Mexico, and elsewhere—rather than purchasing from U.S. suppliers employing Americans. U.S.-based companies even relocated overseas just so that Walmart would purchase their products from them.

The Republican Party's free-market faction wanted more than NAFTA. They hoped to dismantle at least one major component of the New Deal. Texas senator Phil Gramm, the chair of the Senate Banking Committee, pushed the 1999 Gramm-Leach-Biley Act which gutted the Glass-Steagall Act of the early 1930s. With New Deal-era restrictions removed, banks and Wall Street brokerage firms could team up to provide innovative investment opportunities. Banks extended mortgages to high-risk (low-income) home buyers who were likely to default on their payments. Then they bundled these "subprime mortgages" into securities which Wall Street sold to customers. Wall Street speculation fed a housing construction boom reminiscent of the 1920s. Buildings and houses went up, but either remained unoccupied or were repossessed multiple times.

Ideological Combat: The 1990s

Clinton's legislative record, as well as the fact that Perot ran as an independent for the second time, helped him win reelection in 1996. However, Clinton's 49 percent share of the popular vote once again deprived him of a majority. Clinton's political success was due in part to his overtures to corporations, building upon his connections to such Arkansas-based firms as Walmart and Tyson Foods. By the end of the 1990s, the fastest growing bloc of Democratic voters were those earning $200,000 or more. They were largely social liberals who felt repulsed by social conservatives. Not since the New Deal did so many affluent voters support the Democrats. Conversely, the fastest growing bloc of Republican voters in the 1990s were families earning less than $40,000. Such voters were largely southern social conservatives. Republicans were becoming the party of the working class. They had never held that title and did not necessarily want it.

A growing faction of conservatives grew frustrated with Clinton's successes. They believed the Republicans had not done enough to stop Clinton. One such frustrated conservative was **Grover Norquist**, who had been a Washington fixture since the 1980s. Norquist had worked with Oliver North to funnel money to the contras and traveled to South Africa to rally anti-communists behind the white-minority government. In 1985, Norquist founded the libertarian Americans for Tax Reform. He also helped write the 1994 Contract with America.

By the early 1990s, Norquist demanded that Republicans either sign a no-tax pledge or face generously funded party primary challengers. Norquist's rhetoric aroused amusement and anger, depending on the audience. As he liked to observe, "I'm not in favor of abolishing government. I just want to shrink it down to the size where we can drown it in the bathtub."

In addition to his pursuit of ideological purity, Norquist angered many conservatives by urging the Republican Party to back off its support of Israel and recognize that Islam and capitalism were compatible. A few social conservatives and neoconservatives in turn alleged that Norquist received funding from Saudi Arabian religious fundamentalists. Some also attacked his Palestinian wife, insinuating that Norquist had terrorist ties.

Other conservative voices emerged in the 1990s. The Federal Communications Commission (FCC) had repealed a rule known as the Fairness Doctrine in 1987. That rule had required on-air political discussions to feature viewpoints from both sides. The repeal of the Fairness Doctrine opened the way for AM stations to rebuild their market share with talk radio shows which were cheap to produce. Since liberals listened to NPR, if they listened to radio at all, AM talk radio became a conservative preserve.

It helped conservative talk radio that its pioneer, **Rush Limbaugh**, was an experienced disc jockey and sports announcer. More than 15 million people listened to Limbaugh's monologues in the 1990s. Successful political radio shows required hosts who understood the art of communication as much as they grasped policy debates. A legion of conservative talk show radio programs emerged in the 1990s. Although united in their hatred of Clinton, many talk show hosts attacked Gingrich as a liberal collaborator. The proliferation of conservative radio programs exposed how fractured Republicans were on social, economic, and foreign policy.

Australian-born newspaperman **Rupert Murdoch** saw an opportunity to emulate, and expand upon, Clarence Manion's pioneering conservative radio and television shows from the 1950s and 1960s. Murdoch wanted to build a conservative television network and news channel in the U.S. Conservatives did not trust the *New York Times* and mocked the Cable News Network (CNN) as the "Clinton News Network." Murdoch, the owner of 20th Century Fox, enlisted Republican political strategist Roger Ailes in launching the Fox News Channel (FNC) in 1996. Fox News hired conservatives, and a few liberals, as show hosts, co-hosts, or correspondents—including Oliver North of Iran-Contra scandal fame. Libertarians and neoconservatives were well represented, social conservatives often received slots outside prime viewing hours, and Pat Buchanan-Robert Taft isolationists were generally nowhere to be seen.

Murdoch founded the neoconservative magazine, the *Weekly Standard*, in 1995. (He purchased the *Wall Street Journal* in 2007.) Political operative Bill Kristol gave the *Weekly Standard* its editorial direction and cemented its relationship with the American Enterprise Institute. Although the *Weekly Standard* never generated the circulation and advertising revenue to be profitable, its writers performed considerable work for the Fox News Channel. The *Weekly Standard* and the AEI became the talent stables for Fox News. Like conservative talk radio, Fox News and the *Weekly Standard* spent as much time attacking conservatives whom they believed had deviated from the party line as they did condemning Clinton.

Conservative talk radio hosts and magazines fixated on Clinton, convinced that corruption had lined his path to power in Arkansas. In 1994, spurred by multiple stories of dishonest business arrangements in Arkansas, the U.S. Office of the Independent Counsel launched an investigation of Clinton. Ken Starr, a social conservative and former judge, ultimately led the investigation. After four years and $70 million expended, Starr's investigation into Clinton's Arkansas connections yielded nothing.

Starr decided to broaden his investigation to include sexual assault allegations against Clinton. None of those allegations could be proven. Clinton, however, denied, before a grand jury, that he had sexual relations with a young White House intern. Starr could prove otherwise, leading to demands in 1998 to impeach Clinton for lying under oath.

Gingrich had no problem working with Clinton, or with trying to remove him from office, though he had reservations about doing the latter. In part, Gingrich wanted to work with Clinton to reform Social Security and keep the program on a fiscally sound track. There was also the problem that while Starr insisted that a Senate impeachment trial would center on Clinton's act of perjury, Gingrich knew that Clinton would argue that he was being persecuted for committing adultery. Most voters accepted Clinton's interpretation of Starr's investigation and 65 percent opposed impeachment efforts.

In 1998, Pat Robertson informed the Christian Coalition that Clinton had "mocked, demeaned, belittled, and lied" to the American people. Clinton, Robertson preached, had to be removed from office. A few months later, Robertson announced that Clinton had, "from a public relations standpoint," already won and that it was pointless to proceed with a Senate impeachment trial.

Immediately after the 1998 midterm elections in which Republicans lost congressional seats, conservatives ousted Gingrich. They resented Gingrich's willingness to negotiate with Clinton. Gingrich resigned as Speaker, but not before calling his conservative critics "cannibals" devouring one of their own. His departure paved the way for Senator Gramm and his libertarian allies to gut New Deal-era regulations of banking and Wall Street.

It took no time for congressional conservatives to implode. Bob Livingston of Louisiana, who assumed the position of House Speaker after Gingrich's removal, resigned from Congress in disgrace in 1999. Clinton's media allies had revealed Livingston's record of adultery. Illinois congressman Henry Hyde, who had long opposed abortion and same-sex marriage, led the impeachment charge. Hyde, it soon became known, had also committed adultery. Ironically, Livingston's replacement in the House, David Vitter, was, like Hyde, a social conservative intent upon impeaching Clinton. Unlike Hyde, Vitter chose to commit adultery with prostitutes in New Orleans and Washington. Gingrich, who had committed adultery himself, tried to warn conservatives about becoming the morality police.

While Clinton emerged victorious from his 1999 Senate impeachment trial, he had become a punching bag for late-night television comedians. The damage to Clinton's reputation matched the wounds conservatives had inflicted upon themselves. Despite that fact, however, Democratic liberals were not in good spirits. Although Clinton may have been on liberals' side on social issues, his relationship with an intern had placed them in a politically awkward position. Moreover, Clinton's stances on law and order, welfare reform, and tax cuts were too conservative for liberals' tastes. Liberals were also angered by Clinton's partnership with Gingrich. By the end of the 1990s, Republicans moved further to the right and Democrats moved further left.

George W. Bush and the 2000 Election

In the mid-1990s, the *Weekly Standard* promoted a new prospect for the White House: George W. Bush. As the son of President George H.W. Bush, George W. Bush had a "shadow" cabinet and vice president already in place. The younger Bush drew upon his father's foreign policy team, which included Dick Cheney and Donald Rumsfeld. As the governor of Texas, Bush had as much familiarity with foreign policy as Jimmy Carter had in 1976. The difference between Bush and Carter, however, was that the Georgian had the self-confidence to act as his own State Department, while the Texan deferred to his foreign policy advisers.

Bush appeared to be a natural Republican presidential nominee. He had the dynastic background that enthralled most Americans, even as they insisted that they had no use for royalty. Bush also had extensive political connections and, with Texas as a campaign base, sat atop a pile of oil money and electoral votes. He was also shrewder than his critics believed. Looking at the growing Mexican-American population in Texas, Bush learned Spanish.

The younger Bush, however, had many liabilities. During his twenties and early thirties, Bush had fused West Texas Cowboy with Yale Frat Boy. He later alluded only vaguely to his rowdy behavior and, after leaving the Episcopal Church for the Southern Methodist Church, never again drank alcohol.

Unfortunately for Bush, his past caught up with him. Democrats alleged that he had used political connections to enlist in the Texas National Guard and avoid going to Vietnam. They charged that he had drunk-driving arrests that his father had wiped from the public record. As opposition candidates understood, you wait until your rival is nominated, and then you release your allegations one at a time—not all at once—to inflict maximum electoral damage. The Democrats' target audience was social conservatives—not so much as to win them over to their side as to demoralize them so that they did not vote at all.

The 2000 Democratic presidential nominee, Vice President Al Gore, Jr., and Bush had a few things in common—and many differences. Both were part of the Baby Boomer generation and came from political dynasties. Gore, unlike Bush, went to Vietnam, but at his father's insistence. Tennessee senator Al Gore, Sr., faced a difficult 1970 Senate election. He wanted his son to enlist in the military and then film a patriotic campaign commercial with him. Where Gore seemed to have a distant relationship with his father, Bush surrounded himself with family.

Although political pundits had predicted a close presidential election, no one anticipated that it would come down to a few hundred disputed ballots in Florida and require the intervention of the Supreme Court. (Pat Buchanan's entrance into the presidential election as an independent had siphoned votes from Bush, though Gore claimed that elderly Florida voters had meant to vote for him, but chose Buchanan by mistake.) Bush received the electoral votes needed to win, although narrowly losing the popular vote. Not since 1876 had a presidential election been as close and as divisive.

George W. Bush and Domestic Policy, 2001–2003

During the 2000 election, Bush announced that he believed in "compassionate conservatism," which would replace William F. Buckley, Jr.'s, defunct Cold War-era "conservative fusionism." Bush later elaborated on the meaning of "compassionate conservatism" [Document 24: p. 169]. His central point was that "Government cannot solve every problem, but it can encourage people and communities to help themselves and help one another." Libertarians were irate, asserting that the very term "compassionate conservatism" was a repudiation of the Reagan Revolution. CATO Foundation director Edward Crane argued that "Compassionate conservatism is a philosophy closer to that of the New Democrats [Clinton] over at the Progressive Policy Institute than to the Goldwater-Reagan heritage" of the Republican Party.

The legislative centerpiece of "compassionate conservatism" was the No Child Left Behind Act of 2001. To attract liberal support, most especially the endorsement of Massachusetts senator Teddy Kennedy, Bush promised more federal money to public elementary and secondary schools. To conservatives, Bush argued that to receive federal support, public schools would have to implement a standardized testing regime. On a regular basis, at every level of public education, school districts would have to demonstrate consistent improvement in "student learning outcomes."

Bush insisted that assessment would improve public education, especially for minority students who had suffered from "the soft bigotry of low expectations." It quickly became obvious that No Child Left Behind had failed. Student performance on standardized tests, regardless of race, demonstrated little to no improvement. The best predicator of student academic performance was income: children from wealthier school districts scored better than students from working-class districts. Moreover, in those academic subjects not assessed, students lost ground as class time went to studying for what would be on the standardized tests. Poorer school districts, facing a loss of federal funds, had an incentive to falsify test scores, encourage cheating, and expel academically marginal students so they would not be assessed. These were the very districts No Child Left Behind was supposed to help.

Bush's domestic agenda included tax cuts to stimulate the economy. The Economic Growth and Tax Relief Reconciliation Act of 2001 and the Jobs and Growth Tax Relief Act of 2003 were a reaffirmation of 1980s supply-side economic policy. Federal taxes on the profits of investors and businesses—capital gains—went down, as did the income tax. Those in the top 1 percent tax bracket saw their taxes reduced by $570,000. Overall, the tax cuts amounted to $1.3 trillion. Tax savings, in theory, would be invested in expanding businesses and encouraging greater consumer spending.

As in the 1920s, tax cuts stimulated speculation in real estate and in the stock market. Unlike in the 1920s, the federal government had a vast array of federal entitlement programs requiring funding, even as tax revenue declined. Bush, in contrast to Clinton, never had a balanced budget. Indeed, in the eight years of Bush's presidency, the federal budget grew 53 percent, compared with Clinton's 12.5 percent increase. Moreover, Bush added $5.8 *trillion* to the national debt. There was, however, another reason beyond entitlement spending as to why federal outlays rose so dramatically.

George W. Bush and National Security, 2001–2003

During the 2000 election, Bush had focused on domestic policy, secure in the belief, shared by most Americans, that with the end of the Cold War few serious threats to national security remained. Neoconservatives even proclaimed "the end of history," by which they meant that the international order had achieved peace and the world had moved toward embracing democracy. The events of September 11, 2001, in New York City, Pennsylvania, and Washington shocked Americans.

The Soviet withdrawal from Afghanistan sparked wars among various ethnic and tribal groups. One faction, the Pashtun-dominated Taliban, consolidated power in the 1990s. Osama Bin Laden, a wealthy Saudi national and anti-Russian resistance fighter, had allied with the Taliban. Bin Laden and the Taliban shared a fundamentalist interpretation of Islam and viewed Afghanistan as a base for global revolution against secularism, democracy, Israel, America, and "heretical" Muslims. In the 1990s, Bin Laden's organization, Al-Qaeda (The Base), mounted terror attacks in the Middle East and Africa. Al-Qaeda operatives even attempted to knock down one of New York City's World Trade Center towers with a car bomb. President Clinton regarded Al-Qaeda as a nuisance, rather than as a threat to national security. Bush adopted the same stance.

On September 11, 2001, nineteen Al-Qaeda terrorists hijacked four commercial passenger airplanes. They slammed one plane into the Pentagon in Washington, while two planes hit the twin towers of the World Trade Center. The forty passengers and crew on the fourth plane struggled with the terrorists and crashed into a Pennsylvania farm field, likely sparing the White House from destruction. At the Pentagon, 125 died in the building, as well as the fifty-nine crew and passengers on the airplane.

In New York, the collapse of the twin towers took 2,753 lives. The death toll of September 11, 2001, was greater than that of Imperial Japan's attack on the U.S. Pacific Fleet at Pearl Harbor nearly seventy years earlier. Never had a foreign enemy hit the operational heart of America's financial and military centers. The national news media caught part of the attacks live, broadcasting the second plane hitting its tower and both skyscrapers collapsing.

Americans expected Congress to authorize military action in Afghanistan. Many Americans, however, did not expect that the terror attacks would lead to the radical extension of government power *over its own citizens*. In 2001, Congress passed the Providing Appropriate Tools Required to Intercept and Obstruct Terrorism (PATRIOT) Act. Sixty-six House Democrats opposed the PATRIOT Act, which left them open to charges that they were not patriotic. The PATRIOT Act gave the federal government the power to perform secret searches of American homes, intercept emails, install wire taps, and demand phone records of individuals suspected of having terrorist ties.

The CATO Institute's libertarians were initially divided over the PATRIOT Act, but eventually most came to see it as a threat to civil liberties. As for the *National Review*, its libertarians, who could normally be counted upon to express skepticism about the expansion of federal power, were muted. When William F. Buckley, Jr., edged toward retirement, his successors were less able to balance the journals' ideological factions. (Buckley died in 2008.) The neoconservative faction increasingly dominated the *National Review*, aligning its editorials more closely to the *Weekly Standard*.

A handful of conservatives pointed out that sixty years earlier Robert Taft had warned Americans against the drift toward a "garrison State." (In twenty-first-century terms, a "garrison State" would be the same as a "national security State.") Grover Norquist denounced the PATRIOT Act, as did Phyllis Schlafly. Both expressed fear as to what would happen if a

Figure 6.2 World Trade Center, September 11, 2001
Source: Courtesy of the Library of Congress Prints and Photographs Division

liberal ever became president and, asserting national security concerns, used the PATRIOT Act to spy on their political opponents.

Schlafly's days of political influence, however, were behind her—thanks to Reagan's successful efforts to marginalize her. Interventionist conservatives made short work of Norquist, first by ramping up allegations that he had political ties to Saudi Arabia, and then by observing that fifteen of the nineteen September 11 terrorists were Saudi Arabian. A few figures on the Left noted the irony that one faction of conservatives was using "McCarthyite" tactics against another faction of conservatives.

Along with the PATRIOT Act, Congress rushed through the Aviation and Transportation Security Act of 2001. More candid members of Congress, Republican and Democrat, admitted that they had not read either piece of legislation. They were operating in a frantic atmosphere much like their predecessors had during the first 100 days of Franklin Roosevelt's presidency. The Aviation and Transportation Security Act created a new federal agency with fifty-five thousand employees, the Transportation Security Administration (TSA). Passengers boarding air flights would now be funneled through TSA screeners.

In 2002, Bush reorganized the federal bureaucracy to create the Department of Homeland Security (DHS). TSA became part of Homeland Security, as did the Coast Guard, Secret Service, Immigration and Custom Enforcement, and the Federal Emergency Management Agency (FEMA). While Homeland Security agencies devoted to fighting terrorism thrived, FEMA, which aided Americans in the event of natural disasters, drifted.

The most consequential national security initiative Bush undertook after September 11 was to deal with Iraq. After the Persian Gulf War, George H.W. Bush had imposed trade restrictions and a no-fly zone in Iraq to protect anti-regime forces from attack. By 2001, American efforts to isolate Iraq were failing, as nations around the world renewed their commercial ties with Saddam Hussein. It was also costing American taxpayers millions of dollars to monitor Hussein.

Vice President Dick Cheney and Secretary of Defense Donald Rumsfeld concluded that the U.S. needed to pursue a military option against Iraq. White House speechwriter **David Frumm** wove Cheney's and Rumsfeld's talking points into a call for action. Frumm, who had written for the *Weekly Standard* and the *Wall Street Journal*, coined a memorable phrase: "the Axis of Evil." At his 2002 State of the Union Address, Bush called on Congress to oppose terrorist regimes developing "weapons of mass destruction" [Document 25: p. 170]. Iraq, along with Iran and North Korea, Bush warned, was developing nuclear weapons which could someday be used against America. To prevent a future nuclear war, the U.S. needed to wage a preventative conventional war against Iraq.

Journalists Bill Kristol and **Max Boot**—the latter a "Jeane J. Kirkpatrick Senior Fellow" at the neoconservative Council on Foreign Relations—made the case for military intervention in Iraq. The Fox News Channel, the *Weekly Standard*, and the *National Review* warned that Saddam Hussein was stockpiling biological weapons and developing an atomic bomb. The world had failed to stop Hitler from launching World War II. America could prevent the "Axis of Evil" from launching World War III. Moreover, as Kristol and Rumsfeld insisted, the Iraqi people would welcome Americans as "liberators." For his part, Boot argued that "Afghanistan and other troubled lands today cry out for the sort of enlightened foreign administration once provided by self-confident Englishmen in jodhpurs [riding breeches] and pith helmets." President Woodrow Wilson's foreign policy of "making the world safe for democracy" had been reborn.

Congress voted in 2002 to authorize Bush to use force against Iraq. Unlike on the resolution to intervene in Afghanistan, Democrats broke ranks with Republicans. Sixty-one percent of House Democrats and 44 percent of Senate Democrats voted against military intervention in Iraq. While Afghanistan had been a war of necessity, Iraq was a war of "choice." Moreover, anti-American insurgents were still at large in Afghanistan. Many Democrats asked why Bush had started another war before finishing the first war.

When the U.S. invaded Iraq in 2003, conservative critic Pat Buchanan called it an "unnecessary war" against a country that had not been behind the September 11 attacks. He blamed the war on the neoconservatives who, he believed, dominated Bush's foreign policy team. Interventionist conservatives countered that Buchanan had no understanding of foreign relations. They also noted that Buchanan often singled out the Jewish advocates of the Iraqi invasion, while writing less about hawkish Episcopalians and Methodists.

George W. Bush's Reelection and the Foreign Policy Fallout, 2004–2007

The "**War on Terror**," as interventionist conservatives called it, became the centerpiece of Bush's 2004 reelection campaign. As a political construct, the War on Terror seemingly promoted the fusion of different blocs of voters, much as the Cold War had done years earlier. In "exurban counties" outside urban and aging suburban neighborhoods, Bush appealed to voters concerned about the safety of their families. Bush carried ninety-seven of the one hundred upper-middle-class, socially liberal, security-conscious exurban counties. In less affluent "Rustbelt" communities, Bush rallied socially conservative, working-class white voters who, like their exurban counterparts, were concerned with terrorism.

Democratic president nominee John Kerry faced a difficult challenge. The Massachusetts senator emphasized his combat service in the Vietnam War to underscore his patriotism and to provide cover for his opposition to the Iraq War. Kerry's problem, however, was that after his military service had ended, he became a media celebrity due to his leadership in the Vietnam Veterans Against the War. His early political fame, which had elevated him to the Senate, stemmed from his charges that American troops had committed war crimes against the Vietnamese people.

Kerry's campaign wrote off the South and working-class whites in declining industrial communities, believing that both groups had bought into Bush's war rhetoric. Instead, Kerry focused on increasing the African-American vote in inner cities and mobilizing students, faculty, and administrators living in upscale college communities. His strategy nearly worked.

Bush's reelection victory was underwhelming. Just thirty-five electoral votes separated him from Kerry. If Ohio had gone Democratic, Bush would have lost. The close election results underscored the fact that most Democrats had walked away from the War on Terror, joining the unlikely company of libertarians and anti-interventionist conservatives.

The War on Terror was already failing in 2004, but that did not become glaringly evident until after the presidential election. Neoconservatives had pushed for the invasion of Iraq to seize Hussein's weapons of mass destruction, break up the "Axis of Evil," promote democracy in the Middle East, and remove Iraq as a threat to neighboring Afghanistan.

Neoconservatives' premises were wrong. First, there were *no* weapons of mass destruction in Iraq. Second, the American invasion of Iraq encouraged the two other members of the "Axis of Evil," Iran and North Korea, to up their game. Iran infiltrated terrorists into a destabilized Iraq and North Korea accelerated its nuclear missile development program. Third, neither Iraq nor Afghanistan had a democratic tradition. Both countries chose to establish conservative theocracies. Far from welcoming Americans as liberators, many Iraqis joined insurgent organizations to fight the U.S. And fourth, Iran encouraged sectarian war inside Iraq. Iran subsequently extended its political influence throughout the Middle East.

The insurgencies in Iraq and Afghanistan led to mounting casualties. By the end of Bush's second term, over 6,000 Americans had died in Afghanistan and Iraq, with another 50,000 wounded. Many of the wounded were so badly injured that if it had not been for advanced medical technology, they would have died. Tens of thousands of Iraqis and Afghanis died, fighting either with or against the U.S. After spending $3 trillion, the War on Terror had no end in sight.

America's volunteer military experienced increased stress. As had happened in the 1970s, military recruitment quotas were unmet. Defense Secretary Rumsfeld responded with "stop-loss" policies to prevent troops from leaving when their enlistments were up. Troops received multiple combat tours, preventing them from recovering physically and mentally. The military lowered recruitment standards. In 2003, 84 percent of soldiers were high school graduates. By 2007, the percentage of high school graduates in the Army had fallen to 71 percent. This was problematic given the advanced technology troops were expected to use in combat. Unwilling to impose a draft, or significantly increase the size of the military—both of which would have created a political firestorm—Rumsfeld recruited civilian military contractors. In another era, these contractors would have been called "mercenaries."

Americans were losing faith in the architects of U.S. foreign policy. They were also losing their confidence in the ability of the military to fight wars without needlessly sacrificing American lives. As with the Vietnam War, the War on Terror deployed working-class youths into combat, while the upper middle class remained on the sidelines.

George W. Bush and the Domestic Policy Crash, 2005–2008

Bush's second presidential term began badly and ended worse. In 2005, Hurricane Katrina hit Louisiana and Mississippi. At least 1,800 Americans died, all but 300 of them in Louisiana. New Orleans was the center of the human disaster, with Katrina overwhelming the city's levees and leading to massive flooding. The national news media broadcast images of New Orleans residents left homeless, hungry, and seemingly abandoned.

The Federal Emergency Management Agency reacted slowly to the crisis. Americans asked how it was possible for the federal government to ship thousands of tons of supplies across the globe to Iraq, but to be unable to rescue its own people from drowning at home. The public suspected that FEMA had become an unwelcome stepchild in a Department of Homeland Security more concerned with terrorists than dealing with natural disasters.

Katrina shredded what was left of Bush's public credibility. In the 2006 midterm elections, Democrats won back control of the House and the Senate after spending the past twelve years in the minority. James Webb, Reagan's former Navy Secretary, successfully ran for the Senate from Virginia as a *Democrat*. Webb had opposed the invasion of Iraq, just as he had opposed the earlier Persian Gulf War. The disgust Webb had expressed for George H.W. Bush was nothing compared with the hatred he had for George W. Bush. Webb pointedly refused to shake the younger Bush's hand at public receptions.

The final act of Bush's presidency brought the Republican Party, and its reeling conservatives, to their knees. Beginning in 2007, America's housing market began contracting. Because of exploding default rates on subprime mortgages, brokerage firms and banks began collapsing. They had invested in mortgage securities, made possible by the 1999 repeal of the Glass-Steagall Act. Even General Motors had gotten into the subprime mortgage securities field. Originally, the General Motors Acceptance Corporation (GMAC) had provided loans to purchase GM automobiles. GMAC, however, branched off into the housing market and Wall Street securities.

As housing values fell 31 percent between 2007 and 2008, unemployment shot up to 9 percent. Financial corporations and banking institutions began to fail—among them such giants as the American International Group (AIG), Lehman Brothers, J.P. Morgan-Chase, the Bank of America, and Wells Fargo. Soon, General Motors teetered on the brink of bankruptcy, as did Chrysler, which seemed to be caught in America's overall economic collapse. Panic became widespread. Even the stock values for companies that had not invested in subprime mortgage securities lost value on Wall Street. Not since the Great Depression had America seen a financial meltdown as severe.

Bush, with the cooperation of a Democratic Congress, agreed to a solution that left the public outraged. Creating the Troubled Assets Relief Program (TARP), Democratic and Republican leaders compelled the taxpayers to bail out banks, brokerage firms, and automobile makers to the tune of $700 billion. General Motors received $50 billion in TARP money, Wells Fargo claimed $25 billion, and AIG, an insurance company that had gotten into the mortgage securities market through the backdoor, collected $150 billion. Whether these corporations would ever pay back the American people was left up in the air. Voters noticed how the two political parties intervened swiftly to save Wall Street, but did nothing to help middle- and working-class people who had nothing to do with the financial meltdown but who were footing the bills.

Conservatives Flounder, 2008–2010

Republican presidential nominee John McCain was going to lose in 2008 regardless of what he did. Few voters cared about his time in Vietnam as a prisoner of war. Indeed, to young, first-time voters, Vietnam was their *grandfathers*' war—if they had even served in the military. The Arizona senator had few friends in Congress and conservatives resented his willingness to attack them and earn favorable coverage from CNN. He promised the American people a never-ending War on Terror and continued taxpayer bailouts of corporations. Working-class white voters in the Rustbelt, who had twice voted for Bush, chose to stay home, or vote for the Democrat.

Democratic presidential nominee **Barack Obama** had much going for him. As a biracial candidate, Obama inspired large numbers of African-Americans to vote in the primaries and general election, much as John F. Kennedy had excited Catholics in 1960. The Illinois senator was a disciplined candidate, rarely deviating from his script. When he deviated, Obama let slip his contempt for working-class voters who "clung to their guns and religion." That cost him white working-class support in the Pennsylvania Democratic primary. Overall, Obama performed well in the Democratic primaries. Obama shoved aside former First Lady and New York senator Hillary Rodham Clinton. Whether standing beside Hillary Clinton or McCain in debate, Obama seemed young, energetic, and hopeful. In contrast, Hillary Clinton and McCain looked aged, tired, and depressed.

Conservative opposition to Obama in the first two years of his presidency was either ineffective or nonexistent. The Senate's conservative giants, Strom Thurmond and Jesse Helms, were gone. Thurmond had passed away in 2003, while Helms had left the Senate in 2003 and died five years later. As for the House, no conservative leader came forward with Gingrich's organizational skills, imagination, and energy. There was also no Reagan waiting in the wings to run for president. Reagan's death in 2004, like Roosevelt's in 1945, left a political void that proved difficult to fill.

Religious conservatives, who had loomed so large in previous decades, seemed to have disappeared. Conservative donor and activist Joseph Coors had died in 2003, leaving social conservatives without a well-heeled advocate. The Christian Coalition had shown that, at best, it could mobilize a quarter of the electorate—an electorally significant proportion, but not enough to revitalize conservative opposition at the federal or state levels. War and economic collapse had pushed social issues far down voters' list of political priorities.

What little opposition there was to Obama's domestic and foreign policy agendas came from the conservative media. The problem for conservatives was that anyone who listened to Rush Limbaugh, read the *Weekly Standard*, or watched the Fox News Channel was already convinced that President Obama was a disaster. They were not going to convert independents. The conservative media was preaching only to the choir.

Obama's domestic legislative agenda had two major components: economic "stimulus" spending and national health care insurance. The 2009 American Recovery and Reinvestment Action appropriated $787 billion which went toward tax cuts, the extension of unemployment benefits to the long-term jobless, and grants to support infrastructure and education in the states. Congressional Republicans were virtually unanimous in their opposition. The problem with the "economic stimulus," as Democrats called it, was two-fold.

First, primary and secondary schools which accepted the one-time federal infusion of money discovered that their Republican governors had no intention of making the increase in public education funding permanent. Teachers hired with federal stimulus funds were fired once their districts spent the stimulus funds. Second, few Democratic-led states took their stimulus funding and built roads and bridges. What had made the New Deal politically viable had been its commitment to building infrastructure that employed working-class people and led to projects that Democrats pointed out to voters during elections. The failure of stimulus funding to improve the economy gave Limbaugh the opening to brand Obama's initiative as "porkulus." It did not help Obama when conservative journalists observed that politically connected Democrats had received federal stimulus funds but produced few jobs.

The 2010 Affordable Care Act was intended to establish a national health insurance program, mainly by expanding Medicaid coverage. Under the terms of the Affordable Care Act, which congressional Republicans dismissed as "Obamacare," insurance companies had to cover people with preexisting medical problems—an expensive proposition. Youths, who typically declined medical coverage, had to buy it, or face federal financial penalties. This compelled healthier youths to subsidize the medical care of older, likely sicker, Americans. Finally, the states were required to commit more of their budgets to Medicaid to receive federal matching funds. The Obama Administration estimated that health care expansion would only add $940 billion over a ten-year period to the national debt. Medicaid, which had been on financial life support since the 1990s, plunged into a death spiral.

Industrialists Charles and David Koch, along with libertarian activists such as former Texas congressman Dick Armey, encouraged the rise of new conservative organizations to challenge Obama. Collectively, these groups became known as "the Tea Party movement." The Tea Party reference was to the 1773 Boston Tea Party—America's first tax revolt.

One Tea Party group, the Tea Party Patriots, had close ties to the Koch-funded American Legislative Exchange Council (ALEC). Their objective, beyond influencing legislation at the state level, was two-fold: first, advocate for limiting federal power over the states; and second, champion a constitutional amendment requiring that the federal government balance its budget. The rise of the Tea Party secured the Koch brothers' role as the key funders of conservative causes, surpassing both Joseph Coors and J. Howard Pew.

Small-government advocates at the state and local levels were appalled as Obama sped past Bush in spending and debt accumulation. During Obama's two terms, he added another $7.9 *trillion* to the national debt. In the 2010 midterm elections, thanks in part to the libertarian Tea Party revolt, Republicans recaptured the House—taking sixty-three seats away from Democrats. (Republicans captured the Senate in the 2014 midterm elections.) The 2010 midterm elections were among the worst for a president in American history. Obama no longer had a cooperative Congress, leading him down the path of issuing executive orders and extending the power of federal regulatory agencies.

Conservatives Win and Lose, 2011–2016

Democrats were growing bitter after 2010, and not just because they lost the House, along with hundreds of state legislative seats across the country. Liberals had believed that Obama represented a departure from Bush's foreign policy. Their impression was mistaken. Obama reduced the number of American troops in Iraq and Afghanistan. However, not all was as it seemed. He increased defense expenditures. Moreover, Obama substituted drones for soldiers in both Afghanistan and Iraq, killing suspected terrorists by remote control. The remote-controlled War on Terror may not have been receiving the news coverage it once had, but it remained an ongoing operation. In 2008, Obama had pledged to close an American base in Cuba (Guantanamo) where Bush housed and interrogated terrorist prisoners. Obama "studied" the issue for eight years—and then did nothing.

Fortunately for Obama's political prospects, he remained popular, even if his policies were not. Better yet, the Republicans nominated a weak candidate for president in 2012. Former Massachusetts governor Willard "Mitt" Romney was the stereotype of an entitled Republican who was out of touch with the economic concerns of ordinary Americans. The son of a wealthy corporate executive, Romney built his inherited tens of millions of dollars into hundreds of millions of dollars. His vehicle for success had been Bain Capital, a Wall Street brokerage firm that specialized in closing struggling businesses and selling off their assets. Coming just four years after America's financial crash, with millions of Americans continuing to struggle, nominating Romney was sure to repel economically distressed voters.

According to public opinion surveys, half of Republican voters disliked Romney, but thought Obama was worse. Conservatives were harsh in their assessment of Romney. Many noted that he had embraced both sides of every social, economic, and foreign policy issue in the past decade. (Romney did not have president Clinton's, Reagan's, and Roosevelt's political skills to get away with taking all sides of an issue.) Limbaugh told his radio audience that "Romney is not a conservative." Conservative political blogger Erik Erickson was harsher: "[Romney] is neither liberal nor conservative. He is simply unprincipled." A few conservatives also expressed reservations about nominating a Mormon for president—a religious faith which some viewed as a cult. To no one's surprise, Obama won with 332 electoral votes.

Liberal and conservative Washington-based think tanks and opinion journals believed that the 2016 presidential election would be a dynastic rematch: Clinton versus Bush. George W. Bush's brother, former Florida governor John Ellis "Jeb" Bush, was to match political wits with former New York senator and Secretary of State Hillary Rodham Clinton. The rematch did not go as planned.

On the Democratic side, liberals were restless—and convinced that Hillary Clinton was a servant of Wall Street. Vermont senator Bernie Sanders, a self-identified socialist, launched a Democratic primary challenge to Hillary Clinton. Sanders' army of enthusiastic volunteers were young enough to be his grandchildren, but still they flocked to his massive rallies. The Clinton faction of the Democratic Party had to spend millions in campaign funds, and call on every political favor they were owed, to win a hotly contested primary fight. She won the Democratic presidential nomination, but at the cost of alienating a generation of young voters who perceived her to be concerned only for herself.

On the Republican side, Jeb Bush performed miserably in a crowded field. Other contenders did not like the idea that he was to be coronated as dynastic royalty. Panicked libertarian and neoconservative writers at the *Weekly Standard* and the *National Review* looked for an alternative to Jeb Bush. None of the columnists, let alone the Heritage Foundation, CATO, or the American Enterprise Institute, believed that the Republican presidential nomination would go to a New York real estate developer, one-time registered Democrat, and reality television series star.

Donald Trump was crude, rude, and direct. He angered interventionist conservatives by criticizing the invasion of Iraq. He expressed disgust with the waste of American lives and money on the War on Terror. Trump also condemned NAFTA for destroying American jobs and communities, ridiculed the bailout of Wall Street, and attacked the relationship Republican and Democratic politicians had with favor-seeking corporations. (As a real estate developer, Trump had first-hand experience dealing with grasping politicians.) He was the only candidate in the Republican presidential primaries who expressed concern about the escalating number of narcotics overdoses among working-class whites. Trump also pointed to the rising number of homicides in urban America among African-American youths.

Trump roasted liberals and conservatives, giving voters the impression that he thought little had gone right since Reagan left the White House. He called for a fundamental change in the nation's economic and foreign policies, arguing that it was time to put "America First." In response, former Texas governor Rick Perry, who regarded himself as the rightful heir of Reagan, argued that "Donald Trump's candidacy is a cancer on conservatism, and it must be clearly diagnosed, excised, and discarded." Conservative intellectuals tried to build up other candidates to stop Trump, but failed.

Figure 6.3 Donald J. Trump (1946–), President of the United States, 2017–
Source: Courtesy of the Library of Congress Prints and Photographs Division

Some hoped to persuade the Republican Party leadership to disregard the primary results and nominate someone else for president.

During the fall election, congressional Republicans denounced Trump, accusing him of being a sexist and a racist. Such rhetoric was unprecedented in that Democrats typically leveled those charges against Republicans. The boosters of the War on Terror, Max Boot, David Frumm, and Irving Kristol, either championed third-party candidates or announced that they supported Hillary Clinton. Most of the conservative opinion journals spent more time attacking Trump than criticizing Hillary Clinton. Neoconservatives claimed that Trump's policy of putting "America First" was merely an update on the pre-World War II, isolationist, anti-Semitic America First Committee.

To the shock of most political consultants and media commentators, Trump cracked the Democrats' Rustbelt stronghold, taking Michigan, Pennsylvania, and Wisconsin. Hillary Clinton had dismissed Trump's supporters as "a basket of deplorables." Most of those she dismissed were white working-class Democrats who had twice voted for Obama. Then again, Obama's working-class white voters had a peculiar relationship with him. While they liked Obama as a person, working-class white Democrats were just as likely as Republicans to blame black poverty on lifestyle choices rather than on racial discrimination.

Trump, who essentially ran against both the Democratic and Republican parties, recreated much of the Reagan coalition—but without neoconservatives and with a fraction of small-government libertarians. He also recreated the Roosevelt coalition—but without African-Americans. Southern white Protestants, religious conservatives, working-class whites, and Catholics voted for Trump. No traditional Republican or conservative could have won Michigan, Pennsylvania, and Wisconsin in 2016—only Trump. Pat Buchanan had dreamed for years of building a new, working-class electoral majority and he finally saw his vision realized.

The fact was that voters, whether they supported Trump in the general election, or had championed Sanders in the Democratic primaries, were tired of a political system that had failed for the past twenty-five years to deliver rising wages, hope, and peace. Most disturbing to Democrats, African-Americans did not turn out in the numbers that they had for Obama in 2012 or 2008. Their lack of enthusiasm for Hillary Clinton went far beyond the fact that she was not Obama. Many African-Americans believed that the decades-long bipartisan war on crime had unjustly targeted minorities. Hillary Clinton had given no impression that she was going to reform federal law enforcement policy.

In the larger political picture, both the Democratic and the Republican parties had been losing ground for decades. In 1960, 51 percent of voters claimed to be Democrats and 28 percent identified as Republicans. By 2014, only 32 percent of voters admitted to being Democrats and just 23 percent identified as Republicans. The losses both parties suffered bolstered the ranks of independents.

Most Americans had lost faith in the ability of the federal government to accomplish even simple goals. Americans distrusted political parties, churches, members of Congress, FEMA, the Defense Department, the news media, and all levels of public education. Working-class whites were among the most disaffected. Tellingly, by 2016, 54 percent of working-class whites saw no point in borrowing money to go to college. While conservative think tanks and journalists condemned universities for their financial and ideological ties to liberals, working-class whites had a more compelling reason to disdain higher education. Earning a college degree was no longer a path to obtaining a job to support oneself.

The level of economic distress and political alienation felt among the generation born after 1980 was profound. Since the late 1990s, college graduates had assumed student loan debt totaling more than $1 trillion—and had little hope of escaping that debt. This generational cohort, which the news media called "Millennials," stood out politically from its predecessors. According to opinion polls prior to the 2016 election, just 30 percent of Millennials believed that democracy served any useful purpose—compared with 72 percent of the G.I. Generation.

Trump's election had put Republicans in a position where they could no longer blame a Democratic White House for thwarting their policy goals. With both legislative branches under Republican leadership, and with a Republican in the White House, conservatives had the ability to make good all their promises. They could abolish the Affordable Care Act, overhaul the federal tax system, and reform America's immigration system. They had promised to do all this for the previous eight years.

140   *Analysis and Assessment*

Trump's 2017 inaugural address, following the path set by Reagan and Roosevelt, offered hope. However, his discussion of America's problems went beyond the lamentations Reagan and Roosevelt had evoked in their inaugural addresses [Document 26: p. 171]:

> Mothers and children trapped in poverty in our inner cities; rusted-out factories scattered like tombstones across the landscape of our nation; an education system, flush with cash, but which leaves our young and beautiful students deprived of knowledge; and the crime and gangs and drugs that have stolen too many lives and robbed our country of so much unrealized potential.

After their initial shock, conservatives and liberals across Washington reached a horrifying conclusion: Trump had not come to praise a faltering post-Cold War political order, but to bury it.

Part II
Primary Documents

Document 1: Herbert C. Hoover, "Address of President Herbert Hoover Accepting the Republican Nomination for President, August 11, 1932"

… We have maintained the financial integrity of the Government. We have cooperated to restore and stabilize the situation abroad. As a nation we have paid every dollar demanded of us. We have used the credit of the Government to aid and protect our institutions, both public and private. We have provided methods and assurances that none suffer from hunger or cold amongst our people. We have instituted measures to assist our farmers and our homeowners. We have created vast agencies for employment. Above all, we have maintained the sanctity of the principles upon which this Republic has grown great.

… The solution of our many problems which arise from the shifting scene of national life is not to be found in haphazard experimentation or by revolution. It must be through organic development of our national life under these ideals. It must secure that cooperative action which brings initiative and strength outside of the Government. It does not follow, because our difficulties are stupendous, because there are some souls timorous enough to doubt the validity and effectiveness of our ideals and our system, that we must turn to a State-controlled or State-directed social or economic system in order to cure our troubles. That is not liberalism; that is tyranny. It is the regimentation of men under autocratic bureaucracy with all its extinction of liberty, of hope, and of opportunity …

Ofttimes the tendency of democracy in the presence of national danger is to strike blindly, to listen to demagogues and to slogans, all of which destroy and do not save. We have refused to be stampeded into such courses. Ofttimes democracy elsewhere in the world has been unable to move fast enough to save itself in emergency …

… Across the path of the Nation's consideration of these vast problems of economic and social order there has arisen a bitter controversy over the control of the liquor traffic. I have always sympathized with the high purpose of the 18th Amendment, and I have used every power at my command to make it effective over this entire country. I have hoped that it was the final solution of the evils of the liquor traffic against which our people have striven for generations. It has succeeded in great measure in those many communities where the majority sentiment is favorable to it. But in other and increasing numbers of communities there is a majority sentiment unfavorable to it. Laws which are opposed by the majority sentiment create resentments which undermine enforcement and in the end produce degeneration and crime.

Our opponents pledge the members of their party to destroy every vestige of constitutional and effective Federal control of the traffic. That means that over large areas the return of the saloon system with its corruption, its moral and social abuse which debauched the home, its deliberate interference with the States endeavoring to find honest solution, its permeation of political parties, its perversion of legislatures, which reached even to the Capital of the Nation. The 18th Amendment smashed that regime as by a stroke of lightning. I cannot consent to the return of that system again ...

(Herbert C. Hoover, "Address of President Herbert Hoover Accepting the Republican Nomination for President, August 11, 1932," excerpts reprinted with the permission of the Herbert Hoover Papers, University of Iowa Libraries)

Document 2: J. Howard Pew, "Which Road to Take?" Speech delivered in Washington, D.C., for the American Liberty League, 1935

... Our New Dealers have taken the view of the extreme Federalists who wanted to lodge all authority over commerce and industry in the "General Government." That has been plainly been the real objective of New Deal legislation. Had it succeeded, it would have set up a complete economic dictatorship under which the Federal Government could have perpetrated anew the whole series of blunders that were committed in the ancient and medieval world. Fortunately, the Supreme Court has emphatically forbidden this ...

... [However] the New Dealers still persist in their program of complete federalization and establishing authority for economic dictatorship. Some would amend the Constitution; others seek ways to circumvent Constitution and Court. Should they succeed we can only expect a continuation of projects aiming at such a complete Government control over business, industry, and enterprise as they have in Italy; and contemplating an ultimate socialization of wealth, business, industry on the precious model of Russian communism.

In the last three or four years we have heard much prophecy that the capitalistic regime is nearing its close; that democracy has failed and that some new form, whether derived from Italy or Germany or Russia or based on Marxian socialism lay just around the corner. Most of us here in America have regarded this discussion as academic. We have observed what is happening in Europe with a certain mild wonderment, not suspecting that such things could happen here. I have talked with people who had studied the corporative and totalitarian states in Europe, without at all realizing how closely they resembled the organization which the New Deal has sought to impose ...

In my view, state socialism is even now developing on a scale so great and at a tempo so rapid as to warrant grave concern. The Government has invaded countless fields that only a few years ago were entirely without its sphere. Private business and enterprise are rapidly becoming terrorized at the Frankenstein of Governmental competition and control. As these fears move to increased caution, initiative becomes paralyzed, enterprise stagnates, and the task of economic restoration is more and more shouldered over on the

Government. It is a load that Government cannot carry and should not attempt unless it is proposed to completely recast our social forms and go in for a socialistic state ...

... I warn my friends of the lumber, the steel, the cement, and the textile industries to be aware; the eye of economic dictatorship is on them. And after they have been gathered into the fold, the rest will be progressively easier. The railroads are already well on the way into the Government bag and so are the banks. Uncle Sam has become the world's greatest landlord outside of Russia ...

In a word, we have already travelled a long sector of a road toward socialization. We stand today at a critical junction. To the left, marked with gaudy and alluring guideposts, lies the road of adventure into socialization and communism. Straight ahead lies the road by which we have come thus far. Its signboards are weather-beaten and homely, but their directions are dictated by reason, wisdom, and experience ...

(Excerpts reprinted with the permission of the Jouett Shouse Papers, 1899–1967, University of Kentucky Special Collections)

Document 3: Jouett Shouse, "The New Deal vs. Democracy," Speech delivered in Washington, D.C., for the American Liberty League, 1936

... Mr. Roosevelt started upon an orgy of spending which has no counterpart in all history and which continues without the slightest suggestion of cessation and without the slightest consideration of its effect upon the fiscal affairs of the government.

... The New Deal has built up a huge bureaucracy which has shown no regard for the Constitutional rights and liberties of our citizens.

The New Deal has converted the Federal Civil Service into a barefaced spoils system.

The New Deal has used the money of taxpayers of all political parties to build up a propaganda machine to aid its efforts to continue in power.

The New Deal has prostituted the administration of the relief of the unfortunate to the ends of partisan politics.

The New Deal has spent huge sums upon public works, despite grave doubts as to the desirability or usefulness of the projects.

The New Deal has instituted a series of boondoggling enterprises which are as ridiculous as they are unwise.

The New Deal has all but destroyed the export market for American agricultural products.

The New Deal has opened American markets to import of foodstuffs which properly should be supplied by the American farmer.

The New Deal has harassed American business and has entered into competition in almost every possible way with private industry.

The New Deal has misused the Federal taxing power in an effort to promote visionary schemes for the redistribution of wealth.

The New Deal has imposed taxes heavier than were ever before placed upon the nation in time of peace and by reckless borrowing has saddled huge obligations upon generations yet unborn.

The New Deal has led the nation far along the road toward national bankruptcy and has increased the national debt to unprecedented size.

The New Deal has manifested its contempt for constitutional government.

The New Deal has sought to make the Legislative Branch of the government subservient to the will of the Executive.

The New Deal, through its official spokesman, has criticized decisions of the Supreme Court because in the interpretation of the basic law of the land that tribunal held pet New Deal acts unconstitutional.

The New Deal, in the words of Mr. Roosevelt himself, has set up "new instruments of public power," admittedly dangerous in the hands of men who might misuse that power.

In a word, the New Deal has sought to destroy the American system of government composed of three coordinate branches and to upset the dual sovereignty as between state and nation which the Constitution provides.

The New Deal represents the attempt in America to set up a totalitarian government, one which recognizes no sphere of individual or business life as immune from governmental authority and which submerges the welfare of the individual to that of the government.

... The task of the next President of the United States is going to be as severe as any that could be imagined. A man of prudent caution, of hard-headed business sense, of inflexible will and determination is needed for the job. The processes of recovery have begun despite the tinkering of the New Deal, but they must be carried forward with care, with courage, with perseverance ...

(Excerpts reprinted with the permission of the Jouett Shouse Papers, 1899–1967, University of Kentucky Special Collections)

Document 4: Hatton Sumners, "Extension of Remarks of Hon. Hatton W. Sumners of Texas, in the House of Representatives, Monday, March 11, 1946"

I have watched what my own generation, under administration of both parties, has been doing to the greatest system of democratic government ever evolved through the processes of the ages. By ignoring principles and the lessons of history, and accepting the theories of men and political expedience for our guidance, we have made vassals of our States and dependents of our people. By concentration of governmental power and drafts upon the Federal Treasury, we have now a financially "busted," great piled-up mass of governmental confusion beyond human comprehension, impossible of democratic control, extravagant, wasteful, inefficient, and by its nature the instrumentality of favoritism, tyranny, oppression, and corruption, amid the destroyer of the self-reliance and self-respect and governmental capacity of the people, qualities without which no people can remain free. The people are coming to realize what has happened, Republicans and Democrats; people of all stations and political faiths. But they are yet too much depending upon the Congress.

The powers of the Congress are not what they used to be. Largely because of this concentration, even the policy-fixing and legislative power, the most basic of the essential powers of the Congress, have largely been shifted to the executive agencies and organized minorities. The time of the Congressman is now taken up largely as go-between for his constituents and these agencies, writing innumerable letters about their matters, with little time left for attending to even the most important legislative matters, and almost no time for the duties of statesmanship at a time when our circumstances require of us the highest type of statesmanship ever required, perhaps, of any people. There is practically no opportunity for the Member of Congress to be home and explain legislation and defend his position. Clearly this is the people's job.

The most important basic thing that we now need is to be rid of mythological tales as to the origin of our Constitution and bring it within the comprehension of the average citizen. That can be done but not by that sort of book writer whose claim for genius rests upon his ability to unsimplify things.

Effective at the expiration of the present Congress, I tender my services to the States for whatever they may be worth, should they be willing to make an effort to regain their sovereignty and reestablish their power, strip the Federal Government down to Federal business so that it may be operated under laws enacted by the Congress instead of largely by directives emanating from an appointed, unsupervised personnel, and the unnecessary expense of the Federal and State Governments working at the same job be eliminated; and also tender my services to organizations and groups of private citizens who are willing to lay aside class consciousness, personal, and party considerations, and instead of pointing the finger of accusation at each other, admit each to the other a common responsibility for our condition, recognize a common danger and a common duty to bring to bear our united strength in a determined effort to save our democracy from destruction by ourselves.

(Appendix to the *Congressional Record*, House, 79th Congress, Second Session, March 11, 1946, Volume 92, Washington, D.C.: Government Printing Office, 1946, A1282–A1283)

Document 5: Charles Lindbergh, "Who Are the War Agitators?" Speech delivered in Des Moines, Iowa, September 11, 1941

... As I have said, these war agitators comprise only a small minority of our people; but they control a tremendous influence. Against the determination of the American people to stay out of war, they have marshaled the power of their propaganda, their money, their patronage.

Let us consider these groups, one at a time.

First, the British: It is obvious and perfectly understandable that Great Britain wants the United States in the war on her side. England is now in a desperate position. Her population is not large enough and her armies are not strong enough to invade the continent of Europe and win the war she declared against Germany.

Her geographical position is such that she cannot win the war by the use of aviation alone, regardless of how many planes we send her. Even if America entered the war, it is improbable that the Allied armies could invade Europe and overwhelm the Axis powers. But one thing is certain. If England can draw this country into the war, she can shift to our shoulders a large portion of the responsibility for waging it and for paying its cost ...

England has devoted, and will continue to devote every effort to get us into the war. We know that she spent huge sums of money in this country during the last war in order to involve us. Englishmen have written books about the cleverness of its use.

We know that England is spending great sums of money for propaganda in America during the present war. If we were Englishmen, we would do the same. But our interest is first in America; and as Americans, it is essential for us to realize the effort that British interests are making to draw us into their war.

The second major group I mentioned is the Jewish.

It is not difficult to understand why Jewish people desire the overthrow of Nazi Germany. The persecution they suffered in Germany would be sufficient to make bitter enemies of any race.

No person with a sense of the dignity of mankind can condone the persecution of the Jewish race in Germany. But no person of honesty and vision can look on their pro-war policy here today without seeing the dangers involved in such a policy both for us and for them. Instead of agitating for war, the Jewish groups in this country should be opposing it in every possible way for they will be among the first to feel its consequences ...

Their greatest danger to this country lies in their large ownership and influence in our motion pictures, our press, our radio, and our government ...

The Roosevelt administration is the third powerful group which has been carrying this country toward war. Its members have used the war emergency to obtain a third presidential term for the first time in American history. They have used the war to add unlimited billions to a debt which was already the highest we have ever known. And they have just used the war to justify the restriction of congressional power, and the assumption of dictatorial procedures on the part of the president and his appointees ...

(Excerpts reprinted with the permission of the Charles A. Lindbergh Papers, Yale University Library)

Document 6: Robert A. Taft, *A Foreign Policy for Americans*, 1951 (selection)

I think it is fair to say that the State Department has adopted an attitude of hostility toward Congress and an unwillingness to submit any matter to Congress if it thinks it can possibly carry it through without such submission. It shows a complete distrust of the opinion of the people, unless carefully nursed by State Department propaganda.

The matter was brought to an issue by the intervention of the President in the Korean War without even telling Congress what he was doing for several weeks. And it was brought still further to the fore by the proposal that we commit troops to an international army under the control of a council of twelve nations. I do not think that the American people have ever faced a more serious constitutional issue or one which in the end may present a greater threat to their freedom.

In the long run, the question which the country must decide involves vitally not only the freedom of the people of the United States but the peace of the people of the United States. More and more, as the world grows smaller, we are involved in problems of foreign policy. If in the great field of foreign policy, the President has the arbitrary and unlimited powers he now claims, then there is an end to freedom in the United States not only in the foreign field but in the great realm of domestic activity which necessarily follows any foreign commitments. The area of freedom at home becomes very circumscribed indeed.

If the President has unlimited power to involve us in war, then I believe that the consensus of opinion is that war is more likely. History shows that when the people have the opportunity to speak they as a rule decide for peace if possible. It shows that arbitrary rulers are more inclined to favor war than are the people at any time. This question has become of tremendous importance, perhaps greater than any particular problem of troops to Europe or the manner in which the Korean War shall be conducted. The claims made by the President of the United States and by various documents presented to the Senate by the executive representatives far exceed the powers claimed by President Roosevelt during World War II ...

... Some may feel that if the President can do certain things there is no sense in arguing that he has no right to do them. But the division and limitation of powers is the very basis of our constitutional system, and decisions regarding the proper limits of such powers affect the validity of many other actions, such as the right of Congress to pass legislation to restrain the President's authority to send troops abroad in such a way as to involve the country in war. True, the President perhaps cannot be prevented from usurping power, but we can only presume the President will follow constitutional laws passed by the people's representatives ...

(Excerpts from *A Foreign Policy for Americans*, New York: Doubleday, 1951: 22–23, 28. Reprinted with the permission of Penguin-Random House.)

Document 7: Joseph McCarthy, "The History of George Catlett Marshall," remarks delivered during the 82nd Congress, June 14, 1951

We have been reviewing General Marshall's record as it applies to the war in Europe with an eye to his competence and the extent to which he backed up Stalin in political decisions. The Democrats in Denver [at their annual National Committee meeting] proclaimed him "a master of global strategy." The term, of course, implies much more than purely military planning. As we have seen, when you reach the upper levels of command inhabited during the recent war by Marshall, [Winston] Churchill, and Roosevelt, the military decisions blend everywhere with the political. They cannot be dissociated. A war is not conducted merely as a means of killing the enemy, although during the late war Mr. Roosevelt expressed so much joy over Russia's accomplishments in that line that it might be questioned if he always understood the nature of war. We have seen recently in Korea where, beggared of any respectable and intelligent war purpose, our forces have been led to believe from Marshall's testimony that the only objective of that war is to kill the enemy. I leave aside the ethical considerations raised by such an attitude and point out that the enemy's extermination is not enough, Of course, it is necessary to have the enemy's submission. But also, great powers must have some understanding of what that submission portends and what they intend to do with the world over which they will exercise sway once the enemy is defeated.

We have observed what calamities might have befallen the allied cause had Roosevelt accepted Marshall's persistent demand for a "second front now." We have seen the equivocal and dangerous nature of his counsel with reference to the North African invasion. We have observed how closely he fitted his views into those of Stalin over every major issue of the war. We have seen further how in his instructions to General [John R.] Deane, his refusal to exercise foresight over the corridor to Berlin, and his wish that the Russians might first enter that great and shattered city, General Marshall's decisions paralleled the interests of the Kremlin.

The Democrats at Denver may have been correct in their appraisal of General Marshall's attainments as a strategist. The question that arises, after examining the facts we have enumerated and those we shall enumerate, is, in whose interest did he exercise his genius? If he was wholeheartedly serving the cause of the United States, these decisions were great blunders. If they followed a secret pattern to which we do not as yet have the key, they may very well have been successful in the highest degree.

I do not at this time discuss the question of whether General Marshall was aware that he was implementing the will of Stalin in these matters. I do not propose to go into his motives. Unless one has all the tangled and often complicated circumstances contributing to a man's decisions, an inquiry into his motives is often fruitless. I do not pretend to understand General

Marshall's nature and character, and I shall leave that subject to subtler analysts of human personality.

(*Congressional Record*, Senate, 82nd Congress, First Session, June 14, 1951, Volume 97, Part 5, Washington, D.C.: Government Printing Office, 1951, 6566)

Document 8: "Declaration of Constitutional Principles, 1956," (also known as the "Southern Manifesto") delivered during the 84th Congress, March 12, 1956

The unwarranted decision of the Supreme Court in the public-school cases is now bearing the fruit always produced when men substitute naked power for established law.

The Founding Fathers gave us a Constitution of checks and balances because they realized the inescapable lesson of history that no man or group of men can be safely entrusted with unlimited power. They framed this Constitution with its provisions for change by amendment in order to secure the fundamentals of government against the dangers of temporary popular passion or the personal predilections of public officeholders.

We regard the decision of the Supreme Court in the school cases as a clear abuse of judicial power. It climaxes a trend in the Federal Judiciary undertaking to legislate, in derogation of the authority of Congress, and to encroach upon the reserved rights of the States and the people ...

This unwarranted exercise of power by the Court, contrary to the Constitution, is creating chaos and confusion in the States principally affected. It is destroying the amicable relations between the white and Negro races that have been created through 90 years of patient effort by the good people of both races. 1t has planted hatred and suspicion where there has been heretofore friendship and understanding.

Without regard to the consent of the governed, outside agitators are threatening immediate and revolutionary changes in our public-school systems. If done, this is certain to destroy the system of public education in some of the States.

With the gravest concern for the explosive and dangerous condition created by this decision and inflamed by outside meddlers:

We reaffirm our reliance on the Constitution as the fundamental law of the land.

We decry the Supreme Court's encroachments on rights reserved to the States and to the people, contrary to established law, and to the Constitution.

We commend the motives of those States which have declared the intention to resist forced integration by any lawful means.

We appeal to the States and people who are not directly affected by these decisions to consider the constitutional principles involved against the time when they too, on issues vital to them, may be the victims of judicial encroachment.

Even though we constitute a minority in the present Congress, we have full faith that a majority of the American people believe in the dual system of government which has enabled us to achieve our greatness and will in time demand that the reserved rights of the States and of the people be made secure against judicial usurpation. We pledge ourselves to use all lawful means to bring about a reversal of this decision which is contrary to the Constitution and to prevent the use of force in its implementation.

In this trying period, as we all seek to right this wrong, we appeal to our people not to be provoked by the agitators and troublemakers invading our States and to scrupulously refrain from disorder and lawless acts.

(*Congressional Record*, Senate, 84th Session, Second Session, March 12, 1956, Volume 102, Part 4, Washington, D.C.: Government Printing Office, 1956, 4460–4461)

Document 9: Barry Goldwater, *The Conscience of a Conservative*, 1960 (selection)

... Franklin Roosevelt's rapid conversion from Constitutionalism to the doctrine of unlimited government, is an oft-told story. But I am here concerned not so much by the abandonment of States' Rights by the national Democratic Party—an event that occurred some years ago when that party was captured by the socialist ideologues in and about the labor movement—as by the unmistakable tendency of the Republican Party to adopt the same course. The result is that today neither of our two parties maintains a meaningful commitment to the principle of States' Rights. Thus, the cornerstone of the Republic, our chief bulwark against the encroachment of individual freedom by Big Government, is fast disappearing under the piling sands of absolutism.

The Republican Party, to be sure, gives lip-service to States' Rights. We often *talk* about "returning to the states their rightful powers"; the Administration has even gone so far as to sponsor a federal-state conference on the problem. But deeds are what count, and I regret to say that in actual practice, the Republican Party, like the Democratic Party, summons the coercive power of the federal government whenever national leaders conclude that the states are not performing satisfactorily.

Let us focus attention on one method of federal interference—one that tends to be neglected in much of the public discussion of the problem. In recent years the federal government has continued, and in many cases increased, federal "grants-in-aid" to the States in a number of areas in which the Constitution recognizes the exclusive jurisdiction of the States. These grants are called "matching funds" and are designed to "stimulate" state spending in health, education, welfare, conservation, or any other area in which the federal government decides there is a need for national action. If the States agree to put up money for these purposes, the federal government undertakes to match the appropriation according to the ratio prescribed by Congress. Sometimes the ratio is fifty-fifty; often the federal government contributes over half the cost.

There are two things to note about these programs. The first is that they are *federal* programs—they are conceived by the federal government both as to purpose and as to extent. The second is that the "simulative" grants are, in effect, a mixture of blackmail and bribery. The States are told to go along with the program "or else." Once the federal government has offered matching funds, it is unlikely, as a practical matter, that a member of a State Legislature will turn down his State's fair share of revenue collected from all of the States. Understandably, many legislatures feel that to refuse aid would be political suicide. This is an indirect form of coercion, but it is effective nonetheless.

A more direct method of coercion is for the federal government to *threaten* to move in unless state governments take action that Washington deems appropriate ...

... Nothing so could far advance the cause of freedom as for state officials throughout the land to assert their rightful claims to lost state power; and for the federal government to withdraw promptly and totally from every jurisdiction which the Constitution reserved to the states.

(Excerpts from *The Conscience of a Conservative*, Washington, D.C.: Regnery Publishers, 1960: "States' Rights," 24, 25, 30)

Document 10: George C. Wallace, "Inaugural Address of Governor George Wallace, January 14, 1963, Montgomery, Alabama"

... Let us send this message back to Washington by our representatives who are with us today that from this day we are standing up, and the heel of tyranny does not fit the neck of an upright man that we intend to take the offensive and carry our fight for freedom across the nation, wielding the balance of power we know we possess in the Southland that WE, not the insipid bloc of voters of some sections will determine in the next election who shall sit in the White House of these United States ...

Hear me, Southerners! You sons and daughters who have moved north and west throughout this nation we call on you from your native soil to join with us in national support and vote and we know wherever you are away from the hearths of the Southland that you will respond, for though you may live in the farthest reaches of this vast country your heart has never left Dixieland.

And you native sons and daughters of old New England's rock-ribbed patriotism and you sturdy natives of the great Midwest and you descendants of the far West flaming spirit of pioneer freedom we invite you to come and be with us for you are of the Southern spirit and the Southern philosophy you are Southerners too and brothers with us in our fight.

... [Each] race, within its own framework has the freedom to teach to instruct to develop to ask for and receive deserved help from others of separate racial stations. This is the great freedom of our American founding fathers but if we amalgamate into the one unit as advocated by the communist philosophers then the enrichment of our lives the freedom for our development is gone forever. We become, therefore, a mongrel unit of one under a single all-powerful government and we stand for everything and for nothing.

The true brotherhood of America, of respecting the separateness of others and uniting in effort has been so twisted and distorted from its original concept that there is a small wonder that communism is winning the world.

... The liberals' theory that poverty, discrimination and lack of opportunity is the cause of communism is a false theory if it were true the South would have been the biggest single communist bloc in the western hemisphere long ago, for after the great War Between the States, our people faced a desolate land of burned universities, destroyed crops and homes, with manpower depleted and crippled, and even the mule, which was required to work the land, was so scarce that whole communities shared one animal to make the spring plowing. There were no government handouts, no Marshall Plan aid, no coddling to make sure that *our* people would not suffer; instead the South was set upon by the vulturous carpetbagger and federal troops, all loyal Southerners were denied the vote at the point of bayonet ... There was no money, no food, and no hope of either. But our grandfathers bent their knee only in church and bowed their head only to God ...

(Reprinted with the permission of the Alabama Department of Archives and History)

Document 11: Barry Goldwater, "Remarks," delivered at the 88th Congress, June 18, 1964

... The problems of discrimination can never be cured by laws alone; but I would be the first to agree that laws can help—laws carefully considered and weighed in an atmosphere of dispassion, in the absence of political demagoguery, and in the light of fundamental constitutional principles.

... The two portions of this bill to which I have constantly and consistently voiced objections, and which are of such overriding significance that they are determinative of my vote on the entire measure, are those which would embark the Federal Government on a regulatory course of action with regard to private enterprise in the area of so-called public accommodations and in the area of employment—to be more specific, titles II and VII of the bill. I find no constitutional basis for the exercise of Federal regulatory authority in either of these areas; and I believe the attempted usurpation of such power to be a grave threat to the very essence of our basic system of government; namely, that of a constitutional republic in which 50 sovereign

States have reserved to themselves and to the people those powers not specifically granted to the Central or Federal Government.

If it is the wish of the American people that the Federal Government should be granted the power to regulate in these two areas and in the manner contemplated by this bill, then I say that the Constitution should be so amended by the people as to authorize such action in accordance with the procedures for amending the Constitution which that great document itself prescribes. I say further that for this great legislative body to ignore the Constitution and the fundamental concepts of our governmental system is to act in a manner which could ultimately destroy the freedom of all American citizens, including the freedoms of the very persons whose feelings and whose liberties are the major subject of this legislation.

My basic objection to this measure is, therefore, constitutional. But, in addition, I would like to point out to my colleagues in the Senate and to the people of America, regardless of their race, color, or creed, the implications involved in the enforcement of regulatory legislation of this sort. To give genuine effect to the prohibitions of this bill will require the creation of a Federal police force of mammoth proportions. It also bids fair to result in the development of an "informer" psychology in great areas of our national life—neighbors spying on neighbors, workers spying on workers, business spying on businessmen where those who would harass their fellow citizens for selfish and narrow purposes will have ample inducement to do so. These, the Federal police force and an "informer" psychology, are the hallmarks of the police state and landmarks in the destruction of a free society ...

(*Congressional Record*, Senate, 88th Congress, 2nd Session, June 18, 1964, Volume 110, Part 26, Washington, D.C.: Government Printing Office, 1964, 14318–14319)

Document 12: Barry M. Goldwater, "Acceptance Speech, Republican National Convention, July 16, 1964"

... Tonight, there is violence in our streets, corruption in our highest offices, aimlessness among our youth, anxiety among our elderly; and there's a virtual despair among the many who look beyond material success toward the inner meaning of their lives. And where examples of morality, should be set, the opposite is seen. Small men seeking great wealth or power have too often and too long turned even the highest levels of public service into mere personal opportunity.

... The growing menace in our country tonight, to personal safety, to life, to limb and property, in homes, in churches, on the playgrounds and places of business, particularly in our great cities, is the mounting concern—or—should be—of every thoughtful citizen in the United States. Security from domestic violence, no less than from foreign aggression, is the most elementary and fundamental purpose of any government, and a government that cannot fulfill this purpose is one that cannot long command the loyalty of its citizens.

... Now, those who seek absolute power, even though they seek it to do what they regard as good, are simply demanding the right to enforce their own version of heaven on earth, and let me remind you they are the very ones who always create the most hellish tyranny.

... And I needn't remind you—but I will—that it's been during Democratic years that our strength to deter war has been stilled and even gone into a planned decline. It has been during Democratic years that we have weakly stumbled into conflicts, timidly refusing to draw our own lines against aggression, deceitfully refusing to tell even our people of our full participation and tragically letting our finest men die on battlefields unmarked by purpose, unmarked by pride or the prospect of victory.

Yesterday it was Korea; tonight, it is Vietnam. Make no bones of this. Don't try to sweep this under the rug. We are at war in Vietnam. And yet the president, who is the commander in chief of our forces, refuses to say—refuses to say, mind you—whether or not the objective over there is victory, and his secretary of defense continues to mislead and misinform the American people, and enough of it has gone by.

... We Republicans seek a government that attends to its inherent responsibilities of maintaining a stable monetary and fiscal climate, encouraging a free and a competitive economy, and enforcing law and order.

Thus, do we seek inventiveness, diversity, and creative difference within a stable order, for we Republicans define government's role where needed at many, many levels—preferably, though, the one closest to the people involved: our towns and our cities, then our counties, then our states, then our regional contacts, and only then the national government.

... Anyone who joins us in all sincerity, we welcome. Those, those who do not care for our cause, we don't expect to enter our ranks, in any case. And let our Republicanism so focused and so dedicated not be made fuzzy and futile by unthinking and stupid labels.

I would remind you that extremism in the defense of liberty is no vice! And let me remind you also that moderation in the pursuit of justice is no virtue! ...

(Excerpts reprinted with the permission of
Distinctive Collections, Barry M. Goldwater Papers,
Arizona State University Library)

Document 13: Ronald Reagan, "A Time for Choosing," address on behalf of Barry M. Goldwater presidential campaign, October 27, 1964

... I have spent most of my life as a Democrat. I recently have seen fit to follow another course. I believe that the issues confronting us cross party lines. Now, one side in this campaign has been telling us that the issues of this election are the maintenance of peace and prosperity. The line has been used, "We've never had it so good."

But I have an uncomfortable feeling that this prosperity isn't something on which we can base our hopes for the future. No nation in history has ever survived a tax burden that reached a third of its national income. Today, 37 cents of every dollar earned in this country is the tax collector's share, and yet our government continues to spend $17 million a day more than the government takes in. We haven't balanced our budget 28 out of the last 34 years. We have raised our debt limit three times in the last twelve months, and now our national debt is one and a half times bigger than all the combined debts of all the nations in the world ...

As for the peace that we would preserve, I wonder who among us would like to approach the wife or mother whose husband or son has died in South Vietnam and ask them if they think this is a peace that should be maintained indefinitely. Do they mean peace, or do they mean we just want to be left in peace? There can be no real peace while one American is dying some place in the world for the rest of us ...

... If we lose freedom here, there is no place to escape to. This is the last stand on Earth. And this idea that government is beholden to the people, that it has no other source of power except to sovereign people, is still the newest and most unique idea in all the long history of man's relation to man. This is the issue of this election. Whether we believe in our capacity for self-government or whether we abandon the American revolution and confess that a little intellectual elite in a far-distant capital can plan our lives for us better than we can plan them ourselves.

... [Anytime] you and I question the schemes of the do-gooders, we are denounced as being against their humanitarian goals. They say we are always "against" things, never "for" anything. Well, the trouble with our liberal friends is not that they are ignorant, but that they know so much that isn't so. We are for a provision that destitution should not follow unemployment by reason of old age, and to that end we have accepted Social Security as a step toward meeting the problem.

... Those who would trade our freedom for the soup kitchen of the welfare state have told us that they have a utopian solution of peace without victory. They call their policy "accommodation." And they say if we only avoid any direct confrontation with the enemy, he will forget his evil ways and learn to love us. All who oppose them are indicted as warmongers ...

... You and I have the courage to say to our enemies, "There is a price we will not pay." There is a point beyond which they must not advance. This is the meaning in the phrase of Barry Goldwater's "peace through strength" ...

You and I have a rendezvous with destiny. We will preserve for our children this, the last best hope of man on Earth, or we will sentence them to take the last step into a thousand years of darkness ...

(Excerpts from the Ronald Reagan Presidential Library and Museum)

Document 14: Phyllis Schlafly, "What's Wrong with 'Equal Rights' for Women?" 1972

... In the last couple of years, a noisy movement has sprung up agitating for "women's rights." Suddenly, everywhere we are afflicted with aggressive females on television talk shows yapping about how mistreated American women are, suggesting that marriage has put us in some kind of "slavery," that housework is menial and degrading, and—perish the thought—that women are discriminated against. New "women's liberation" organizations are popping up, agitating, and demonstrating, serving demands on public officials, getting wide press coverage always, and purporting to speak for some 100,000,000 American women. It's time to set the record straight. The claim that American women are downtrodden and unfairly treated is the fraud of the century ... The proposed Equal Rights Amendment states: "Equality of rights under the law shall not be denied or abridged by the United States or by any state on account of sex." So, what's wrong with that? Well, here are a few examples of what's wrong with it. This Amendment will absolutely and positively make women subject to the draft. Why any woman would support such a ridiculous and un-American proposal as this is beyond comprehension. Why any Congressman who had any regard for his wife, sister or daughter would support such a proposition is just as hard to understand. Foxholes are bad enough for men, but they certainly are not the place for women—and we should reject any proposal which would put them there in the name of "equal rights." It is amusing to watch the semantic chicanery of the advocates of the Equal Rights Amendment when confronted with this issue of the draft. They evade, they sidestep, they try to muddy up the issue, but they cannot deny that the Equal Rights Amendment will positively make women subject to the draft ... The Equal Rights literature argues that this would be good for women, so they can achieve their "equal rights" in securing veterans' benefits. Another bad effect of the Equal Rights Amendment is that it will abolish a woman's right to child support and alimony, and substitute what the women's libbers think is a more "equal" policy, that "such decisions should be within the discretion of the Court and should be made on the economic situation and need of the parties in the case." Under present American laws, the man is always required to support his wife and each child he caused to be brought into the world. Why should women abandon these good laws—by trading them for something so nebulous and uncertain as the "discretion of the Court"? The law now requires a husband to support his wife as best as his financial situation permits, but a wife is not required to support her husband (unless he is about to become a public charge). A husband cannot demand that his wife go to work to help pay for family expenses. He has the duty of financial support under our laws and customs ... This is our special privilege because of the high rank that is placed on motherhood in our society ...

(Excerpts from *Phyllis Schlafly Reports*, 7, February 1972. Reprinted with the permission of the Eagle Forum Trust.)

Document 15: Jude Wanniski, "Taxes, Revenues, and the 'Laffer Curve,'" 1978

... When the tax rate is 100 percent, all production ceases in the money economy (as distinct from the barter economy, which exists largely to escape taxation). People will not work in the money economy if all the fruits of their labors are confiscated by the government. And because production ceases, there is nothing for the 100-percent rate to confiscate, so government revenues are zero.

On the other hand, if the tax rate is zero, people can keep 100 percent of what they produce in the money economy. There is no governmental "wedge" between earnings and after-tax income, and thus no governmental barrier to production. Production is therefore maximized, and the output of the money economy is limited only by the desire of workers for leisure. But because the tax rate is zero, government revenues are again zero, and there can be no government. So, at a 0-percent tax rate the economy is in a state of anarchy, and at a 100-percent tax rate the economy is functioning entirely through barter.

In between lies the curve. If the government reduces its rate to something less than 100 percent, say to point A, some segment of the barter economy will be able to gain so many efficiencies by being in the money economy that, even with near-confiscatory tax rates, after-tax production would still exceed that of the barter economy. Production will start up, and revenues will flow into the government treasury. By lowering the tax rate, we find an increase in revenues.

... Most judgments regarding tax rates and expenditures are made by individual politicians. Andrew Mellon became a national hero for engineering the rate reductions of the 1920's, and was called "the greatest Treasury Secretary since Alexander Hamilton ..."

... The worst mistakes in history are made by political leaders who, instead of realizing that revenues could be gained by lowering tax rates, become alarmed at the fall in revenues that results when citizens seek to escape high tax rates through barter and do-it-yourself labor. Their impulse is to impose taxes that cannot be escaped ...

... Another timeless remedy of governments that find revenues falling in the face of rising tax rates is to increase the numbers and powers of the tax collectors. Invariably, this method further reduces the flow of revenues to the treasury ...

... Because Mellon was successful in persuading Republican Presidents—first Warren G. Harding and then Calvin Coolidge—of the truth of his ideas the high wartime tax rates were steadily cut back. The excess-profits tax on industry was repealed, and the 77-percent rate on the highest bracket of personal income was rolled back in stages, so that by 1925 it stood at 25 percent. As a result, the period 1921–29 was one of phenomenal economic expansion ...

... Politicians who understand the curve will find that they can defeat politicians who do not, other things being equal. Electorates all over the world always know when they are unnecessarily perched along the upper edge of the "Laffer curve," and will support political leaders who can bring them back down ...

(Excerpts from *The Public Interest*, 33, Fall 1978: 3–16. Reprinted with the permission of National Affairs, Inc.)

Document 16: Jerry Falwell, *Listen, America! The Conservative Blueprint for America's Moral Rebirth*, 1980 (selection)

I believe the 1980s will be a decade of destiny. During the crucial years of the 1980s it will be determined whether we continue to exist as a free people. It is now past time for the moral people of America to fight against those forces that would destroy our nation. No other nation on the face of the earth has been blessed by God Almighty like the people of the United States of America, but we have taken this for granted for many years.

It is time we face reality. We are in trouble as a nation. We are very quickly moving toward an amoral society where nothing is absolutely right or absolutely wrong. Our absolutes are disappearing, and with this disappearance we must face the sad fact that our society is crumbling.

I cannot keep silent about the sins that are destroying the moral fiber of our nation. As a minister of the Gospel I have seen the grim statistics on divorce, broken homes, abortion, juvenile delinquency, promiscuity, and drug addiction. I have witnessed firsthand the human wreckage and the shattered lives that statistics can never reveal in their totality.

With the dissolving of our absolutes, America now has a high crime rate that cost the taxpayer $2 billion a year. In the past ten years violent crimes have increased 174 percent in America. Murder is up 129 percent. Aggravated assault is up 139 percent. A serious crime is committed every 3.5 seconds. One robbery is committed every 83 seconds. One murder is committed every 27 minutes.

Drug addiction and alcoholism are in pandemic proportions. Suicide is growing at a frightening pace. More than 400,000 heroin addicts live in the United States. (Sixty thousand in California alone.) And 22 million Americans smoke marijuana. The number one drug and health problem is alcohol, and there are more than 9 million alcoholics in the United States. Retail sales of alcohol in one recent year totaled $32.5 billion.

We have teenagers who are experimenting with sex in the most vile form, while teenage pregnancies, incest, and sexual child abuse are rampant problems. Gonorrhea is now contracted by more than 2 million Americans each year. It is the most common infection recorded by public-health officials, and it is increasing so rapidly among the nation's young people that medical authorities are desperately searching for a vaccine against it. About 65,000 women become infertile each year because of its infection.

... The strength of America has been in her righteousness, in her walk with God. Now we see national sins that are permeating our nation, and we find that our citizens are without remorse, without regret, or repentance, and we are not far from judgment of God upon this great nation of ours. With our erosion from the historic faith of our fathers, we are seeing the erosion in our stability as a nation. We have already shown that we are economically, politically, and militarily sick because our country is morally sick …

(Excerpts from *Listen, America! The Conservative Blueprint for America's Moral Rebirth*, New York: Doubleday, 1980: 101–103. Reprinted with the permission of Penguin-Random House.)

Document 17: Ronald Reagan, "Neshoba County Fair Speech," delivered August 3, 1980

… I know, people have been telling me that Jimmy Carter has been doing his best. And that's our problem.

The President lately has been saying that I am irresponsible. And you know, I'll admit to that if he'll confess he's responsible.

We've had the New Deal, and then Harry Truman gave us the Fair Deal, and now we have a misdeal.

… But probably the worst thing is what had been done to this country on the international scene. This once proud country, this country that all the world turned to and looked to as the shelter, as the safety and as the anchor to windward. Today, our friends don't know whether they can trust us, and certainly our enemies have no respect for us.

Our young men are told to pre-register in the event that we need a draft. May I suggest something I think we need much more than that, because I don't believe we need a peacetime draft. What we need is to recognize what we're asking of the young people of this country who are in the volunteer military and then provide a pay scale and benefits commensurate.

… Sure, it's right that we should say we want, too, to do something about unemployment, and about inflation, about the value of our money and to get this country moving again. But I think even more important on a broader scale [is] in doing that, what we will have to do is to bring back to this country what is so evident here: Bring back the recognition that the people of this country can solve the problems, that we don't have anything to be afraid of as long as we have the people of America.

[In] more recent years with the best intention, they have created a vast bureaucracy, or a bureaucratic structure—bureaus and departments and agencies—to try and solve all the problems and eliminate all the things of human misery that they can. They have forgotten that when you create a government bureaucracy, no matter how well intentioned it is, almost instantly its top priority becomes preservation of the bureaucracy.

… I believe that there are programs like that, programs like education and others, that should be turned back to the states and the local communities with the tax sources to fund them, and let the people [applause drowns out end of statement].

I believe in state's rights; I believe in people doing as much as they can for themselves at the community level and at the private level. And I believe that we've distorted the balance of our government today by giving powers that were never intended in the constitution to that federal establishment. And if I do get the job I'm looking for, I'm going to devote myself to trying to reorder those priorities and to restore to the states and local communities those functions which properly belong there.

I'm going to try also to change federal regulations in the tax structure that has made this once powerful industrial giant in this land and in the world now with a lower rate of productivity than any of the other industrial nations, with a lower rate of savings and investment on the part of our people and put us back where we belong ...

(Transcribed by Stanley Dearman for the *Neshoba Democrat*. Reprinted by the *Neshoba Democrat*, November 15, 2007. Excerpts reprinted with the permission of James E. Prince III, editor and publisher of the *Neshoba Democrat*.)

Document 18: Ronald W. Reagan, "Presidential Inaugural Address, January 20, 1981"

... These United States are confronted with an economic affliction of great proportions. We suffer from the longest and one of the worst sustained inflations in our national history. It distorts our economic decisions, penalizes thrift, and crushes the struggling young and the fixed-income elderly alike. It threatens to shatter the lives of millions of our people.

Idle industries have cast workers into unemployment, human misery, and personal indignity.

Those who do work are denied a fair return for their labor by a tax system which penalizes successful achievement and keeps us from maintaining full productivity. But great as our tax burden is, it has not kept pace with public spending. For decades we have piled deficit upon deficit, mortgaging our future and our children's future for the temporary convenience of the present. To continue this long trend is to guarantee tremendous social, cultural, political, and economic upheavals.

... The economic ills we suffer have come upon us over several decades. They will not go away in days, weeks, or months, but they will go away. They will go away because we as Americans have the capacity now, as we've had in the past, to do whatever needs to be done to preserve this last and greatest bastion of freedom.

In this present crisis, government is not the solution to our problem; government is the problem. From time to time we've been tempted to believe that society has become too complex to be managed by self-rule, that government by an elite group is superior to government for, by, and of the people. Well, if no one among us is capable of governing himself, then who among us has the capacity to govern someone else? All of us together, in and out of government, must bear the burden. The solutions we seek must be equitable, with no one group singled out to pay a higher price.

We hear much of special interest groups. Well, our concern must be for a special interest group that has been too long neglected. It knows no sectional boundaries or ethnic and racial divisions, and it crosses political party lines. It is made up of men and women who raise our food, patrol our streets, man our mines and factories, teach our children, keep our homes, and heal us when we're sick—professionals, industrialists, shopkeepers, clerks, cabbies, and truckdrivers. They are, in short, "We the people," this breed called Americans.

Well, this administration's objective will be a healthy, vigorous, growing economy that provides equal opportunities for all Americans with no barriers born of bigotry or discrimination. Putting America back to work means putting all Americans back to work. Ending inflation means freeing all Americans from the terror of runaway living costs. All must share in the productive work of this "new beginning," and all must share in the bounty of a revived economy. With the idealism and fair play which are the core of our system and our strength, we can have a strong and prosperous America, at peace with itself and the world.

(Excerpts reprinted from the Ronald Reagan Presidential Library and Museum)

Document 19: Ronald W. Reagan, "Address to the Nation on the Economy, October 13, 1982"

… Tonight, in homes across this country, unemployment is the problem uppermost on many people's minds. Getting Americans back to work is an urgent priority for all of us and especially for this administration. But remember, you can't solve unemployment without solving the things that caused it, the out-of-control government spending, the skyrocketing inflation, and interest rates that led to unemployment in the first place. Unless you get at the root causes of the problem—which is exactly what our economic program is doing—you may be able to temporarily relieve the symptoms, but you'll never cure the disease. You may even make it worse.

I have a special reason for wanting to solve this problem in a lasting way. I was 21 and looking for work in 1932, one of the worst years of the Great Depression. And I can remember one bleak night in the thirties when my father learned on Christmas Eve that he'd lost his job. To be young in my generation was to feel that your future had been mortgaged out from under you, and that's a tragic mistake we must never allow our leaders to make again. Today's young people must never be held hostage to the mistakes of the past. The only way to avoid making those mistakes again is to learn from them.

The pounding economic hangover America's suffering from didn't come about overnight. And there's no single instant cure. In recent weeks, a lot of people have been playing what I call the "blame game." The accusing finger has been pointed in every direction of the compass, and a lot of time and hot air have been spent looking for scapegoats. Well, there's plenty of blame to go around.

... Now, I don't pretend for a moment that, in 21 months, we've been able to undo all the damage to our economy that has built up over more than 20 years. The first part of our program has been in the books only 1 year and 13 days. Much of the legislation we need has still not been enacted. We've still got a long way to go before we restore our prosperity. But what I can report to you tonight, my fellow Americans, is that at long last your government has a program in place that faces our problems and has already started solving them.

... Together we've chosen a new road for America. It's a far better road. We need only the courage to see it through. I know we can. Throughout our history, we Americans have proven again and again that no challenge is too big for a free, united people. Together, we can do it again. We can do it by slowly but surely working our way back to prosperity that will mean jobs for all who are willing to work, and fulfillment for all who still cherish the American dream.

We can do it, my fellow Americans, by staying the course ...

(Excerpts reprinted from the Ronald Reagan Presidential Library and Museum)

Document 20: Ronald W. Reagan, "Address to the Nation on Defense and National Security, March 23, 1983"

... Since the dawn of the atomic age, we've sought to reduce the risk of war by maintaining a strong deterrent and by seeking genuine arms control. "Deterrence" means simply this: making sure any adversary who thinks about attacking the United States, or our allies, or our vital interests, concludes that the risks to him outweigh any potential gains. Once he understands that, he won't attack. We maintain the peace through our strength; weakness only invites aggression.

This strategy of deterrence has not changed. It still works. But what it takes to maintain deterrence has changed. It took one kind of military force to deter an attack when we had far more nuclear weapons than any other power; it takes another kind now that the Soviets, for example, have enough accurate and powerful nuclear weapons to destroy virtually all of our missiles on the ground. Now, this is not to say that the Soviet Union is planning to make war on us. Nor do I believe a war is inevitable—quite the contrary. But what must be recognized is that our security is based on being prepared to meet all threats.

... For 20 years the Soviet Union has been accumulating enormous military might. They didn't stop when their forces exceeded all requirements of a legitimate defensive capability. And they haven't stopped now. During the past decade and a half, the Soviets have built up a massive arsenal of new strategic nuclear weapons—weapons that can strike directly at the United States.

... This is why I'm speaking to you tonight—to urge you to tell your Senators and Congressmen that you know we must continue to restore our military strength. If we stop in midstream, we will send a signal of decline, of lessened will, to friends and adversaries alike. Free people must voluntarily, through open debate and democratic means, meet the challenge that totalitarians pose by compulsion. It's up to us, in our time, to choose and choose wisely between the hard but necessary task of preserving peace and freedom and the temptation to ignore our duty and blindly hope for the best while the enemies of freedom grow stronger day by day.

... After careful consultation with my advisers, including the Joint Chiefs of Staff, I believe there is a way. Let me share with you a vision of the future which offers hope. It is that we embark on a program to counter the awesome Soviet missile threat with measures that are defensive. Let us turn to the very strengths in technology that spawned our great industrial base and that have given us the quality of life we enjoy today.

What if free people could live secure in the knowledge that their security did not rest upon the threat of instant U.S. retaliation to deter a Soviet attack, that we could intercept and destroy strategic ballistic missiles before they reached our own soil or that of our allies?

I know this is a formidable, technical task, one that may not be accomplished before the end of this century. Yet, current technology has attained a level of sophistication where it's reasonable for us to begin this effort. It will take years, probably decades of effort on many fronts. There will be failures and setbacks, just as there will be successes and breakthroughs. And as we proceed, we must remain constant in preserving the nuclear deterrent and maintaining a solid capability for flexible response. But isn't it worth every investment necessary to free the world from the threat of nuclear war? We know it is ...

(Excerpts reprinted from the Ronald Reagan Presidential Library and Museum)

Document 21: Ronald W. Reagan, "Remarks at the Veterans Day Ceremony at the Vietnam Veterans Memorial, November 11, 1988"

... We're gathered today, just as we have gathered before, to remember those who served, those who fought, those still missing, and those who gave their last full measure of devotion for our country. We're gathered at a monument on which the names of our fallen friends and loved ones are engraved, and with crosses instead of diamonds beside them, the names of those whose fate we do not yet know. One of those who fell wrote, shortly before his death, these words: "Take what they have left and what they have taught you with their dying and keep it with your own. And take one moment to embrace those gentle heroes you left behind."

Well, today, Veterans Day, as we do every year, we take that moment to embrace the gentle heroes of Vietnam and of all our wars. We remember those who were called upon to give all a person can give, and we remember those who were prepared to make that sacrifice if it were demanded of them in the line of duty, though it never was. Most of all, we remember the devotion and gallantry with which all of them ennobled their nation as they became champions of a noble cause.

I'm not speaking provocatively here. Unlike the other wars of this century, of course, there were deep divisions about the wisdom and rightness of the Vietnam War. Both sides spoke with honesty and fervor. And what more can we ask in our democracy? And yet after more than a decade of desperate boat people, after the killing fields of Cambodia, after all that has happened in that unhappy part of the world, who can doubt that the cause for which our men fought was just? It was, after all, however imperfectly pursued, the cause of freedom; and they showed uncommon courage in its service. Perhaps at this late date we can all agree that we've learned one lesson: that young Americans must never again be sent to fight and die unless we are prepared to let them win.

... For too long a time, they stood in a chill wind, as if on a winter night's watch. And in that night, their deeds spoke to us, but we knew them not. And their voices called to us, but we heard them not. Yet in this land that God has blessed, the dawn always at last follows the dark, and now morning has come. The night is over. We see these men and know them once again—and know how much we owe them, how much they have given us, and how much we can never fully repay. And not just as individuals but as a nation, we say we love you ...

(Excerpts reprinted from the Ronald Reagan Presidential Library and Museum)

Document 22: Ronald W. Reagan, "Remarks on East–West Relations at the Brandenburg Gate in West Berlin, June 12, 1987"

... Behind me stands a wall that encircles the free sectors of this city, part of a vast system of barriers that divides the entire continent of Europe. From the Baltic, south, those barriers cut across Germany in a gash of barbed wire, concrete, dog runs, and guard towers. Farther south, there may be no visible, no obvious wall. But there remain armed guards and checkpoints all the same—still a restriction on the right to travel, still an instrument to impose upon ordinary men and women the will of a totalitarian state. Yet it is here in Berlin where the wall emerges most clearly; here, cutting across your city, where the news photo and the television screen have imprinted this brutal division of a continent upon the mind of the world. Standing before the

Brandenburg Gate, every man is a German, separated from his fellow men. Every man is a Berliner, forced to look upon a scar.

... In the 1950's, [Soviet leader Nikita] Khrushchev predicted: "We will bury you." But in the West today, we see a free world that has achieved a level of prosperity and well-being unprecedented in all human history. In the Communist world, we see failure, technological backwardness, declining standards of health, even want of the most basic kind—too little food. Even today, the Soviet Union still cannot feed itself. After these four decades, then, there stands before the entire world one great and inescapable conclusion: Freedom leads to prosperity. Freedom replaces the ancient hatreds among the nations with comity and peace. Freedom is the victor.

And now the Soviets themselves may, in a limited way, be coming to understand the importance of freedom. We hear much from Moscow about a new policy of reform and openness. Some political prisoners have been released. Certain foreign news broadcasts are no longer being jammed. Some economic enterprises have been permitted to operate with greater freedom from state control. Are these the beginnings of profound changes in the Soviet state? Or are they token gestures, intended to raise false hopes in the West, or to strengthen the Soviet system without changing it? We welcome change and openness; for we believe that freedom and security go together, that the advance of human liberty can only strengthen the cause of world peace.

There is one sign the Soviets can make that would be unmistakable, that would advance dramatically the cause of freedom and peace. General Secretary Gorbachev, if you seek peace, if you seek prosperity for the Soviet Union and Eastern Europe, if you seek liberalization: Come here to this gate! Mr. Gorbachev, open this gate! Mr. Gorbachev, tear down this wall!

... In Europe, only one nation and those it controls refuse to join the community of freedom. Yet in this age of redoubled economic growth, of information and innovation, the Soviet Union faces a choice: It must make fundamental changes, or it will become obsolete. Today thus represents a moment of hope. We in the West stand ready to cooperate with the East to promote true openness, to break down barriers that separate people, to create a safer, freer world ...

(Excerpts reprinted from the Ronald Reagan Presidential Library and Museum)

Document 23: Newt Gingrich, "Contract with America, 1994"

... On the first day of the 104th Congress, the new Republican majority will immediately pass the following major reforms, aimed at restoring the faith and trust of the American people in their government:

- **FIRST**, require all laws that apply to the rest of the country also apply equally to the Congress;

- **SECOND,** select a major, independent auditing firm to conduct a comprehensive audit of Congress for waste, fraud, or abuse;
- **THIRD,** cut the number of House committees, and cut committee staff by one-third;
- **FOURTH,** limit the terms of all committee chairs;
- **FIFTH,** ban the casting of proxy votes in committee;
- **SIXTH,** require committee meetings to be open to the public;
- **SEVENTH,** require a three-fifths majority vote to pass a tax increase;
- **EIGHTH,** guarantee an honest accounting of our Federal Budget by implementing zero base-line budgeting.

Thereafter, within the first 100 days of the 104th Congress, we shall bring to the House Floor the following bills, each to be given full and open debate, each to be given a clear and fair vote and each to be immediately available this day for public inspection and scrutiny.

1. **THE FISCAL RESPONSIBILITY ACT:** A balanced budget/tax limitation amendment and a legislative line-item veto to restore fiscal responsibility to an out-of-control Congress, requiring them to live under the same budget constraints as families and businesses.
2. **THE TAKING BACK OUR STREETS ACT:** An anti-crime package including stronger truth-in-sentencing, "good faith" exclusionary rule exemptions, effective death penalty provisions, and cuts in social spending from this summer's "crime" bill to fund prison construction and additional law enforcement to keep people secure in their neighborhoods and kids safe in their schools.
3. **THE PERSONAL RESPONSIBILITY ACT:** Discourage illegitimacy and teen pregnancy by prohibiting welfare to minor mothers and denying increased AFDC [Aid to Families with Dependent Children] for additional children while on welfare, cut spending for welfare programs, and enact a tough two-years-and-out provision with work requirements to promote individual responsibilities.
4. **THE FAMILY REINFORCEMENT ACT:** Child support enforcement, tax incentives for adoption, strengthening rights of parents in their children's education, stronger child pornography laws, and an elderly dependent care tax credit to reinforce the central role of families in American society.
5. **THE AMERICAN DREAM RESTORATION ACT:** A $500 per child tax credit, begin repeal of the marriage tax penalty, and creation of American Dream Savings Accounts to provide middle-class tax relief.
6. **THE NATIONAL SECURITY RESTORATION ACT:** No U.S. troops under U.N. command and restoration of the essential parts of our national security funding to strengthen our national defense and maintain our credibility around the world.

7. **THE SENIOR CITIZENS FAIRNESS ACT:** Raise the Social Security earnings limit which currently forces seniors out of the work force, repeal the 1993 tax hikes on Social Security benefits and provide tax incentives for private long-term care insurance to let Older Americans keep more of what they have earned over the years.
8. **THE JOB CREATION AND WAGE ENHANCEMENT ACT:** Small business incentives, capital gains cut and indexation, neutral cost recovery, risk assessment/cost–benefit analysis, strengthening the Regulatory Flexibility Act and unfunded mandate reform to create jobs and raise worker wages.
9. **THE COMMON SENSE LEGAL REFORM ACT:** "Loser pays" laws, reasonable limits on punitive damages and reform of product liability laws to stem the endless tide of litigation.
10. **THE CITIZEN LEGISLATURE ACT:** A first-ever vote on term limits to replace career politicians with citizen legislators ...

(Excerpts reprinted from the U.S. House of Representatives website)

Document 24: George W. Bush, "Fact Sheet: Compassionate Conservatism, April 30, 2002"

... Government cannot solve every problem, but it can encourage people and communities to help themselves and one another. *The truest kind of compassion is to help citizens build better lives of their own.*

We do not believe in a sink-or-swim society. The policies of our government must heed the universal call of all faiths to love our neighbors as we would want to be loved ourselves. We are using an active government to promote self-government.

... The President believes the truest kind of compassion doesn't only come from more government spending, but from helping citizens build lives of their own. The aim of this philosophy is not to spend less money, or to spend more money, but to spend only on what works. The measure of compassion is more than good intentions—it is good results. Sympathy is not enough—we need solutions.

The President's vision of compassionate conservatism effectively tackles some of society's toughest assignments—*educating our children, fighting poverty at home and aiding poor countries around the world.*

Educating our Children. Compassionate conservatism places great hope and confidence in public education. Public schools are America's great hope, and making them work for every child is America's great duty. The President's new education reform is compassionate because it requires schools to meet new, high standards of performance in reading and math. The new reforms also give local schools and teachers the freedom, resources, and training to meet their needs. It is conservative to let local communities chart their own path to excellence. *It is compassionate to make sure that no child is left behind.*

Fighting Poverty at Home. Compassionate conservatism offers a new vision for fighting poverty in America. For many Americans, *welfare* once was a static and destructive way of life. In 1996 welfare was reformed to include work and time limits and since that time America's welfare rolls have been cut by more than half. More importantly, many lives have been drastically improved. *Millions of Americans once on welfare are finding that a job is more than a source of income—it is also a source of dignity. By encouraging work, we practice compassion.*

Government should promote the work of charities, community groups and faith-based institutions. Government should view Americans who work in faith-based charities as partners, not as rivals. When it comes to providing resources, the government should not discriminate against these groups that often inspire life-changing faith in a way that government never should.

Helping Poor Countries Around the World. Nearly half of the world's people live on less than two dollars a day. *When we help them we show our compassion, our values, and our belief in universal human dignity.* Yet the old way of pouring vast amounts of money into development aid without any concern for results has failed—often leaving behind more misery, poverty, and corruption.

... It is compassionate to increase our international aid. It is conservative to require the hard reforms that lead to prosperity and independence.

(Excerpts reprinted from the George W. Bush White House website)

Document 25: George W. Bush, "President Delivers State of the Union Address, January 29, 2002"

... We last met in an hour of shock and suffering. In four short months, our nation has comforted the victims, begun to rebuild New York and the Pentagon, rallied a great coalition, captured, arrested, and rid the world of thousands of terrorists, destroyed Afghanistan's terrorist training camps, saved a people from starvation, and freed a country from brutal oppression.

... Our nation will continue to be steadfast and patient and persistent in the pursuit of two great objectives. First, we will shut down terrorist camps, disrupt terrorist plans, and bring terrorists to justice. And, second, we must prevent the terrorists and regimes who seek chemical, biological, or nuclear weapons from threatening the United States and the world.

... Our second goal is to prevent regimes that sponsor terror from threatening America or our friends and allies with weapons of mass destruction. Some of these regimes have been pretty quiet since September the 11th. But we know their true nature. North Korea is a regime arming with missiles and weapons of mass destruction, while starving its citizens.

Iran aggressively pursues these weapons and exports terror, while an unelected few repress the Iranian people's hope for freedom.

Iraq continues to flaunt its hostility toward America and to support terror. The Iraqi regime has plotted to develop anthrax, and nerve gas, and nuclear weapons for over a decade. This is a regime that has already used poison gas to murder thousands of its own citizens—leaving the bodies of mothers huddled over their dead children. This is a regime that agreed to international inspections—then kicked out the inspectors. This is a regime that has something to hide from the civilized world.

States like these, and their terrorist allies, constitute an axis of evil, arming to threaten the peace of the world. By seeking weapons of mass destruction, these regimes pose a grave and growing danger. They could provide these arms to terrorists, giving them the means to match their hatred. They could attack our allies or attempt to blackmail the United States. In any of these cases, the price of indifference would be catastrophic.

We will work closely with our coalition to deny terrorists and their state sponsors the materials, technology, and expertise to make and deliver weapons of mass destruction. We will develop and deploy effective missile defenses to protect America and our allies from sudden attack. And all nations should know: America will do what is necessary to ensure our nation's security.

We'll be deliberate, yet time is not on our side. I will not wait on events, while dangers gather. I will not stand by, as peril draws closer and closer. The United States of America will not permit the world's most dangerous regimes to threaten us with the world's most destructive weapons.

Our war on terror is well begun, but it is only begun. This campaign may not be finished on our watch—yet it must be, and it will be, waged on our watch ...

(Excerpts reprinted from the George W. Bush White House website)

Document 26: Donald J. Trump, "Inaugural Address, January 20, 2017"

... For too long, a small group in our nation's Capital has reaped the rewards of government while the people have borne the cost.

Washington flourished—but the people did not share in its wealth.

Politicians prospered—but the jobs left, and the factories closed.

The establishment protected itself, but not the citizens of our country.

Their victories have not been your victories; their triumphs have not been your triumphs; and while they celebrated in our nation's Capital, there was little to celebrate for struggling families all across our land.

That all changes—starting right here, and right now, because this moment is your moment: it belongs to you.

It belongs to everyone gathered here today and everyone watching all across America.

This is your day. This is your celebration.

And this, the United States of America, is your country.

What truly matters is not which party controls our government, but whether our government is controlled by the people.

January 20th, 2017, will be remembered as the day the people became the rulers of this nation again.

The forgotten men and women of our country will be forgotten no longer.

Everyone is listening to you now.

You came by the tens of millions to become part of a historic movement the likes of which the world has never seen before.

At the center of this movement is a crucial conviction: that a nation exists to serve its citizens.

Americans want great schools for their children, safe neighborhoods for their families, and good jobs for themselves.

These are the just and reasonable demands of a righteous public.

But for too many of our citizens, a different reality exists: Mothers and children trapped in poverty in our inner cities; rusted-out factories scattered like tombstones across the landscape of our nation; an education system, flush with cash, but which leaves our young and beautiful students deprived of knowledge; and the crime and gangs and drugs that have stolen too many lives and robbed our country of so much unrealized potential.

This American carnage stops right here and stops right now.

We are one nation—and their pain is our pain. Their dreams are our dreams; and their success will be our success. We share one heart, one home, and one glorious destiny.

The oath of office I take today is an oath of allegiance to all Americans.

For many decades, we've enriched foreign industry at the expense of American industry;

Subsidized the armies of other countries while allowing for the very sad depletion of our military;

We've defended other nation's borders while refusing to defend our own;

And spent trillions of dollars overseas while America's infrastructure has fallen into disrepair and decay.

We've made other countries rich while the wealth, strength, and confidence of our country has disappeared over the horizon.

One by one, the factories shuttered and left our shores, with not even a thought about the millions upon millions of American workers left behind.

The wealth of our middle class has been ripped from their homes and then redistributed across the entire world.

But that is the past. And now we are looking only to the future ...

From this day forward, a new vision will govern our land.

From this moment on, it's going to be America First.

(Excerpts reprinted from the Donald J. Trump White House website)

Glossary

America First Committee: Founded in 1940 by conservative isolationists to oppose U.S. aid to Great Britain, which was fighting Nazi Germany. Aviation pioneer Charles Lindbergh was America First's most prominent speaker. Organization disbanded shortly after Imperial Japan's attack on the U.S. Pacific Fleet at Pearl Harbor in December 1941.

American Enterprise Association: America's first conservative domestic policy think tank, established originally in New York in 1938. Later relocated to Washington, D.C., and renamed the American Enterprise Institute. Closely associated with neoconservatives.

Americans for Democratic Action (ADA): Organization of labor leaders and political office holders who in 1947 wanted to save the Democratic Party from anti-communist conservative attack while supporting the Truman Doctrine and civil rights. ADA activists who later gained national office included Ronald Reagan.

Boll Weevils: Label used by liberals to describe southern white Democrats who supported Ronald Reagan's legislative agenda in the 1980s. The boll weevil was a parasite that nearly destroyed southern cotton in the early twentieth century.

CATO Institute: Libertarian, Washington-based think tank founded in 1977 by such activists as the industrialist Charles Koch.

Chicken Hawks: *see* Doves, Hawks, and Chicken Hawks.

Cold War: How American journalists and foreign policy experts characterized the increasingly frosty relations between the U.S. and the Soviet Union after World War II. Ended with the collapse of the Soviet Union in 1990.

Conservative Fusionism: Ideological construct developed in the 1950s by William F. Buckley, Jr., and the conservatives grouped around the *National Review*. Conservative Fusionism called upon members of the post-World War II Right to find common ground in their opposition to growing federal power. Social conservatives, libertarians, and anti-communist defense hawks could join in their shared dislike of radicalism and overreaching federal domestic powers. Robert Taft isolationists were not welcome. Anti-communism was the glue that held the conservative fusionists together. When the Cold War ended, conservatives reverted to factional warfare.

Dixiecrat: Name journalists gave to States' Rights Party presidential nominee Strom Thurmond in 1948. A Dixiecrat was a southern Democrat who rejected the party's embrace of civil rights and labor unions.

Doves, Hawks, and Chicken hawks: In the 1960s journalists described opponents of the Vietnam War as doves, those who advocated military escalation were known as hawks, and conservatives who supported the Vietnam War, but who were unwilling to fight, were chicken hawks.

G.I. Generation: Literally, "Government Issued" Generation. Refers to the generation of Americans who came of age during the Great Depression and World War II and became devoted New Deal Democrats.

Hawks: *see* Doves, Hawks, and Chicken Hawks.

Heritage Foundation: Conservative, Washington-based think tank founded in 1973 with funding from such activists as Colorado beer baron Joseph Coors. The Heritage Foundation formulated numerous economic and defense policies in the 1970s, many of which Ronald Reagan embraced as president.

Isolationism: Isolationism became a general political sentiment in reaction to U.S. intervention in World War I. While most Americans disliked Nazi Germany and Imperial Japan in the 1930s, 80 percent did not want to participate in World War II. Senator Robert Taft of Ohio led the isolationist conservative faction in Congress and continued to do so until the early 1950s, when interventionist Modern Republicans triumphed. After the collapse of the Soviet Union, isolationism regrouped within the conservative movement.

Libertarians: Ideological tagline for conservatives who, to varying degrees, oppose federal regulation of the marketplace and the extension of federal power over the states and over individuals. Libertarians typically condemn federal regulation of the boardroom and the bedroom, making an electoral alliance with social conservatives difficult.

McCarthyism: A term derived from the actions of Republican senator Joseph McCarthy of Wisconsin in the early 1950s. McCarthyism is the practice of slandering opponents and making wild accusations without evidence or any consideration of due process.

Mellon Plan: Tax reduction/economic stimulus plan developed by Secretary of the Treasury Andrew Mellon in the 1920s. Precursor to 1980s supply-side economics.

Modern Republicans: President Dwight Eisenhower, in the 1950s, argued that the Republican Party had to become a "modern" party, accepting the New Deal's legacy entitlement programs and legislation, while embracing civil rights and communist containment. Modern Republicans are also known as liberal Republicans.

Neoconservatives: Ideological tagline for New Deal-Cold War Democrats who felt repulsed by their party's opposition to the Vietnam War and its inability, or unwillingness, to address mounting urban crime. After 1972, such Democrats moved into the Republican Party and became anti-communist and law-and-order conservatives.

New Deal: Catchphrase for a variety of federal programs and legislative initiatives during the Great Depression. President Franklin Roosevelt's New Deal represented a profound expansion of federal power and fundamentally changed American politics.

New Deal Democrats: Term for the electoral coalition that supported the New Deal's social-welfare and labor legislation and farm programs. Coalition members included southern white Protestants, northern black Protestants, Catholics, Jews, and industrial workers.

Prohibition: The ratification of the Eighteenth Amendment to the Constitution in 1919 prohibited the production, sale, and transport of alcohol. Ratification of the Twenty-First Amendment in 1933 repealed Prohibition.

Reagan Democrats: Media label given to white working-class voters in the North and South who remained New Deal Democrats but rejected post-1960s social liberalism. Reagan Democrats voted Republican at the presidential level but often continued to vote for Democrats down the ticket.

Rustbelt: Formerly known as the Industrial Heartland. The Rustbelt included states which claimed large numbers of Catholics, Jews, and union members. No Democrat after 1932 could generally expect to win the White House without carrying at least three of the five following states: Illinois, Michigan, New York, Ohio, and Pennsylvania. Wisconsin is also included in the Rustbelt.

Silent Majority: Term which President Richard Nixon and White House staffer Patrick Buchanan used to describe white, working-class Democrats who reacted against their party's toleration of campus and urban disruption. Nixon and Buchanan believed that the Republican Party could build an electoral majority by recruiting disaffected New Deal-Cold War Democrats.

Social conservatives: Ideological tagline for moral, often religious, conservatives. Social conservatism in the U.S. has always run deep among southern white Protestants and rural northern Protestants. White working-class Catholics joined forces with Protestant social conservatives over such issues as abortion and crime. Both the Moral Majority of the 1980s and the Christian Coalition of the 1990s were socially conservative organizations.

Southern Manifesto: Also known as the "Declaration of Constitutional Principles." Term given to the statement of principles nearly all southern Democrats in Congress issued in 1956 pledging resistance against racial integration.

Southern Strategy: In the 1950s, some conservatives urged the Republican Party to abandon support for civil rights and pursue the support of disaffected southern white Democrats. The Southern Strategy gained momentum among Republicans following George Wallace's disruptive independent presidential run in 1968. Richard Nixon embraced the Southern Strategy after 1968.

Stagflation: An economic description of what happens when a nation experiences both high levels of unemployment and inflation. Liberal economists had argued since the New Deal that economic reality was an either/or proposition: that either a nation had a stagnant economy with high unemployment or an overheated economy with high inflation, but that you could not have both simultaneously. That formulation appeared correct until the 1970s.

Supply-side economics: Economic policies evolved from the Mellon Plan and refined in the 1970s by conservative economist Arthur Laffer. President Ronald Reagan embraced many tenets of supply-side economics, most especially reducing taxes to stimulate economic expansion.

Truman Doctrine: Foreign policy principles drawn up in 1947 by President Harry Truman calling for the U.S. to contain communist expansion in Europe. The outbreak of the Korean War in 1950 led to the extension of the Truman Doctrine to Asia.

War on Terror: The name George W. Bush's advisers gave to the American military response to the terrorist attacks of September 11, 2001. The 2003 U.S. invasion of Iraq became part of America's War on Terror.

Further Reading

The literature on American politics and conservatism in the twentieth century is extensive—and divided into numerous subfields.

The Roosevelt Legacy

Franklin D. Roosevelt's policies spawned a multi-generational Democratic electoral coalition, as well as a multi-generational conservative reaction. For excellent overviews of the Roosevelt legacy, four books are indispensable: William E. Leuchtenburg, *In the Shadow of FDR: From Harry Truman to Barack Obama* (Ithaca, N.Y.: Cornell University Press, 2009); Steve Fraser and Gary Gerstle, eds., *The Rise and Fall of the New Deal Order, 1930–1980* (Princeton, N.J.: Princeton University Press, 1990); Allan J. Lichtman, *White Protestant Nation: The Rise of the American Conservative Movement* (N.Y.: Atlantic Monthly Press, 2008); and Michael Barone, *Our Country: The Shaping of America from Roosevelt to Reagan* (New York: The Free Press, 1992).

New Deal Democrats Join the Conservative Coalition

The transformation of southern white Democrats into conservative Republicans is discussed in: Kari Frederickson, *The Dixiecrat Revolt and the End of the Solid South, 1932–1968* (Chapel Hill: University of North Carolina Press, 2001); Joseph Crespino, *Strom Thurmond's America: A History* (New York: Hill and Wang, 2013); Dan Carter, *The Politics of Rage: George Wallace, The Origins of the New Conservatism, and the Transformation of American Politics* (Baton Rouge: Louisiana University Press, 2000); and Stephan Lesher, *George Wallace: An American Populist* (Reading, M.A.: Addison-Wesley, 1994).

Northern urban Catholics' disaffection with the Democratic Party after World War II, and their attraction to Richard Nixon and Ronald Reagan, has been chronicled in: Kenneth D. Durr, *Behind the Backlash: White Working-Class Politics in Baltimore, 1940–1980* (Chapel Hill: University of North Carolina Press, 2003); Thomas J. Sugrue, *The Origins of the Urban*

Crisis: Race and Inequality in Postwar Detroit (Princeton, N.J.: Princeton University Press, 2014); and Vincent Cannato, *The Ungovernable City: John Lindsay and the Struggle to Save New York* (New York: Basic Books, 2002).

Divisions over U.S. Foreign Policy

Discussions of the ideological divisions over American foreign policy since 1945 include such works as: Kenneth J. Heineman, *Campus Wars: The Peace Movement at American State Universities in the Vietnam Era* (New York: New York University Press, 1994); Robert Timberg, *The Nightingale's Song* (New York: The Free Press, 1996); Charles DeBenedetti, *An American Ordeal: The Antiwar Movement of the Vietnam Era* (Syracuse, N.Y.: Syracuse University Press, 1990); and Tom Wells, *The War Within: America's Battle over Vietnam* (Berkeley: University of California Press, 1994).

Social Conservatism/Religious Right

Social conservatism has drawn the attention of: Leo P. Ribuffo, *The Old Christian Right: The Protestant Far Right from the Great Depression to the Cold War* (Philadelphia, P.A.: Temple University Press, 1983); Kenneth J. Heineman, *God is a Conservative: Religion, Politics, and Morality in Contemporary America* (New York: New York University Press, 2005); Donald T. Critchlow, *Phyllis Schlafly and Grassroots Conservatism: A Woman's Crusade* (Princeton, N.J.: Princeton University Press, 2008); William Martin, *With God on Our Side: The Rise of the Religious Right in America* (New York: Broadway Books, 1996); and Daniel K. Williams, *God's Own Party: The Making of the Christian Right* (New York: Oxford University Press, 2010).

Libertarians

Libertarians have been examined in: Kim Phillips-Fein, *Invisible Hands: The Making of the Conservative Movement from the New Deal to Reagan* (New York: W.W. Norton, 2009); Michael W. Miles, *The Odyssey of the American Right* (New York: Oxford University Press, 1980); and Jason Stahl, *Right Moves: The Conservative Think Tank in American Political Culture Since 1945* (Chapel Hill: University of North Carolina Press, 2016).

Neoconservatives

The best discussion of neoconservatives is: John Ehrman, *The Rise of Neoconservatism: Intellectuals and Foreign Affairs, 1945–1994* (New Haven, C.T.: Yale University Press, 1995).

Conservative Media

The indispensable book on American conservative media is: Nicole Hemmer, *Messengers of the Right: Conservative Media and the Transformation of American Politics* (Philadelphia: University of Pennsylvania Press, 2016). A classic examination of 1930s conservative radio broadcasting is Alan Brinkley, *Voices of Protest: Huey Long, Father Coughlin, and the Great Depression* (New York: Random House, 1983). For a first-hand discussion of conservative media, see, Patrick J. Buchanan, *Right from the Beginning* (New York: Little, Brown, and Co., 1988). The best biography of conservative journalist William F. Buckley, Jr., is John B. Judis, *William F. Buckley, Jr.: Patron Saint of the Conservatives* (New York: Simon and Schuster, 1988).

Sunbelt Conservatives

The rise of the New Right in the American West is treated in: Michelle Nickerson and Darren Dochuk, eds., *Sunbelt Rising: The Politics of Space, Place, and Region* (Philadelphia: University of Pennsylvania Press, 2011); and Lisa McGirr, *Suburban Warriors: The Origins of the New American Right* (Princeton, N.J.: Princeton University Press, 2015).

Barry Goldwater and Ronald Reagan

Biographies of Barry Goldwater and Ronald Reagan include: Matthew Dallek, *The Right Moment: Ronald Reagan's First Victory and the Decisive Turning Point in American Politics* (New York: The Free Press, 2000); Lou Cannon, *President Reagan: The Role of a Lifetime* (New York: Public Affairs Press, 2000); John Ehrman, *The Eighties: America in the Age of Reagan* (New Haven, C.T.: Yale University Press, 2005); John P. Diggins, *Ronald Reagan: Fate, Freedom, and the Making of History* (New York: W.W. Norton, 2007); Robert Alan Goldberg, *Barry Goldwater* (New Haven, C.T.: Yale University Press, 1995); and Rick Perlstein, *Before the Storm: Barry Goldwater and the Unmaking of the American Consensus* (New York: Nation Books, 2009).

Conservatism as an Intellectual and Political Movement

For American conservatism as an intellectual and political movement see: Gregory L. Schneider, *The Conservative Century: From Reaction to Revolution* (Lanham, M.D.: Rowman and Littlefield, 2009); Michael Kazin, *The Populist Persuasion: An American History* (New York: Basic Books, 1995); Donald T. Critchlow, *The Conservative Ascendancy: How the Republican Right Rose to Power in Modern America* (Lawrence: University Press of Kansas, 2011); Michael Bowen, *The Roots of Modern Conservatism: Dewey, Taft, and the Battle for the Soul of the Republican*

Party (Chapel Hill: University of North Carolina Press, 2011); and, Jerome L. Himmelstein, *To the Right: The Transformation of American Conservatism* (Berkeley: University of California Press, 1990).

Conservative Youth

The academic literature on the post-World War II student Right has grown, but still lags in comparison with studies devoted to the 1960s student Left. Two books on young conservatives are indispensable: Gregory L. Schneider, *Cadres for Conservatism: Young Americans for Freedom and the Rise of the Contemporary Right* (New York: New York University Press, 1999), and Rebecca E. Klatch, *A Generation Divided: The New Left, the New Right, and the 1960s* (Berkeley: University of California Press, 1999).

References

Archives

Goldwater, Barry M. "Acceptance Speech, Republican National Convention." July 16, 1964. Distinctive Collections, Barry M. Goldwater Papers, FM MAA-1, Box 135, Folder 48, Arizona State University Library.

Hoover, Herbert C. "Address of President Herbert Hoover Accepting the Republican Nomination for President, August 11, 1932." Herbert Hoover Papers, Box 2, University of Iowa Libraries.

Lindbergh, Charles. "Who Are the War Agitators?" Des Moines, Iowa, Speech, September 11, 1941. Charles A. Lindbergh Papers, Box 204, Yale University Library.

Pew, J. Howard. "Which Road to Take?" No. 53. Washington, D.C.: American Liberty League, 1935. Jouett Shouse Papers, 1899–1967, University of Kentucky Special Collections.

Shouse, Jouett. "The New Deal vs. Democracy." No. 128, Washington, D.C.: American Liberty League, 1936. Jouett Shouse Papers, 1899–1967, University of Kentucky Special Collections.

Wallace, George C. "Inaugural Address of Governor George Wallace, January 14, 1963, Montgomery, Alabama." File Q20276-Q20290, Alabama Department of Archives and History.

Books

Allitt, Patrick. *The Conservatives: Ideas and Personalities through American History*. New Haven, C.T.: Yale University Press, 2014.

Appy, Christian G. *Working-Class War: American Combat Soldiers and Vietnam*. Chapel Hill: University of North Carolina Press, 1993.

Barone, Michael. *Hard America, Soft America: Competition vs. Coddling and the Battle for the Nation's Future*. New York: Crown Publishing, 2004.

Barone, Michael. *Our Country: The Shaping of America from Roosevelt to Reagan*. New York: The Free Press, 1992.

Bell, Daniel. *The Radical Right*. Piscataway, N.J.: Transaction, 1964.

Bowen, Michael. *The Roots of Modern Conservatism: Dewey, Taft, and the Battle for the Soul of the Republican Party*. Chapel Hill: University of North Carolina Press, 2011.

Brinkley, Alan. *Voices of Protest: Huey Long, Father Coughlin, and the Great Depression.* New York: Random House, 1983.

Buchanan, Patrick J. *Right from the Beginning.* New York: Little, Brown, and Co., 1988.

Buckley, William F., Jr., and Bozell, L. Brent, Jr. *McCarthy and His Enemies: The Record and Its Meaning.* Chicago: Henry Regnery Co., 1954.

Cannato, Vincent. *The Ungovernable City: John Lindsay and the Struggle to Save New York.* New York: Basic Books, 2002.

Cannon, Lou. *President Reagan: The Role of a Lifetime.* New York: Public Affairs Press, 2000.

Carter, Dan. *The Politics of Rage: George Wallace, The Origins of the New Conservatism, and the Transformation of American Politics.* Baton Rouge: Louisiana University Press, 2000.

Carty, T. *A Catholic in the White House? Religion, Politics, and John F. Kennedy's Presidential Campaign.* New York: Palgrave Macmillan, 2004.

Chambers, Whittaker. *Witness.* Washington, D.C.: Regnery Publishing, 2014.

Courtright, David T. *No Right Turn: Conservative Politics in a Liberal America.* Cambridge, M.A.: Harvard University Press, 2010.

Crespino, Joseph. *Strom Thurmond's America.* New York: Hill and Wang, 2012.

Critchlow, Donald T. *The Conservative Ascendancy: How the Republican Right Rose to Power in Modern America.* Lawrence: University Press of Kansas, 2011.

Critchlow, Donald T. *Phyllis Schlafly and Grassroots Conservatism: A Woman's Crusade.* Princeton, N.J.: Princeton University Press, 2008.

Dallek, Matthew. *The Right Moment: Ronald Reagan's First Victory and the Decisive Turning Point in American Politics.* New York: The Free Press, 2000.

Davies, Gareth. *From Opportunity to Entitlement: The Transformation and Decline of Great Society Liberalism.* Lawrence: University of Kansas Press, 1996.

DeBenedetti, Charles. *An American Ordeal: The Antiwar Movement of the Vietnam Era.* Syracuse, N.Y.: Syracuse University Press, 1990.

Diggins, John P. *Ronald Reagan: Fate, Freedom, and the Making of History.* New York: W.W. Norton, 2007.

Durr, Kenneth D. *Behind the Backlash: White Working-Class Politics in Baltimore, 1940–1980.* Chapel Hill: University of North Carolina Press, 2003.

Ehrman, John. *The Eighties: America in the Age of Reagan.* New Haven, C.T.: Yale University Press, 2005.

Ehrman, John. *The Rise of Neoconservatism: Intellectuals and Foreign Affairs, 1945–1994.* New Haven, C.T.: Yale University Press, 1995.

Falwell, Jerry. *Listen, America! The Conservative Blueprint for America's Moral Rebirth.* New York: Doubleday, 1981.

Fein-Phillips, Kim. *Invisible Hands: The Making of the Conservative Movement from the New Deal to Reagan.* New York: W.W. Norton, 2009.

Fraser, Steve, and Gerstle, Gary, eds. *The Rise and Fall of the New Deal Order, 1930–1980.* Princeton, N.J.: Princeton University Press, 1989.

Frederickson, Kari. *The Dixiecrat Revolt and the End of the Solid South, 1932–1968.* Chapel Hill: University of North Carolina Press, 2001.

Fried, Albert. *FDR and His Enemies.* New York: Palgrave, 1999.

Friedman, Milton, and Friedman, Rose. *Free to Choose: A Personal Statement.* New York: Harcourt, Brace, and Co., 1979.

Gellman, Irwin F. *The Contender: Richard Nixon, the Congress Years, 1946–1952*. New York: The Free Press, 1999.

Ginsburg, Benjamin. *The Fatal Embrace: Jews and the State*. Chicago, I.L.: University of Chicago Press, 1993.

Goldberg, Robert Alan. *Barry Goldwater*. New Haven, C.T.: Yale University Press, 1995.

Goldwater, Barry. *The Conscience of a Conservative*. Washington, D.C.: Regnery Publishers, 1960.

Gould, Lewis L. *Grand Old Party: A History of Republicans*. New York: Random House, 2003.

Grantham, Dewey W. *The South in Modern America: A Region at Odds*. New York: HarperCollins, 1994.

Grem, Darren E. *The Blessings of Business: How Corporations Shaped Conservative Christianity*. New York: Oxford University Press, 2016.

Hart, Jeffrey. *The Making of the Conservative Mind: The National Review and Its Times*. Wilmington, D.E.: Intercollegiate Studies Institute, 2005.

Heineman, Kenneth J. *Campus Wars: The Peace Movement at American State Universities in the Vietnam Era*. New York: New York University Press, 1993.

Heineman, Kenneth J. *A Catholic New Deal: Religion and Reform in Depression Pittsburgh*. University Park: Pennsylvania State University Press, 1999.

Heineman, Kenneth J. *God Is a Conservative: Religion, Politics, and Morality in Contemporary America*. New York: New York University Press, 2005.

Heineman, Kenneth J. "Religiously Informed Social Reform and Reaction in the Era of the Great Depression,'" in, Stephen J. Stein, ed., *The Cambridge History of Religions in America, 1790–1945*, 3 vols., Cambridge: Cambridge University Press, 2012.

Hemmer, Nicole. *Messengers of the Right: Conservative Media and the Transformation of American Politics*. Philadelphia: University of Pennsylvania Press, 2016.

Himmelstein, Jerome L. *To the Right: The Transformation of American Conservatism*. Berkeley: University of California Press, 1990.

Hunter, James Davison. *Culture Wars: The Struggle to Define America*. New York: Basic Books, 1991.

Jenkins, Philip. *Decade of Nightmares: The End of the Sixties and the Making of Eighties America*. New York: Oxford University Press, 2006.

Judis, John B. *William F. Buckley, Jr.: Patron Saint of the Conservatives*. New York: Simon and Schuster, 1988.

Kazin, Michael. *The Populist Persuasion: An American History*. New York: Basic Books, 1995.

Klatch, Rebecca E. *A Generation Divided: The New Left, the New Right, and the 1960s*. Berkeley: University of California Press, 1999.

Kotkin, Joel. *The Next Hundred Million: America in 2050*. New York: Penguin, 2010.

Ladd, Everett Carll, Jr. *Where Have all the Voters Gone? The Fracturing of America's Political Parties*. New York: W.W. Norton, 1978.

Lasch, Christopher. *The Revolt of the Elites and the Betrayal of Democracy*. New York: W.W. Norton, 1995.

Lesher, Stephan. *George Wallace, American Populist*. Reading, M.A.: Addison-Wesley, 1994.

Leuchtenburg, William E. *Franklin D. Roosevelt and the New Deal, 1932–1940*. New York: HarperCollins, 1963.

Leuchtenburg, William E. *In the Shadow of FDR: From Harry Truman to Barack Obama.* Ithaca, N.Y.: Cornell University Press, 2009.

Levy, Peter B. *America in the Sixties, Right, Left, and Center: A Documentary History.* Westport, C.T.: Praeger, 1998.

Lichtman, Allan J. *White Protestant Nation: The Rise of the American Conservative Movement.* New York: Atlantic Monthly Press, 2008.

MacPherson, Myra. *Long Time Passing: Vietnam and the Haunted Generation.* Bloomington: Indiana University Press, 2009.

Martin, William. *With God on Our Side: The Rise of the Religious Right in America.* New York: Broadway Books, 1996.

McGirr, Lisa. *Suburban Warriors: The Origins of the New American Right.* Princeton, N.J.: Princeton University Press, 2001.

Miles, Michael W. *The Odyssey of the American Right.* New York: Oxford University Press, 1980.

Minchin, Timothy J. *Empty Mills: The Fight Against Imports and the Decline of the U.S. Textile Industry.* Lanham, M.D.: Rowman and Littlefield, 2012.

Nadasen, Primella. *Welfare Warriors: The Welfare Rights Movement in America.* New York: Routledge, 2014.

Nichols, David A. *Ike and McCarthy: Dwight Eisenhower's Secret Campaign against Joseph McCarthy.* New York: Simon and Schuster, 2017.

Nickerson, Michelle, and Dochuk, Darren, eds. *Sunbelt Rising: The Politics of Space, Place, and Region.* Philadelphia: University of Pennsylvania Press, 2011.

Parmet, Herbert S. *Richard Nixon and His America.* Boston, M.A.: Little, Brown, and Co., 1990.

Perlstein, Rick. *Before the Storm: Barry Goldwater and the Unmaking of the American Consensus.* New York: Nation Books, 2009.

Radosh, Ronald. *Divided they Fell: The Demise of the Democratic Party, 1964–1996.* New York: The Free Press, 1996.

Ribuffo, Leo. *The Old Christian Right: The Protestant Far Right from the Great Depression to the Cold War.* Philadelphia, P.A.: Temple University Press, 1983.

Schlafly, Phyllis. *A Choice, Not an Echo: The Inside Story of How American Presidents Are Chosen.* Washington, D.C.: Regnery Publishing, 2014.

Schneider, Gregory L. *Cadres for Conservatism: Young Americans for Freedom and the Rise of the Contemporary Right.* New York: New York University Press, 1999.

Schneider, Gregory L. *Conservatism in America Since 1930: A Reader.* New York: New York University Press, 2003.

Schneider, Gregory L. *The Conservative Century: From Reaction to Revolution.* Lanham, M.D.: Rowman and Littlefield, 2009.

Sparrow, Bartholomew. *The Strategist: Brent Scowcroft and the Call of National Security.* New York: PublicAffairs, 2015.

Stahl, Joshua. *Right Moves: The Conservative Think Tank in American Political Culture Since 1945.* Chapel Hill: University of North Carolina Press, 2016.

Sugrue, Thomas J. *The Origins of the Urban Crisis: Race and Inequality in Postwar Detroit.* Princeton, N.J.: Princeton University Press, 1996.

Surbrug, Robert. *Beyond Vietnam: The Politics of Protest in Massachusetts, 1974–1990.* Amherst: University of Massachusetts Press, 2009.

Taft, Robert A. *A Foreign Policy for Americans.* New York: Doubleday, 1951.

Timberg, Robert. *The Nightingale's Song.* New York: The Free Press, 1996.

Wells, Tom. *The War Within: America's Battle over Vietnam.* Berkeley: University of California Press, 1994.

Williams, Daniel K. *God's Own Party: The Making of the Christian Right.* New York: Oxford University Press, 2010.

Magazine and Journal Articles

Ames, Mark. "Independent and Principled? Behind the CATO Myth." *The Nation*, April 20, 2012. www.thenation.com/article/independent-and-principled-behind-cato-myth/

"Bailout Recipients." *ProPublica: Journalism in the Public Interest*, October 31, 2017. https://projects.propublica.org/bailout/list

Ball, Molly. "Grover Norquist, the Happiest Man in Washington." *The Atlantic*, April 8, 2017. www.theatlantic.com/politics/archive/2017/04/grover-norquist-the-happiest-man-in-washington/523206/

Bennett, Laurie. "The Koch's Aren't the Only Funders of CATO." *Forbes*, March 13, 2012. www.forbes.com/sites/lauriebennett/2012/03/13/the-kochs-arent-the-only-funders-of-cato/#6ddfb7420964

"'Boll Weevil' Economics." *Christian Science Monitor*, September 17, 1981. www.csmonitor.com/1981/0917/091719.html

Bork, Robert. "Civil Rights—A Challenge." *The New Republic*, 21 (August 31, 1963): 21–24.

Buckley, William F., Jr. "Statement of Principles and Credenda." *National Review*, 1 (November 19, 1955): 1–3.

Erickson, Erik. "Mitt Romney as the Nominee: Conservatism Dies and Barack Obama Wins." *RedState*, November 8, 2011. www.redstate.com/erick/2011/11/08/mitt-romney-as-the-nominee-conservatism-dies-and-barack-obama-wins/

FitzGerald, Frances. "A Disciplined, Charging Army." *The New Yorker*, 57 (May 18, 1981): 53–144.

Foer, Franklin. "Fevered Pitch: Grover Norquist's Strange Alliance with Radical Islam." *The New Republic*, November 11, 2001. https://newrepublic.com/article/83799/norquist-radical-islam-cair

Friedersdorf, Connor. "Iraq Hawks Don't Realize They're to Blame for America's War Weariness." *The Atlantic*, March 25, 2013. www.theatlantic.com/politics/archive/2013/03/iraq-hawks-dont-realize-theyre-to-blame-for-americas-war-weariness/274311/

Hackett, George. "1990: The Bloodiest Year Yet?" *Newsweek*, July 15, 1990. www.newsweek.com/1990-bloodiest-year-yet-206532

Hawkins, John. "Five Reasons So Many Grassroots Conservatives Don't Like Mitt Romney." *Townhall.com*, January 31, 2012. https://townhall.com/columnists/johnhawkins/2012/01/31/five-reasons-so-many-grassroots-conservatives-dont-like-mitt-romney-n1298196

Heineman, Kenneth J. "Asserting States' Rights, Demanding Federal Assistance: Texas Democrats in the Era of the New Deal," *Journal of Policy History*, 28 (2016): 342–374.

Heineman, Kenneth J. "Catholics, Communists, and Conservatives: The Making of Cold War Democrats on the Pittsburgh Front," *U.S. Catholic Historian*, 34 (Fall 2016): 25–54.

Heineman, Kenneth J. "Iron City Trinity: The Triumph and the Trials of Catholic Social Activism in Pittsburgh, 1932–1972," *U.S. Catholic Historian*, 22 (Spring 2004): 121–145.

Hemmer, Nicole. "How Conservative Media Learned to Play Politics." *Politico Magazine*, August 30, 2016. www.politico.com/magazine/story/2016/08/conservative-media-history-steve-bannon-clarence-manion-214199

Hoge, Dean R. "Mainline Churches: The Real Reason for the Decline." *First Things*, March 1993. www.firstthings.com/article/1993/03/mainline-churches-the-real-reason-for-decline

"Is Pat Buchanan Anti-Semitic?" *Newsweek*, December 22, 1991. www.newsweek.com/pat-buchanan-anti-semitic-201176

Kaplan, Fred. "Dumb and Dumber: The U.S. Army Lowers Recruitment Standards ... Again." *Slate*, January 24, 2008. www.slate.com/articles/news_and_politics/war_stories/2008/01/dumb_and_dumber.html

Kaplan, Fred. "The Dumbing Down of the Army." *Slate*, October 4, 2005. www.slate.com/articles/news_and_politics/war_stories/2005/10/the_dumbingdown_of_the_us_army.html

Kirkpatrick, Jeane. "Dictatorships and Double Standards." *Commentary*, 68 (November 1979): 34–54.

Limbaugh, Rush. "Romney is Not a Conservative." *Real Clear Politics*, October 12, 2011. www.realclearpolitics.com/video/2011/10/12/rush_limbaugh_romney_is_not_a_conservative.html

Lord, Jeffrey. "Reagan's 1986 Election." *The American Spectator*, October 16, 2006. https://spectator.org/46321_reagans-1986-election/

McCarthy, Daniel. "Secret Origins of the 'Southern Strategy.'" *The American Conservative*, April 3, 2008. www.theamericanconservative.com/2008/04/03/secret-origins-of-the-southern-strategy/

Muravchik, Joshua. "Patrick J. Buchanan and the Jews." *Commentary*, 91 (January 1991): 29–37.

Newman, Stephen A. "From John F. Kennedy's 1960 Campaign Speech to Christian Supremacy: Religion in Modern Presidential Politics." New York Law School, *Law Review*, 53 (2008–2009): 691–733.

Olsen, Henry. "Reagan: FDR's True Heir." *Real Clear Politics*, July 2, 2017. www.realclearpolitics.com/articles/2017/07/02/reagan_fdrs_true_heir_134354.html

Patton, Mike. "The Growth of Government: 1980 to 2012." *Forbes*, January 24, 2013. www.forbes.com/sites/mikepatton/2013/01/24/the-growth-of-the-federal-government-1980-to-2012/#186ba67017b6

Ribuffo, Leo P. "The Discovery and Rediscovery of American Conservatism Broadly Conceived." *OAH Magazine of History*, 17 (January 2003): 5–10.

Sarasohn, David. "Patriots vs. the Patriot Act." *The Nation*, 77 (September 4, 2003): 23.

Semuels, Alana. "The End of Welfare as We Know It." *The Atlantic*, April 1, 2016. www.theatlantic.com/business/archive/2016/04/the-end-of-welfare-as-we-know-it/476322/

Utley, Jon Basil. "The Untold Story of Antiwar Conservatives." *The American Conservative*, April 18, 2013. www.theamericanconservative.com/articles/the-untold-story-of-the-conservatives-against-war/

Wanniski, Jude. "Taxes, Revenues, and the 'Laffer Curve,'" *The Public Interest*, 33 (Fall 1978): 3–16.

"Why the South Must Prevail." *National Review*, 3 (August 24, 1957): 148–149.

Newspaper Articles

Adair, Bill. "He [Rudy Giuliani] Ignores Bipartisan Support for Defense Cuts." *PolitiFact*, January 5, 2008.

Baker, Peter. "Arthur Laffer's Theory of Tax Cuts Comes to Life Once More." *New York Times*, April 25, 2017.

Barnes, Bart. "Coach Tom Landry Dies." *Washington Post*, February 13, 2000.

Binder, David. "Soviet Turmoil: The Cuban-Soviet Connection—31-Year Irritant to the U.S." *New York Times*, September 12, 1991.

Blake, Aaron. "Who is Grover Norquist?" *Washington Post*, November 26, 2012.

Bowman, Tom. "Reagan Guided Huge Buildup in Arms Race." *Baltimore Sun*, June 8, 2004.

Buchanan, Patrick J. "Blacks and Republicans." *New York Times*, April 5, 1977.

Cannon, Lou. "Reagan Campaigning from County Fair to Urban League." *Washington Post*, August 4, 1980.

Cannon, Lou. "Tapping the Little Guy." *Washington Post*, March 6, 1977.

Clymer, Adam. "Barry Goldwater, Conservative and Individualist, Dies at 89." *New York Times*, May 29, 1998.

Confessore, Nicholas. "Quixotic '80 Campaign Gave Birth to Koch's' Powerful Network." *New York Times*, May 17, 2014.

"Conservatives, Liberals, Align against the Patriot Act." *Washington Times*, June 14, 2005.

Cooperman, Alan. "Openly Religious, to a Point: Bush Leaves the Specifics of His Faith to Speculation." *Washington Post*, September 16, 2004.

Cove, Peter. "Get Able-Bodied Americans off the Couch." *Wall Street Journal*, July 4, 2017.

Cushman, John H. "James Webb's New 'Fields of Fire.' " *New York Times*, February 28, 1988.

Daley, Steve. "Perot's Dig at Persian Gulf War Exposes Soft Underbelly of Bush's Victory." *Chicago Tribune*, June 14, 1992.

Dionne, E.J., Jr. "Reopening an Old Wound; Quayle's Guard Duty in Vietnam War Era Puts the Focus Again on." *New York Times*, August 23, 1988.

Douglas, Martin. "Phyllis Schlafly, 'First Lady' of a Political March to the Right, Dies at 92." *New York Times*, September 5, 2016.

Halloran, Richard. "ROTC Shunned No More, Grows Increasingly Selective." *New York Times*, July 20, 1987.

Healy, Melissa. "Clinton Defense Budget Cuts into Troops, Ships." *Los Angeles Times*, March 27, 1993.

Hinds, Michael deCourcy. "Number of Killings Soars in Big Cities Across U.S." *New York Times*, July 18, 1990.

Holmes, Steven A. "Jesse Helms Dies at 86; Conservative Force in the Senate." *New York Times*, July 5, 2008.

Kliff, Sarah. "How the Republican Party became Pro-Life." *Washington Post*, March 10, 2012.

Kotkin, Joel. "A New Way Forward on Trade and Immigration." *Orange County Register*, August 20, 2017.

Lindsey, Robert. "Rehnquist in Arizona: A Militant Conservative in 60's Politics." *New York Times*, August 4, 1986.

Lyons, Richard D. "Karl Hess, a Republican Aide Who Became an Anarchist, 70." *New York Times*, April 27, 1994.

McFadden, Robert D. "William Rusher, Champion of Conservatism, Dies at 87." *New York Times*, April 18, 2011.

McGill, Brian. "Catholicism in the U.S." *Wall Street Journal*, September 18, 2015.

Newport, Frank. "In U.S., Four in 10 Report Attending Church in Last Week." *Gallup News*, December 24, 2013.

"Pat Robertson Calls for Clinton's Impeachment." *Los Angeles Times*, September 20, 1998.

Pearson, Richard. "Former Ala. Gov. George C. Wallace Dies." *Washington Post*, December 14, 1998.

Roberts, Steven V. "Senate Approves Reagan's Request to Help Contras." *New York Times*, March 28, 1986.

Reagan, Ronald W. "Neshoba County Fair Speech." *Neshoba Democrat*, August 3, 1980.

"Ross Barnett, Segregationist, Dies; Governor of Mississippi in 1960's." *New York Times*, November 7, 1987.

Routledge, Gray. "Why are Millennials Wary of Freedom?" *New York Times*, October 14, 2017.

Salpukas, Agis. "1980 Car Sales at a 19-Year Low." *New York Times*, January 8, 1981.

Sciolino, Elaine, and Gordon, Michael R. "Confrontation in the Gulf: U.S. Gave Iraq Little Reason Not to Mount Kuwait Assault." *New York Times*, September 23, 1990.

Secter, Bob. "1988 Republican National Convention: Robertson Returns to TV but Still Can Be Force in the GOP." *Los Angeles Times*, August 16, 1988.

Shields, Mark. "Correcting the Record." *Creators Syndicate*, February 28, 2015.

Siler, Martin. "Robert Welch, Founder of the John Birch Society, Dies at 85." *Los Angeles Times*, January 8, 1985.

Sokolove, Michael. "Dick Armey is Back on the Attack." *New York Times*, November 4, 2009.

Steinfels, Peter. "Moral Majority to Dissolve; Says Mission Accomplished." *New York Times*, June 12, 1989.

Thomas, Robert, Jr. "Henry Regnery, 84, Ground-Breaking Conservative Publisher." *New York Times*, June 23, 1996.

Thurow, Lester C. "Beware of Reagan's Military Spending." *New York Times*, May 31, 1981.

Weaver, Warren, Jr. "Democrats' Platform Shows a Shift from Liberal Positions of 1976 and 1980." *New York Times*, July 22, 1984.

Weil, Martin. "Karl Hess, 70, Dies." *Washington Post*, April 26, 1994.

Weiner, Rachel. "How ALEC Became a Political Liability." *Washington Post*, April 24, 2012.

Weiner, Tim. "Jeane Kirkpatrick, Reagan's Forceful Envoy, Dies." *New York Times*, December 9, 2006.

Williams, Timothy. "Roger Milliken, Conservative Tycoon, Dies at 95." *New York Times*, December 31, 2010.

Think Tank and Policy Center Reports

"2004 Presidential Race." *Center for Responsive Politics*, OpenSecrets.org.

Allen, Jodie T. "How a Different America Responded to the Great Depression." *Pew Research Center*, December 14, 2010.

"America's Changing Religious Landscape." *Pew Research Center*, May 12, 2015.
Auxier, Richard C. "Reagan's Recession." *Pew Research Center*, December 14, 2010.
Baker, Spring. "Clinton's 'No-Win' Defense Budget." *Heritage Foundation*, February 14, 1997.
Coffey, Bentley, McLaughlin, Patrick A., and Peretto, Pietro. "The Cumulative Cost of Regulations." *Mercatus Working Paper*, April 2016.
Crane, Edward. "The Dangers of Compassionate Conservatism." *CATO Institute*, May/June 2001.
De Rugy, Veronique. "1920s Income Tax Cuts Sparked Economic Growth and Raised Federal Revenues." *CATO Institute*, March 4, 2003.
De Rugy, Veronique. "Spending Under President George W. Bush." *Mercatus Center*, Working Paper, March 2009.
"Fact Sheet Trends in U.S. Corrections [1925–2015]." *The Sentencing Project*, 2015.
McKenzie, Richard. "The Reagan Defense Budget: Failing to Meet the Threat." *Heritage Foundation*, July 14, 1982.
Metzger, Kurt, and Booza, Jason. "African-Americans in the United States, Michigan, and Metropolitan Detroit." *Center for Urban Studies*, February 2002, Working Paper Series, No. 8.
Phillips, James. "The Soviet Invasion of Afghanistan." *Heritage Foundation*, January 9, 1980.
Schlafly, Phyllis. "What's Wrong with 'Equal Rights' for Women?" *Phyllis Schlafly Reports*, no. 7 (February 1972). Eagle Forum.
"Trends in Party Identification, 1939–2014." *Pew Research Center*, April 7, 2015.

U.S. Government

Beck, Allen J., and Gilliard, Darrell K. "Prisoners in 1994." U.S. Department of Justice, *Bureau of Justice Statistics Bulletin*, August 1995.
Bush, George W. "Fact Sheet: Compassionate Conservatism, April 30, 2002." Excerpts George W. Bush White House website.
Bush, George W. "President Delivers State of the Union Address, January 29, 2002." George W. Bush White House website.
Cooper, Alexia, and Smith, Erica L. "Homicide Trends in the United States, 1980–2008." U.S. Department of Justice, *Bureau of Justice Statistics*, November 2011.
"Declaration of Constitutional Principles, 1956." *Congressional Record*, Senate, 84th Congress, Second Session, March 12, 1956, Volume 102, Part 4. Washington, D.C.: Government Printing Office, 1956, 4460–4461.
Gingrich, Newt. "Contract with America, 1994." U.S. House of Representatives website.
Goldwater, Barry. "Remarks." *Congressional Record*, Senate, 88th Congress, 2nd Session, June 18, 1964, Volume 110, Part 26. Washington, D.C.: Government Printing Office, 1964, 14318–14319.
McCarthy, Joseph. "The History of George Catlett Marshall." *Congressional Record*, Senate, 82nd Congress, First Session, June 14, 1951, Volume 97, Part 5. Washington, D.C.: Government Printing Office, 1951, 6566.
"Officer Commissioning Programs: Costs and Officer Performance." Congressional Budget Office, *CBO Papers*, June 1990.
Reagan, Ronald W. "Address to the Nation on Defense and National Security, March 23, 1983." Ronald Reagan Presidential Library and Museum.

190 *References*

Reagan, Ronald W. "Address to the Nation on the Economy, October 13, 1982." Ronald Reagan Presidential Library and Museum.

Reagan, Ronald W. "Presidential Inaugural Address, January 20, 1981." Ronald Reagan Presidential Library and Museum.

Reagan, Ronald W. "Remarks at the Veterans Day Ceremony at the Vietnam Veterans Memorial, November 11, 1988." Ronald Reagan Presidential Library and Museum.

Reagan, Ronald W. "Remarks on East–West Relations at the Brandenburg Gate in West Berlin, June 12, 1987." Excerpts reprinted from the Ronald Reagan Presidential Library and Museum.

Reagan, Ronald W. "A Time for Choosing." Address on Behalf of Barry M. Goldwater Presidential Campaign, October 27, 1964. Ronald Reagan Presidential Library and Museum.

Sumners, Hatton. "Extension of Remarks of Hon. Hatton W. Sumners of Texas." Appendix to the *Congressional Record*, House, 79th Congress, Second Session, March 11, 1946, Volume 92. Washington, D.C.: Government Printing Office, 1946, A1282–A1283.

Trump, Donald J. "Inaugural Address, January 20, 2017." Donald J. Trump White House website.

Websites

The American Conservative. www.theamericanconservative.com/
American Enterprise Institute (AEI), Washington, D.C. www.aei.org/
American Legislative and Exchange Council (ALEC) Arlington, V.A. www.alec.org/
The American Presidency Project, University of California, Santa Barbara. www.presidency.ucsb.edu/index.php
The American Spectator. https://spectator.org/
CATO Institute, Washington, D.C. www.cato.org/
Center for Responsive Politics, Washington, D.C. www.opensecrets.org/
Commentary. www.commentarymagazine.com/
Congressional Record. www.govinfo.gov/app/collection/crecb
Donald J. Trump White House website. www.whitehouse.gov/briefing-room/presidential-actions
George W. Bush White House website. https://georgewbush-whitehouse.archives.gov/
Heritage Foundation, Washington, D.C. www.heritage.org/
Mercatus Center, George Mason University. www.mercatus.org/
The National Interest. http://nationalinterest.org/
National Review Online. www.nationalreview.com/
Real Clear Politics. www.realclearpolitics.com/
RedState. www.redstate.com/
Ronald Reagan Presidential Foundation and Institute, Simi Valley, C.A. www.reaganfoundation.org/
The Sentencing Project, Washington, D.C. www.sentencingproject.org/
Townhall.com. https://townhall.com/
U.S. Department of Justice, Federal Bureau of Investigation (FBI), Uniform Crime Reporting Statistics. https://ucr.fbi.gov/
U.S. House of Representatives. www.house.gov/
The Weekly Standard. www.weeklystandard.com/

Index

Note: Numbers in *italics* refer to figures.

Agnew, Spiro 76
agricultural sector: Agricultural Adjustment Act (1933) 14; federal assistance for 14; Great Depression, impact on 10; Rural Electrification Administration, impact on 14
Al-Qaeda 128; attacks mounted by 128; September 11 attack 127–129, *129*
America First Committee: founding of 26; Lindbergh, Charles, role in 26, 27–28; Manion, Clarence E., role in 42; Regnery, William, role in 26
American Enterprise Association (AEA) 20–21, 77, 109; Schlafly, Phyllis, role at 21
American Enterprise Institute: Goldwater, Barry, support for 58; New Deal, and view of 21; *Weekly Standard* (magazine), link with 124; *see also* American Enterprise Association
American Legislative Exchange Council (ALEC) 96
American Liberty League: Pew, J. Howard, speech to (1935) 144–145; Shouse, Jouett, speech to (1936) 145–146
Americans for Democratic Action (ADA) 47
Americans for Tax Reform 123
Anderson, John B. xvii; presidential candidate (independent) 95, 96; presidential primaries (1980) 93; Reagan, Ronald W., view of 94
Arizona Republican Party 57; Rehnquist, William, leader of 56
Atwater, Lee 113

banking: Banking (Glass-Steagall) Act 1933, 13; collapse of (1933) 12–13; credit and lending (1920s levels of) 8; sub-prime scandal and collapse (2007–2008) 133
Barnett, Ross 53
Biden, Joe, 110
Bin Laden, Osama 105; September 11 terror attack 127–128
Boot, Max xvii; Iraq, and call for military action against 130
Bork, Robert xvii, 56; Democratic opposition to 109–110
Bozell, L. Brent, Jr. xvii; *Conscience of a Conservative, The* 49, 152–153; *McCarthy and His Enemies* 38
Brookings Institute 20
Brown, Pat 68
Bryan, William Jennings 14, 15
Buchanan, Patrick J. xvii; newspaper column, and conservative views of 78; Persian Gulf War, view of 115; presidential primaries (1992) 116
Buckley, William F., Jr. xvii, 34, *44*, 56; "conservative fusionism" 4; *McCarthy and His Enemies* 38; *National Review* (magazine), founding of 44
Buckley, William F., Sr. 34
Bush, George Herbert Walker ("H.W.") xvii; conservatives' view of 113; national security, measures for 113–114; presidential and vice-presidential nominations 113; presidential primaries (1980) 93; views and ideals of 94
Bush, George W. xviii; background of 125–126; banking collapse (2007/08),

and impact of 133; credit and lending, and levels of debt 8; domestic policies of 126–127, 132–133; "Fact Sheet: Compassionate Conservatism" (2002) 169–170; Iraq, and call for military action against 130–131; presidential nomination and election of 125, 131; "State of the Union Address" (2002) 170–171; Texas National Guard, role in 64–65; "War on Terror," and impact of 131–132
Bush, Jeb 137

Carter, Jimmy: background of 81; Carter Doctrine 87; neoconservatives, and opposition to 86–87; presidential election and reelection campaign 92–93, 95–96; public view of 81; Reagan, Ronald W., view of 95; religious schools (South), review of and reaction to 91
Catholic Church: divisions within, 23; New Deal, and criticism of 23–24; and support for union membership 17–18
CATO Institute 126; establishment of 88; PATRIOT Act (2001), view of 128
Chambers, Whittaker xviii; House Committee on un-American Activities, testimony of 30–31, 32; Soviet spying 30–31
Cheney, Dick 125, 130
Christian Anti-Communist Crusade 42
Christian Broadcasting Network 90
Christian Coalition 116
Christianity Today (magazine) 42
civil rights: Civil Rights Act (1957) 41; Civil Rights Act (1964) and federal legislation 57–58; Civil Rights Commission, establishment of 41; demonstrations in support of (1960s) 53–54, 54; education, and racial segregation in schools 40–41; Eisenhower, Dwight D., support for 40; Executive Order 9981 34; military service, and African-American personnel 33–34; National Association for the Advancement of Colored People (NAACP) 40; Parks, Rosa, actions of and impact on 49; post-World War II view of 33; race relations, and in northern cities 33–34, 54–55; southern Democratic opposition to 45; "Southern Manifesto" (Declaration of Constitutional Principles) 45; University of Mississippi, riots at 53, 54
Civil Works Administration (CWA) 13
Clark, Ed 94
Clifford, Clark 97
Clinton, Hillary Rodham xviii; background of 68; "Goldwater Girl" 68; national health insurance program, support for 118; presidential nomination of 137
Clinton, William Jefferson ("Bill") xviii, 120; Democratic Leadership Council (DLC), role in 117; presidential nomination and election of 117, 122; Starr investigation into 124; welfare legislation, implementation of 120
coal industry 9–10
Community Block Grant Act (1974) 83
Congress of Industrial Organizations (CIO) 17; National Association of Manufacturers, opposition to 21; Roosevelt, Franklin D., support of 17
Connally Hot Oil Act (1935) 88
"conservative fusionism" 4
Coors, Joseph xviii; Heritage Foundation, and founding of 77
Coughlin, Charles 23–24
Crane, Edward 126

Democratic Leadership Council (DLC) 117
Democratic Party: 1912 presidential election success 15; 1960 election 50–52; anti-communist views, and divisions of 32–33; Civil Rights Act (1957), support for 41; civil rights, and divisions relating to 34; cultural divisions of 15, 22; divisions within (1970s) 81; employment shifts, and cultural impact on 74–75; and G.I. Generation 34–35; nomination process, reforms to 73–74; Southern Democrats, and position of post-World War I 15–16, 22; "Southern Manifesto," signed by southern members of Congress 45; and union influences 17
Department of Homeland Security: establishment of 130; Federal Emergency Management Agency 130; Federal Emergency Relief

Administration (FERA) 132–133; Transportation Security Administration 129
Dewey, Thomas 33; background and views of 35–36
Dies, Martin, Jr. xviii, 21
domestic policy: Affordable Care Act (2010) 135; AIDS epidemic, and reaction to 106; Aviation and Transportation Security Act (2001) 129; Bush (George W.) Administration 126–127; crime rates and law enforcement 106–107, 121; Department of Homeland Security 130; and federal regulation and expenditure 83; inflation, and "stagflation" as a result of 83–84; motor industry, and impact of foreign imports 82–83; No Child Left Behind Act (2001) 126–127; Obama administration 135; PATRIOT Act (2001) 128–129; post-World War II economy, and impact on 82; and public health 106; and social decline 84; taxation levels (1970s) 84
Drug Enforcement Agency (DEA), establishment of 73

Eagle Forum 78
economic conservatism: pre-Great Depression, and limitations of 6–9; views and ideals of 4
economic policy 88–89; 1970s approach to 88–89; 1982 recession, and impact on 102; banking collapse (2007/2008), and impact of 133; Economic Growth and Tax Relief Reconciliation Act (2001) 127; Economic Recovery Tax Act (1981) 100; industry, impact on (1980s) 100–101; Jobs and Growth Tax Relief Act (2003) 127; and national debt (1980s) 102; Omnibus Budget Reconciliation Act (1981) 100; and political capitalism 88; and savings and loans crisis (1980s) 111; Tax Equity and Fiscal Responsibility Act (1982) 102; and taxation levels 89; Troubled Assets Relief Program 133
Eisenhower, Dwight D. xviii, 40–41; presidential nomination and election of 38–39
employment levels: economic changes (1980s), and impact on 102; Great Depression, impact on 9; and welfare relief 13
Environmental Protection Agency (EPA) 73
Equal Employment Opportunity Commission (EEOC) 57–58
Equal Rights Amendment (ERA) 78–79

Fair Labor Standards Act (1938) 14
Falwell, Jerry 90; background and views of 90–91; *Listen, America!* manifesto 91, 160–161; Moral Majority, foundation of 91; Reagan, Ronald W., view of 105
Faubus, Oval 40–41
Federal Aid Highway Act (1956) 40
Federal Communications Commission (FCC) 123
Federal Deposit Insurance Corporation (FDIC) 13
Federal Emergency Relief Administration (FERA) 13
film industry, and impact on popular culture 108
Fish, Hamilton 10
Ford, Betty 81
Ford, Gerald R. xviii, 76
Ford, Henry 6
foreign policy: Afghanistan, and assistance given to 105; and Carter Doctrine 87; and national security and defense 103–104, 118, 127–128; Neutrality Act (1935 & 1937) 24; New Deal, and threats to 24; Obama administration 136; oil industry and supply, impact of 84–85; Persian Gulf War, intervention in 115–116; September 11, events and impact of 127–128; and Soviet tensions 85; "Truman Doctrine" 33, 36; "War on Terror," and impact of 131–132; World War II, threat of and impact on 24–25
Franco, Francisco 24
Friedman, Milton 109; *Free to Choose* 109
Frumm, David xviii–xix; "Axis of Evil" 130

Gannon, Robert (Father) 23
Garner, John 15, 21
G.I. Generation 34; Vietnam War, and view of draft for 66

Gingrich, Newt 96, *120*; "Contract with America" initiative (1994) 118, 167–169; foreign policy (Reagan administration), and criticism of 104; Speaker of the House, and resignation of 118–119, 124–125

Goldwasser family *see* Goldwater, Barry

Goldwater, Barry xix, 3, *57*; Acceptance Speech (Republican National Convention, 1964) 155–156; *Choice, Not and Echo, A* (Schlafly, Phyllis) 58; civil rights legislation, and opposition to 58; *Conscience of a Conservative, The* (Bozell, L. Brent, Jr.) 49, 152–153; and "Daisy Girl" TV commercial 60; McCarthy, Joseph R., view of 38; New Deal, view of 22, 58, 60; presidential nomination of 46, 49, 59–60; Remarks (to 88th Congress, 1964) 154–155; Republican National Convention, speech to 59–60; University of Mississippi riots, view of 56

Gorbachev, Mikhail xix; Afghanistan, and Soviet withdrawal from 114

Gore, Al, Jr. 126

Graham, Billy xix, 42; Watergate scandal, view of 76

Gramm, William ("Phil") xix; Gramm-Leach-Bailey Act (1999) 122; Reagan, Ronald W., support of 100

Great Depression: agricultural sector, impact on 10; industry, impact on 9–10; unemployment levels 9

"Great Society" 61–62

Grove City College (Pittsburg) 41

Hearst, William Randolph 18

Helms, Jesse xix, *80*; election to the Senate 77; Reagan, Ronald W., support of 79, 104

Heritage Foundation: expansion of 109; founding of 77; Soviet invasion of Afghanistan, and reaction to 87

Hess, Karl xix; American Enterprise Association (AEA/AEI), member of 49; Goldwater, Barry, support for 58

Hiss, Alger xix, 31

Hoover, Herbert xix, 10; address, accepting Republican nomination for President 143–144

House Committee on un-American Activities: Chambers, Whittaker, testimony of 30–31, 32; Dies, Martin, Jr., role in 21; establishment of 21; "Hollywood Hearings" 30; Nixon, Richard Milhouse, role in 30; post-World War II activities of 29–30; Thomas, J. Parnell, chair of 30; World War II, activities of 29

Human Events (journal) 26, 28, 43

Humphrey, Hubert 71; Americans for Democratic Action (ADA), role in 47

Hyde, Henry 125

immigration 7; Republican Party, view of and approach to 16–17; and voting patterns relating to 16–17

industry: construction, and overproduction (1920s) 8–9; economic policy (1980s), and impact on 100–101; Great Depression, impact on 9; and immigrant workforce 7; motor industry, and impact of foreign imports 82–83; steel industry, and impact of Great Depression on 9; tax policies, effect on 6; union membership, and impact on 21, 101

Iran-Contra scandal 110–111

John Birch Society (JBS) 43; *American Opinion* (magazine of) 43; Manion, Clarence E., role in 43; supporters of 43, 58

Johnson, Lyndon B. xix–xx; Civil Rights Act (1957), support for 41; and "Daisy Girl" TV commercial, 60; domestic programs, and failure of 61–62; Great Society pledge 61; Gulf of Tonkin Resolution and intervention in Vietnam 63–64; presidential role and vice-presidential nomination 50, 57, 61; War on Poverty, programs for and impact of 62

Kennedy, Edward ("Teddy") 92–93

Kennedy, John F. xx; assassination, and impact of 57; background of 50; foreign policy, focus of 53; presidential nomination of 50, 52; *Profiles in Courage* 50–51; religious views, and political problems of 51

Kennedy, Joseph P. 50

Kerry, John 131

King, Martin Luther, Jr. xx, 42; arrest and imprisonment of 51;

assassination, and impact of 71; Montgomery Bus Boycott, spokesman for 49; Southern Christian Leadership Conference, role in 49
Kirkpatrick, Jeane xx; Carter Doctrine, view of 87; foreign policy, and influence on 99; neoconservative views of 86
Klu Klux Klan 15
Knox, Frank 26
Koch, Charles xx, 43; CATO Institute, establishment of 88
Koch, David xx, 43, 95; CATO Institute, establishment of 88; vice-presidential nomination, campaign for 94, 96
Koch, Fred 43
Korean War 36; U.S. intervention in 39
Kristol, Irving xx, 75; neoconservative views of 86
Kristol, William ("Bill") xx; Iraq, and call for military action against 130; Persian Gulf War, view of 115; *Weekly Standard* (magazine), editorial of 124

Laffer, Arthur xx, 88–89
Landon, Alfred ("Alf") xx, 20
Libertarian Party 94; libertarians, views and ideals of 4
Liberty League 19, 23
Limbaugh, "Rush" Hudson III xx; radio broadcasts of 123
Lindbergh, Charles xxi, 26, 27; America First Committee, role in 26, 27–28; Nazi Germany, view of 27; Roosevelt, Franklin D., view of 26–27; "Who Are the War Aviators," speech in Des Moines, Iowa (1941) 147–149
Livingston, Bob 125

Manion, Clarence E. xxi; America First Committee, role in 42; civil rights, and views of white voters 57; John Birch Society (JBS), role in 43; *Manion Forum* 43
Marshall, George 37; Marshall Plan, 33
Marshner, Connie 91; Reagan, Ronald W., view of 105
Matthews, J.B. 42; *American Opinion* (magazine), editorial role 43
McCain, John 134
McCarthy, Joseph R. xxi, 29, 37; Arizona election (1952) 38; censure of 40; communists, identification of 36–37; Goldwater, Barry, support of 38; "History of George Catlett Marshall, The," remarks to Congress (1951) 150–151; Marshall, George, criticism by 37; "McCarthyism" 37–38
McFarlane, Robert 110–111
McGovern, George 33; Democratic nomination process, reform of 73–74; presidential nomination, running for 74–75
Medicare and Medicaid 61
Mellon, Andrew xxi, 6
Mellon Plan 6, 8, 9
military service; personnel numbers, and reductions in 118; recruitment problems (1970s) 85–86; Reserve Officer Training Corps (ROTC) 108; standard of recruits, and improvements in 103–104; Vietnam War, and impact of 86; "War on Terror," and impact of 132
Milliken, Roger 49; Heritage Foundation, and founding of 77; political capitalism, support for 88
Mondale, Walter 107, 109
Moral Majority: closure of 116; decline of 112–113; founding of 91; Reagan, Ronald W., support to 105
Murdoch, Rupert xxi; Fox News Channel, and launch of 123–124; *Weekly Standard* (magazine), founding of 124
Murray, Phillip 47

National Association for the Advancement of Colored People (NAACP) 40; racial segregation in schools, action against 40–41
National Association of Evangelicals 51
National Association of Manufacturers 21
National Labor Relations Board (NLRB) 13–14
National Review (magazine): Civil Rights Act (1957), opposition to 45–46, 49; founding of 44; remit of 44–45; states' rights, and support of 56
National Youth Administration (NYA) 13
"neoconservatives" 75
Neutrality Act (1935 & 1937) 24

New Deal: 1938 midterm elections, and impact on 21; Arizona, expenditure in and impact on 22; Catholic Church, and criticism of 23–24; and federal expenditure 18–19; foreign policy, and risks to 24; introduction of 3, 11; media coverage of 18; New Deal Democrats 3; southern Democratic criticism of 22–23; tax liabilities for business 19

Nixon, Richard Milhouse xxi, 29, 73; federal regulatory functions, and expansion of 73; House Committee on un-American Activities, role in 30, 31–32; presidential nomination of, and background to 50, 71–72; reelection of 75–76; Vietnam War, strategies relating to 72–73; Watergate scandal and resignation 76

Norquist, Grover xxi, 123; PATRIOT Act (2001), view of 128–129

North, Oliver L. xxi, *110*; Iran-Contra scandal, role in 110–111

North American Free Trade Agreement (NAFTA) 121; and immigration concerns 121–122

North Atlantic Treaty Organization (NATO) 36

Obama, Barack H. ("Barry") xxi–xxii; Affordable Care Act (2010) 135; domestic policies of 135; foreign policies of 136; presidential nomination and election of 134, 137; Tea Party Movement, and opposition to 135–136

Occupational Safety and Health Administration (OSHA) 73

O'Connell, William (Cardinal) 23

Office of Economic Opportunity 61

O'Neill, Thomas Phillip ("Tip"), Jr. xxii; Iran-Contra scandal, view of 110; Reagan, Ronald W., view of 97–98

Organization of Petroleum Exporting Countries (OPEC) 84–85

Parks, Rosa 49
PATRIOT Act (2001) 128–129
Perot, Henry ("Ross") xxii; Bush, George Herbert Walker, view of 116; presidential nomination of 116, 117
Persian Gulf Wars: Iraq, and 2003 invasion of 130–131; U.S. intervention in 115–116

Pew, J. Howard xxii, 19, *20*, 26, 41, 43; American Liberty League, speech to (1935) 144–145; death of 77; education and media, conservative approach to 41–42; Reagan, Ronald W., support of 77

Podhoretz, Norman 75; defense policy (Reagan administration), and view of 104

Pollard, Ramsey 51

Posse Comitatus Act (1878) 56

Professional Air Traffic Controllers Organization (PATCO) 99

Progressive Party 33

Prohibition 6–7, 8, 12

Pulliam, Eugene 56

Pure Food and Drug Act (1906) 88

Reagan, Nancy 48

Reagan, Ronald W. xxii, 3, *98*; acting career 46–47; "Address to the Nation on Defense and National Security" (1983) 164–165; "Address to the Nation on the Economy" (1982) 163–164; AIDS epidemic, and reaction to 106; Americans for Democratic Action (ADA), role in 47; anti-communist conservative views of 48; assassination attempt 100; background of 18, 46; California governor, election as and programs of 70; defense policy of 103–104; Economic Recovery Tax Act (1981), introduction of 100; federal regulation, and view of 94, 97; *GE Theater*, host of 48; Inaugural Address (1981) 97, 162–163; Iran-Contra scandal 111; legacy of 4; Moral Majority, support from 105; "Neshoba County Fair Speech" (1980) 94, 161–162; Omnibus Budget Reconciliation Act (1981), introduction of 100; personal life of 47–48; presidential nomination, campaign and election of 79–80, 94, 95–96, 107–108; "Reagan Democrats" 96; "Remarks at the Veterans Day Ceremony" (1988) 165–166; "Remarks on East-West Relations" (West Berlin, 1987) 166–167; Roosevelt, Franklin D., support for 18; Screen Actors Guild, role in 30, 47, 99; Strategic Defense Initiative (SDI), introduction of 103;

"Time for Choosing, A" (TV appeal) 68, 156–157; views and ideals of 93–94
Reconstruction Finance Corporation 10
Regnery, Henry xxii
Regnery, William: America First Committee, role in 26; *McCarthy and His Enemies*, publication of 38
Rehnquist, William xxii, 56
religion: Bakker scandal, and impact on Religious Right 112; and declining religiosity 106; Religious Right, public perception and decline of 3–4, 112–113; *see also* Catholic Church
Republican Party: 1932 election, southern blacks and support for 16; 1964 election results 60; 1970s, decline of 76–77; Civil Rights Act (1957), support for 41; communist containment, and policies relating to 39; and conservative fusionists 45; education and media, conservative approach to 41–43; immigration, view of and approach to 16–17; "Modern Republicans," and views of 40, 41, 50; post-World War II resurgence of 29; Republican National Convention 80; "Southern Strategy," and conservatives' approach to 57
Revenue Act (1935) 19
Robertson, Marion Gordon ("Pat") xxii, *112*; background of 90; Christian Broadcasting Network, founding of 90; Christian Coalition, launch of 116; Clinton, William Jefferson ("Bill"), view of 124; presidential primaries (1988) 112
Rockefeller, Nelson 58–59
Romney, Mitt 136–137
Roosevelt, Franklin D. xxiii, *12*; Congress of Industrial Organizations (CIO), support from 17; election of 3; illness and disability 11; legacy of 4; New Deal policies 3, 11; presidential election, 11; radio appearances 18; Reagan, Ronald W., support of 18; rise of 11–12; Supreme Court, and judicial "reform" 23; World War II, and US involvement in 25
Rumsfeld, Donald 125, 130
Rusher, William 57

Sanders, Bernie 137
Schlafly, Phyllis xxiii, *79*; American Enterprise Association (AEA), member of 21; *Choice, Not and Echo, A* 58; Eagle Forum, establishment of 78; Equal Rights Amendment (ERA), view of 78; Goldwater, Barry, support for 58; PATRIOT Act (2001), view of 128–129; Reagan, Ronald W., view of 105–106; "What's Wrong with Equal Rights for Women?" (1972) 158
Schwarz, Fred 42
Scranton, William 59
Securities and Exchange Commission (SEC) 13
September 11 terror attack (9/11) 127–129, *129*; PATRIOT Act (2001), as result of 128–129
Servicemen's Readjustment Act (1944) 38
Shouse, Jouett, American Liberty League, speech to (1936) 145–146
"Silent Majority": Republican Party, and shift towards 75; Vietnam War, and view of 73
Smith, Al: Democratic presidential nominee 15; Liberty League, role in 23
social conservatism: pre-Great Depression, and limitations of 6–9; views and ideals of 3–4
social policy 90–92; Conference on the Family (1976), and reaction to 91; national health insurance programs (Clinton administration) 118; Personal Responsibility and Work Opportunity Reconciliation Act (1996) 120; *see also* domestic policy
Social Security Act (1935) 13
South Baptist Convention 51
Southeast Asian Treaty Organization (SEATO) 39
Southern Christian Leadership Conference 49–50
Southern Manifesto (84th Congress, 1956) 151–152; signed by southern members of Congress 45
Soviet Union: Afghanistan, intervention in 85; atomic weapons, development of 39; breaking up of 114; Brezhnev Doctrine 85; Chambers, Whittaker, spying for 30–31; Cold War, and ending of 114; Hiss, Alger, spying for 31; Korean War, role in 39; Progressive

Party, supported by 33; and US relations, post-World War II 32–33
Spanish Civil War 24
Starr, Ken 124
Stimson, Henry, 26
Strategic Defense Initiative (SDI) 103
Students for a Democratic Society (SDS): founding of 66; United Automobile Workers (UAW), support from 66–67; views and ideals of 68; Zionism, view of 67
Sumners, Hatton xxiii; anti-civil rights view 23; Extension of Remarks of, House of Representatives speech (1946) 146–147; New Deal, view of 22–23
Sun Oil 21
Swope, Gerard 19

Taft, Robert A. xxiii, 30; death of 39; *Foreign Policy for Americans, A* (1951) 149; New Deal, view of 25, 36; noninterventionist views of 25–26
Taft-Hartley Act (1947) 29
tax policies: Mellon Plan 6; supply-side economics 6; *see also* economic policies
Taylor, Myron 19
Tea Party Movement 135–136
Thomas, J. Parnell: "Hollywood Hearings" 30; House Committee on un-American Activities, chair of 30
Thurmond, Strom xxiii, 35; Civil Rights Act (1957), opposition to 45–46; conservative fusionism, view of 46; racial integration, and view of 34
Thurow, Lester 104
Truman, Harry S. xxiii; House Committee on un-American Activities, denouncement of 31; presidential election (1948) 34–35; Soviet Union, view of 32; "Truman Doctrine" 33, 36
Trump, Donald J. xxiii, 138; "America First" policy 137; background of 137; Inaugural Address (2017) 171–172, 140; presidential nomination and election of 137–139

unions: Catholic Church, support for 17–18; Democratic Party, influences of 17; threats posed by 21; union movement, and growth of 17
United Automobile Workers (UAW) 54–55; Students for a Democratic Society (SDS), support for 66–67

Vietnam War 63–66; background to 63; Gulf of Tonkin Resolution 63; Tet Offensive 71; U.S. intervention in 64–66
Viguerie, Richard xxiii–xxiv, 72; Reagan, Ronald W., support of 79–80
Vitter, David 125

Wagner, Robert: Fair Labor Standards Act (1938) 14; Social Security, and support for 13–14; Wagner Act (1935) 13–14
Wallace, George xxiv, 72; assassination attempt 75; Catholic politicians, view of 32; civil rights and racial segregation, view of 55–56; Inaugural Address (1963) 153–154; New Deal, support for 55; presidential nomination of, and attempt at 71–72, 75; Progressive Party, and presidential campaign 33; Secretary of Commerce, and dismissal of 33
Walmart 122
Wanniski, Jude, "Taxes, Revenues, and the 'Laffer Curve'" (1978) 159–160
Warren, Earl 40
Webb, James: Bush, George W., view of 133; Persian Gulf War, view of 115
Welch, Robert 43
welfare: Social Security Act (1935) 13; and unemployment benefits 13; *see also* social policy
Willkie, Wendell 26
Wilson, Woodrow 15
Works Progress Administration (WPA) 13
World War II: America First Committee, and resistance to involvement in 27–28; U.S. involvement in, and noninterventionist views 25, 28

Young, Andrew 86
Young Americans for Freedom (YAF): "Sharon Statement" 67; views and ideals of 67–68
youth movement: Berkeley protests (California) 69–70; Students for a Democratic Society (SDS) 66; Young Americans for Freedom (YAF) 67